STORIED PROPERTY

STORIED PROPERTY
María Cordova's Casa

LYDIA R. OTERO

PLANET EARTH PRESS
TUCSON, ARIZONA

Planet Earth Press
Tucson, Arizona
© Lydia R. Otero, 2025.

ISBN: 978-1-7341180-4-9 (paperback)
ISBN: 978-1-7341180-5-6 (ebook)

Cover Photo: Arizona Historical Society, PC 1000: Tucson General Photo Collection: Places-Tucson-Historic Buildings, No. 28499.
Cover and interior design by Sara Thaxton

No part of this book may be reproduced, stored in a retrieval system, or transmitted in any form or by any means, including electronic, mechanical, photocopying, or recording, without prior written permission from the author. This excludes brief quotations used in reviews, critical works, or scholarly publications.

Instructors, librarians, and community educators may reproduce short excerpts for noncommercial educational purposes, as long as the material is properly cited and not altered. For all other uses, please contact the author.

Supplemental materials accessed through the QR code and website are copyrighted and may not be downloaded, redistributed, or modified without permission. Linking to these materials for educational purposes is permitted when proper attribution is given.

Library of Congress Cataloging-in-Publication Data
Names: Otero, Lydia R., author.
Title: Storied property : María Cordova's casa / by Lydia R. Otero.
Description: Includes bibliographical references and index. | Tucson, AZ: Planet Earth Press, 2025.
Identifiers: LCCN: 2025915047 | ISBN: 978-1-7341180-4-9
Subjects: LCSH Cordova, Maria Navarrete. | Historic sites—Arizona—Tucson. | Historic buildings—Arizona—Tucson. | BISAC HISTORY / Hispanic & Latino | HISTORY / United States / General
Classification: LCC F819.T943 .O84 2025 | DDC 979.101—dc23

*Dedicated to my friend, Pancho Medina (1941–2022),
who would have loved this book.*

I am grateful our paths crossed.

For me, forgiveness and compassion are always linked: how do we hold people accountable for wrongdoing and yet at the same time remain in touch with their humanity enough to believe in their capacity to be transformed?

—bell hooks, in conversation with Maya Angelou

CONTENTS

	List of Illustrations	*xi*
	Introduction	5
1.	María Navarrete Cordova and the "Set" She Refused to Be Part Of	17
2.	Location! Location! Location!	41
3.	Rallying for Home: The Press, History, and the Courts	69
4.	Caught in the Crosshairs: A Bullseye on the Cordovas	93
5.	A House Preserved, A Home Lost	117
6.	La Casa Cordova: A Storied Property, Restored to Forget	143
	Conclusion	163
	Acknowledgements	*177*
	Notes	*181*
	Bibliography	*213*
	Index	*221*

ILLUSTRATIONS

I.1	Aerial View of Downtown Tucson with Site Index	2–3
I.2	La Casa Cordova, 2025	6
I.3	La Casa Cordova historic marker, 2025	7
I.4	Gadsden Purchase stamp, 1953	12
I.5	Book QR Code	15
1.1	Family tree	19
1.2	Telesfora Navarrete in wedding dress	21
1.3	Severin and Refugio Rambaud	27
1.4	Layout of houses	28
1.5	Rambaud residence and rental units, 2025	30
1.6	Restaurant advertisement	32
1.7	Layout of Cordova residence	38
2.1	Sketch of Presidio	43
2.2	Fergusson map detail, 1862	45
2.3	Pre-1965 map of Meyer Avenue	49
2.4	María Cordova in her living room, 1951	52
2.5	María Cordova's Presidio painting	54
2.6	Girl Scouts with Presidio painting, 1962	55
2.7	Presidio wall and features map	57
2.8	1953 Pima County redevelopment map	59
2.9	Proposed downtown high-rise, 1961	64
3.1	Arizona Album: First train in Sonora	71
3.2	"Proud Owner" image of María Cordova	75
3.3	Approximate boundary of Presidio Land Grant	79
3.4	Foreman map detail, 1872	90
4.1	TMA name changes	94

4.2	Residential Emphasis in Hummel Plan	97
4.3	Arizona Savings and Loan	100
4.4	Urban renewal includes Historic Block	104
4.5	Historic Block and TCC Site	105
4.6	Painting in Cinco de Mayo exhibition	110
4.7	María Cordova pointing to her painting	113
5.1	Resolution 6874, City of Tucson	121
5.2	Demolition of Jacobs Mansion	123
5.3	María Cordova with her adult children	127
5.4	Fish-Stevens Mansion?	129
5.5	Archeological digs near Cordova Home	130
5.6	Cordova interior photos, 1972	141
6.1	Art Center construction in 1974	145
6.2	Permit: E. D. Herreras restoration	152
6.3	Restored exterior of Cordovas' Home	153
6.4	"Pure" and Genuine Restoration	154
6.5	Interior staging at La Casa Cordova	158
6.6	María Luisa Tena with her nacimiento (2007)	160
6.7	Nacimiento	161
C.1	Limited access to La Casa Cordova	164
C.2	TMA campus layout in 2025	166
C.3	Recorded owners of La Casa Cordova	171
C.4	La Casa Cordova reopening, 2017	174

STORIED PROPERTY

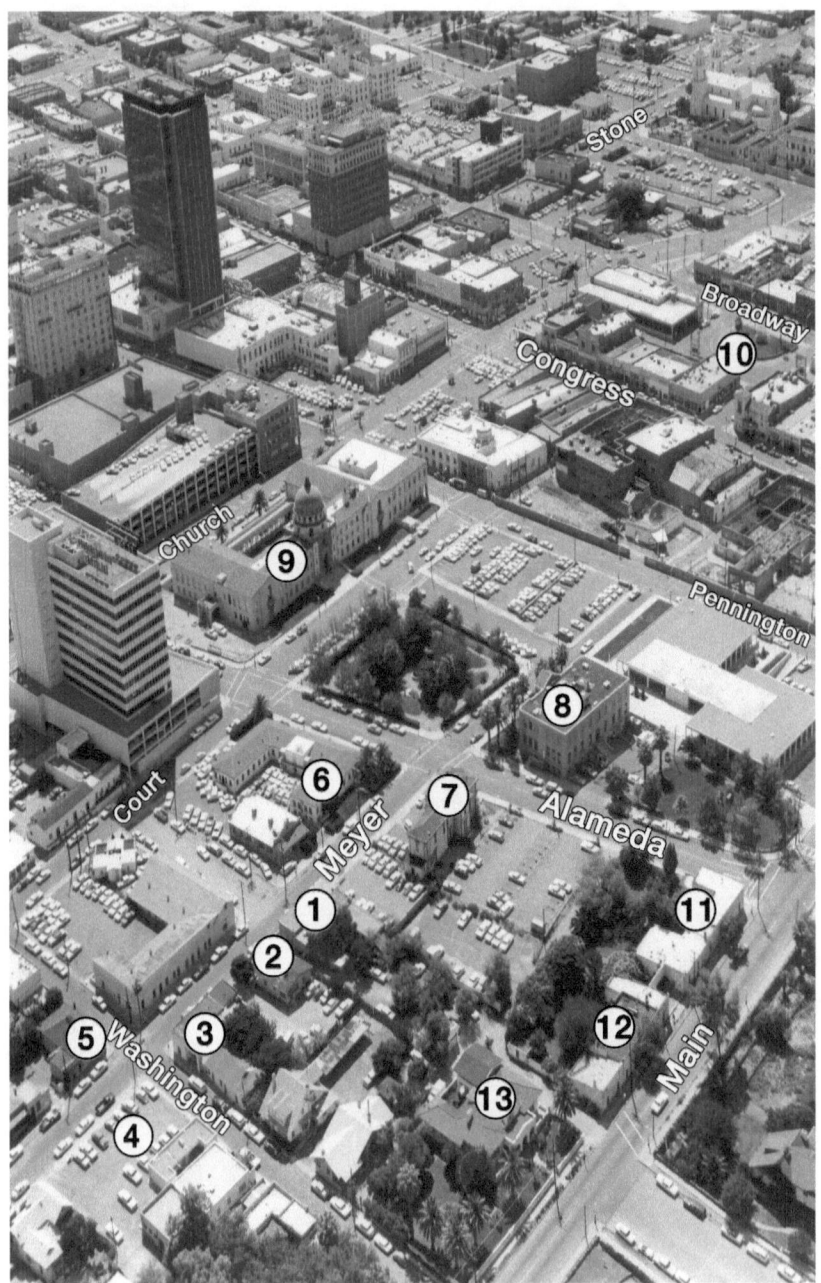

FIGURE I.1 This aerial photograph, taken around 1966, shows downtown Tucson before major redevelopment. Numbers have been added to identify locations referenced throughout the book, including the proximity of María Cordova's home to City Hall. Used with permission from the Arizona Historical Society, PC 200: Above Downtown Tucson View–SE, File 2A.

Sites Near La Casa Cordova

1. Maria Cordova's Casa
   Now part of the TMA's Historic Block as La Casa Cordova.
   171–177 North Meyer Avenue
2. Former Refugio Rambaud Home
   189–191 North Meyer Avenue
3. Former Severin and Refugio Rambaud Home
   Now part of the TMA's Historic Block as Romero House.
   103 West Washington Street
4. Former site of Toy S. Don's (Jeff's) Washington Market
   213 North Meyer Avenue
5. El Rapido Molino de Nixtamal
   220 North Meyer Avenue
6. Former Police/ Health/ City Courts Building
   Now the TMA's Chaiten Baker Center for Art.
   Leased to TMA by City of Tucson in 1988.
   150 West Alameda Street
7. Former Barron Jacobs Mansion
   149 North Meyer Avenue
8. Former City Hall
   109 North Meyer Avenue
9. Pima County Historic Courthouse
   115 North Church Avenue
10. La Placita
    119 West Broadway Boulevard
11. E.N. Fish House
    Now part of the TMA's Historic Block; historic name retained.
    119–121 North Main Avenue
12. Stevens/Duffield House
    Now part of the TMA's Historic Block; historic name retained.
    123–155 North Main Avenue
13. J. Knox Corbett House
    Now part of the TMA's Historic Block; historic name retained.
    180 North Main Avenue

Introduction

La Casa Cordova stands at 173 North Meyer Avenue in Tucson, Arizona, a building visible yet rarely noticed (see Figure I.2).[1] When viewed from the street, a gray concrete driveway with a bright blue tiled sign for the Tucson Museum of Art (TMA) sits to the left, and an asphalt parking lot entrance lies to the right. With its flat roof, minimal ornamentation, and adobe walls coated in plaster, architects would refer to the house's style as a Sonoran row house.[2] The three evenly spaced doors and windows give the façade a clean, symmetrical look. The house appears taller than other row houses of its kind on the block, a visual effect heightened by the uninterrupted height of the off-white wall. Drainpipes are mounted above each door and window, added during restoration to control water runoff and preserve the plastered surface. The stone foundation has been exposed and reinforced, signaling its restoration rather than its original construction.

There is no sidewalk in front of the house. A wide stone path runs directly along the building's edge, flush with the street. The windows are covered from the inside and nothing in front of the house invites people to linger. The three light blue doors are shut, unmarked by even an address. Recently, a pair of planters with greenery were placed out front. Still, the structure remains largely indifferent to passersby.

A bronze marker is mounted on the left side of the wall. It is modest in size, easy to miss, and positioned low enough that it does not command attention. The marker states "Historic Site" in capital letters at the top, but it is often tagged with someone's name (see Figure I.3). Within the outline of Arizona, carefully centered, "La Casa Cordova" dominates the top, and the rest reads:

This adobe house incorporates portions of one of the oldest standing structures in Tucson. The two west rooms are believed to have been built before the Gadsden Purchase of 1854.

The house was named for María Navarette Cordova, whose family acquired it in 1896. It was restored by the Junior League of Tucson, Inc., for the Tucson Museum of Art in 1975 and is listed in the National Register of Historic Places.

At the bottom of the plaque, the Tucson-Pima County Historical Commission and the Arizona Historical Society take credit for the marker and its contents.[3]

Each sentence on the marker reflects a central tension explored in *Storied Property*. These include: a portion of a structure at 173 North Meyer Avenue that may have stood before the Gadsden Purchase, a woman who claimed it as her family home, and a restoration project led by a women's volunteer group for the Tucson Museum of Art (TMA) in the early 1970s. One sentence in particular stands out to anyone interested in history, especially those who rely on official city markers for historical information: "The two west rooms *are believed* to have been built before

FIGURE I.2 La Casa Cordova, 173 North Meyer Avenue, Tucson, Arizona. Taken by the author, 2025.

Introduction   7

FIGURE I.3   La Casa Cordova historic marker, taken in 2025. Courtesy of Karina Kedansky.

the Gadsden Purchase of 1854" *(emphasis added)*. Here, historians and preservationists deliberately used vague language to lend authority without providing evidence or risking the responsibility of naming a source.

María Navarrete Cordova was the source of that claim. In her first newspaper appearance, more than three decades before the historical marker was installed, she stated that the house had been built before 1854. That the experts who approved the marker kept her assertion yet erased its source reveals the selective memory at work.

Storied Property traces how power circulates, how memory is constructed, and how people like María Cordova—who was far from ordinary—get pushed out of history even as their homes become monuments. What we call history is often crafted by those with institutional power, social capital, and access to City Hall. This book does more than document what happened. It seeks to unsettle the official version that allows a house to stand, and for people to walk by, or even through it, without asking deeper questions about legal battles, eviction notices, or the people who once wanted to stay in their homes but had no real choice in the matter.

As the bronze marker also shares, María Cordova's home was listed in the National Register of Historic Places, which recognizes sites of historical and cultural value. Yet the story of how this recognition came about reveals how official acknowledgment can obscure the very struggles that made the property significant in the first place.[4] The house's historical marker states, "The house was named for María Navarrete Cordova, whose family acquired it in 1896." Yet it leaves out her subversive actions and efforts to resist the power of eminent domain (the legal process that allows the government to take private property for what they claim is the public good), which forced her from her home. Almost three years after her home appeared on the National Register, María died on January 3, 1975, harboring resentment toward the new owners of La Casa Cordova for their efforts to erase her from the site's future.

Little has been written about María Cordova or the house that bears her name.[5] Despite its official designation as a historic site, La Casa Cordova has never been the subject of sustained historical analysis. Most accounts are brief, institutional, and focused primarily on its architecture. María herself is often reduced to a name in passing or omitted altogether. *Storied Property* responds to that absence. It takes seriously the life she and her family built in the house, the stories she told, the resistance she enacted, the changes that befell her neighborhood, and the contested meanings assigned to the property before and after it became a museum.

Centering María Cordova opens up an examination of women as preservationists, operating from different positions of ethnicity, class, and cultural authority. None of the women featured in *Storied Property* were passive participants. Cordova asserted her connection to history through storytelling, memory, and legal resistance. Other local preservation networks, like the Junior League of Tucson, relied on power brokers for support and on male experts or collaborators to legitimize the work.

Yet even within those constraints, these women were active participants in shaping how the past was remembered and presented. Their combined efforts influenced the preservation of heritage and the construction of historical narratives in Tucson during the latter half of the twentieth century.

Beginnings

In 1895,⁶ María Navarrete Cordova's story begins in San Miguel de Horcasitas, a town in the state of Sonora, Mexico. Nearly 150 years earlier, in 1749, New Spain had established a presidio, or fort, in the region and called it San Miguel de Horcasitas. It served as the provincial capital for nearly three decades. This colonial settlement relied on military force to subjugate the Indigenous Opata people, and its economy came to depend on their labor to raise cattle and sustain agriculture. As the town developed beyond the presidio and Mexico gained independence from Spain, it retained historical significance as a former seat of power in the state of Sonora.

María was born into a family that had distinguished itself under the colonial system by acquiring large landholdings and exercising political acumen. Both of her parents came from the prestigious classes. She never referenced any biological connection to Indigenous people or an Indigenous past, but when she reminisced about her childhood in Mexico, Indigenous people were always present in the background. Economic scholars Diego Castañeda Garza and Alice Krozer's analysis of wills from the Sonoran upper classes (1871–1910) provides valuable insight into the wealth inequality and social structure of the Mexican society María Navarrete was born into. The dynamics of settler colonialism clearly were in play. As the scholars argue, "The expansion of the agrarian frontier increased inequality due to the violent land grabbing and expropriation of natural resources from the indigenous population that accompanied it. The resulting concentration of land and, importantly, the control of the rivers in Sonora allowed large landowners to increase the yields of their properties and therefore to accumulate more wealth."⁷

The 1854 Gadsden Purchase made Tucson part of the United States, separating it from Sonora. A little more than fifty years later, in 1911, sixteen-year-old María Navarrete, along with her immediate family, crossed the border and established their new home in Tucson. By then, the Mexican Revolution had disrupted the elite systems of wealth and social stability in Sonora. Later in life, María Navarrete Cordova, by then married, recounted moving to a different country but avoided mention of the massive insurrection that shaped her family's departure. The unseating of the thirty-year dictator Porfirio Díaz and the ideological goals of "Tierra y Libertad" ("Land and Liberty") espoused by revolutionary leader Emiliano Zapata were absent from her narratives.[8] Instead, María strategically framed the Navarrete family's migration not as displacement, but as a return to a familiar territory that her family had helped establish. This deliberate portrayal reinforced her sense of ownership and continuity, suggesting that the Navarrete presence in Tucson was not as newcomers but as rightful inhabitants reclaiming historical space.

One of the first people to welcome María Navarrete to Tucson was her great-aunt, Refugio Días (sometimes spelled Díaz). Born in San Miguel de Horcasitas around 1855, Refugio had moved to Tucson in the 1870s, where she acquired multiple properties. It was through this familial connection that María Navarrete Cordova and her children inherited property in Tucson, including La Casa Cordova.

The pages that follow examine María Cordova's efforts to navigate systems of power, historical authority, and belonging within the United States. The pathways that led to privilege were not unfamiliar to her, as they closely mirrored those she had observed in Mexico, where status, land, and reputation shaped one's place in society. As an adult and mother of five children, Cordova managed to inject herself into the chronicles of local history and make a decent living for herself, yet she desired much more. She put her understanding of power and narrative into action, seeking advantage within a settler colonial framework that valued property, historical legitimacy, and cultural fluency. At times, this meant manipulating facts or embellishing historical claims to benefit herself and her family.

Settler Colonial Framework

Understanding how María Cordova positioned herself within that framework requires looking more closely at how settler colonialism operated in a place like Tucson. Defined by its ongoing structure and logic, particularly its goal of "eliminating the Native" in order to gain control of land, settler colonialism provides essential historical context for the conditions Cordova encountered and responded to. The scholar most often looked to on this topic, Patrick Wolfe, writes, "settler colonialism is inherently eliminatory but not invariably genocidal. The primary object of elimination is not the Indigenous population but the settler colonial society's access to territory."[9] While these theories have been widely applied in contexts such as North America, Australia, and Israel/Palestine, there has been little effort to analyze and compare the legacies of colonialism in a specific location such as Tucson, situated about sixty miles from the U.S.–Mexico border.[10] During the 1960s and 1970s, preservation debates in Tucson often centered on land use and legal ownership, particularly the meaning and authority of deeds, issues which are central to *Storied Property*.

After Tucson was incorporated into the U.S. through the Gadsden Purchase in 1854, Mexicans and Native Americans remained the majority population until around 1920, when white residents outnumbered them.[11] The migration of white settlers to Tucson from other parts of the U.S. exemplifies the dynamics of settler colonialism (see Figure I.4). These settlers introduced new mechanisms that controlled how land was distributed, sold, and recorded. In doing so, they created systems that allowed them to take ownership of the land. They removed Indigenous people and displaced the vast majority of the Mexican population from the upper tiers of social and economic life, minimizing their landownership and influence.

Settler colonialism always required local intermediaries, and in Tucson, a few members of the local population were rewarded for enabling the shift in land and power. The ongoing processes of displacement, marginalization, and cultural erasure of Indians and Mexicans that occurred

FIGURE I.4 Three-cent stamp commemorating the 100th anniversary of the Gadsden Purchase, issued by the U.S. Post Office on December 30, 1953. The stamp depicts white settlers arriving in territory that had belonged to Mexico's northern state of Sonora. Courtesy of the Smithsonian National Postal Museum.

in Tucson and across the U.S. Southwest are hallmarks of settler colonialism.[12] Historian Patrick Wolfe's assertion that "invasion is a structure, not an event" underscores that settler colonialism is a process shaped by policies and decisions that are continually reproduced in different forms, not simply something confined to the past.[13] This ongoing structure continues to shape land, power, and belonging.

Federal policies of removal and containment established reservations in Southern Arizona for the Tohono O'odham through a series of executive orders, with major designations in 1874 and 1916. Other Indigenous communities, such as the Apache, were also confined during this period. Some groups, like the Opata and Pima, were absorbed into dominant populations or were subject to shifting forms of tribal recognition. While the creation of reservations is often seen as a later phase of settler colonial control, the process was not over. The post–World War II influx of white settlers into Tucson, many of whom arrived to claim land and opportunity, shows how the settler project continued to reshape the region well into the twentieth century, particularly through urban renewal and urban redevelopment initiatives.

The aim here is not to conflate two distinct forms of dispossession. The forced removal of Native peoples to reservations was part of a larger project of territorial seizure that began with invasion and continues through the present. Urban renewal, while different in scope and origin, also resulted in the displacement of local and historically rooted populations, particularly Mexican Americans or Tucsonenses, a term used by many Mexicans and Mexican Americans to identify themselves, from their homes and the destruction of their barrios.[14] Referencing both is meant to highlight the ongoing processes of removal and control that define settler colonialism, while fully acknowledging that this land first and always belonged to Indigenous peoples.

In the United States, María Cordova fell into the nonwhite category not necessarily because of her phenotype, but because she had migrated from Mexico. Newspaper reports that featured her often emphasized her outsider status and noted that she spoke English with a thick accent. After inheriting her great-aunt Refugio's property, Cordova converted two of her properties into rentals and established a small business. She worked hard to present herself as a model citizen with a distinguished historical past. However, in response to looming urban renewal plans that threatened her livelihood and home, Cordova engaged in a risky strategy.[15]

Far from a radical, Cordova identified with the Republican Party and held conservative views. She voted regularly and even campaigned for Barry Goldwater, the Arizona senator and 1964 Republican presidential nominee. Her sons joined the military. Because she was born in Mexico and came from an upper-class background, Cordova may have embraced a hyper-patriotic stance in response to being viewed as an outsider. Her alignment with conservative ideologies could have been a means to assert belonging, demonstrate loyalty, or claim the respectability she so desired.[16]

In some ways, María Cordova's trajectory echoes that of Juan Seguín, a Tejano military and political leader during and after the Texas Revolution of 1835–1836. He fought alongside Anglo Texans against Mexico, believing in the promise of inclusion and shared governance. But after independence, he was devalued, harassed, and eventually forced to flee Texas. Both Seguín and, more than a century later, Cordova were displaced by the very systems they believed in and helped build. They aligned themselves with dominant powers in pursuit of recognition and opportunity, only to be pushed aside once their presence no longer served those in control, or, in Cordova's case, once it threatened that system. Seguín is remembered mostly as a street name or historical footnote, not for the complexity of his struggle. María's name is etched into a house and a bronze plaque, yet her resistance has been minimized or left out entirely.[17]

Purposefully a Tucson Story

Although she remains central to the narrative, this book is not a biography of María Cordova. With fifty years having passed since her death, there is little room to speculate about her private experiences or emotions. *Storied Property* draws from legal documents, court records, oral histories, newspaper articles, and institutional archives. It uses María Córdova's story not as a fixed truth but as a lens to examine power, displacement, and memory.

This is a Tucson book. It was written by someone born and raised here who still calls the city home. *Storied Property* speaks to others who live here or care about this place. That grounding gives this history its weight. It is based on the understanding that history is always shaped by choices, by what is included and what is left out. It also calls on readers to recognize their role in how Tucson's past is remembered and to pause when walking by La Casa Cordova to ask deeper questions or consider the woman and family who once lived there.

This book does not aim to judge individuals, including María Cordova, but to examine how power operated, who exercised it, and what the consequences were. It critiques systems made up of people—people who made decisions that shaped the city, even if a few later came to regret them. The focus is on the outcomes of those decisions and the ways they continue to reverberate through the built environment, public memory, and the lives of those displaced. *Storied Property* also challenges the authority of the written record, particularly the weight given to property deeds, legal claims, and preservation reports. These documents may confirm ownership, but they cannot fully capture occupancy, presence, or meaning.

María Cordova was not part of any formal civil rights, Chicane/x/o, or social justice movement. It is questionable whether she even aligned with those perspectives. But the tension between her personal motivations and the broader impact of her actions is what makes her so compelling. She defended her property in a system designed to silence and dispossess people like her; ultimately, her actions took on a meaning that extended far beyond her own intent. In Tucson, as in many places, land ownership was a central battleground in settler colonialism and urban renewal. By refusing to surrender her home, she pushed back on the logic of dispossession that displaced thousands. Even if she was fighting for herself, her stance and actions represent a broader struggle. María Navarrete Cordova's insistence on being seen, on preserving her family's story, and on claiming authority over space and history is part of a larger historical reckoning. More than fifty years after her death, we are left to wonder how she might feel about being called subversive. Perhaps, after all she endured in the final years of her life, she would welcome the recognition. Or maybe she would reject the label outright, just as she refused to let anyone define her then, and as her uneven historical record makes it hard to define her now.

www.planetearthpressaz.com/storiedpropertygateway

FIGURE I.5 This QR code and website provide access to selected supplemental materials, including court cases, archival documents, and news items relevant to the first edition of *Storied Property*.

CHAPTER 1

María Navarrete Cordova and the "Set" She Refused to Be Part Of

María Navarrete Cordova, who was born around 1895, experienced wealth and privilege beyond most born in Mexico at that time. Private tutors provided more than just reading and writing lessons in Spanish and English; she learned to sing, play the piano, speak French and paint. Although many of these cultural and economic advantages diminished when she moved to the U.S. in 1911, Cordova was never merely a Mexican woman who immigrated to the United States. Such a compartmentalized view would fail to capture the complexity of her transnational identity. With forceful determination, María Cordova was a twentieth-century transnational woman who was both shaped by and shaped the history of the U.S.-Mexico borderlands.[1] The house where she once lived at 173 North Meyer Avenue, designated as La Casa Cordova, once stood within the historic presidio. María's actions helped safeguard her family's legacy and contributed to the survival of her cherished home. La Casa Cordova stands as a proxy for María, ensuring that she remains an enduring influence on the region's history.

Brief Background of Shifting Geopolitical Boundaries

The Spanish colony of Tucson was established in 1775 as the San Agustín del Tucsón presidio, or fort, in a vast desert populated mainly by Tohono O'odham, Sobaipuri, Apache, and Pima peoples. The colonists adapted the name for their new fort from the Sobaipuri O'odham who had long referred to the area as *S-cuk Shon*, meaning "black base," a name that to Spanish ears sounded like Tucson.[2] After Mexican Independence, the struggling presidio, where settlers waged war against the Apaches and learned the skills needed to survive in the harsh desert environment, became an integral part of the Mexican state of Sonora. It remained connected to Mexican culture, governance, and neighboring towns to the south for support.

The Mexican American War and the Gadsden Purchase established new boundaries and changes associated with U.S. colonization. In 1846, driven by land expansion and settler colonial ambitions, the U.S. sought a pretext to initiate a long-anticipated conflict with Mexico. Historical scholarship has determined that President James K. Polk's claim that "American blood was shed on American soil" was a fabrication designed to manufacture consent for this war.[3] This false assertion has been recognized by scholars as a deliberate pretext to rally public and Congressional support for U.S. expansionism. The episode also reveals how misleading narratives have long served settler colonial agendas by legitimizing territorial acquisition and justifying invasions. Such actions were routinely sanctioned and celebrated as rightful.

The 1848 Treaty of Guadalupe Hidalgo concluded a war that dramatically redrew the region's boundaries. Mexico ceded vast territories, including much of northern Mexico, to the United States. Tucson, however, remained a part of Sonora, Mexico. Only six years later, in 1854, motivated by plans for a southern transcontinental railroad and newly discovered mineral wealth, the U.S. acquired more land through the Gadsden Purchase. This shifted the U.S.-Mexico border southward, transferring Tucson and the surrounding region into U.S. hands. It became part of the U.S. Territory of New Mexico, and later, the Arizona Territory. Through it all, the presidio survived largely because of the alliances it formed with local Indian tribes. Even after the walls that once surrounded the fort had been compromised, the area where it stood continued to represent Tucson's colonial origins.[4]

Transnational Families: The Navarrete's and Fortes

Understanding the broad contours of María Cordova's family history adds depth to her relationship with both the U.S. and Mexico. In the latter half of the nineteenth century, some of her ancestors were among

Sonora and Baja California's most influential power brokers (see Figure 1.1). The Baja California peninsula, a Mexican territory west of Sonora and bounded by the Gulf of California to the east and the Pacific Ocean to the west, was a region marked by instability, much like the rest of Mexico at the time.[5]

It was during this turbulent period that María's paternal grandfather, Pedro Magaña Navarrete, briefly served as *jefe político*, or Governor of Baja California, first for a month in 1862 and again for four months in 1866.[6] His leadership came at a time when Mexico was grappling with the French occupation and Benito Juárez was striving to assert his legitimacy as the nation's president. In this climate of political turbulence and uncertainty, Pedro Magaña Navarrete's tenure was short-lived, and he was ultimately expelled from Baja California. According to historian Adrián Valadés, Navarrete sought refuge in Northern California and never returned.[7]

Seeking respite, Pedro Magaña Navarrete established connections to the landed Mexican elite in Northern California. His wife, Margarita Angulo, whom he married around 1857, was related to and remained close with one of the most influential Californios, Mariano Vallejo. The

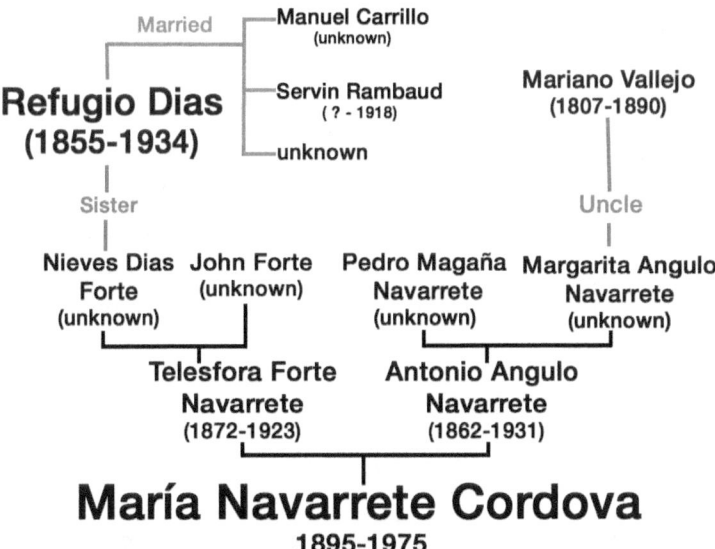

FIGURE 1.1 Select genealogical overview of María Navarrete Cordova's lineage, highlighting key family connections.

fortunes of these Mexican colonizers were already in decline when Navarrete returned to California. White settlers who had arrived during the 1849 Gold Rush were taking over the lands that the Californios had previously wrested from Indigenous peoples.[8]

In 1862, Margarita gave birth to Antonio Angulo Navarrete, María Cordova's father.[9] As an adult, Antonio Angulo Navarrete worked on expanding the railroad system in Mexico. His duties took him across the country, though he spent most of his time in Sonora, connecting the port of Guaymas to Nogales and eventually to the United States. Many towns emerged as the railroad extended its reach, establishing new stops along the route. Carbó, Sonora, was one such town, founded with the arrival of the railroad. In 1887, while Navarrete worked to establish the station there, he encountered fifteen-year-old Telesfora Forte. She had been born around 1872 in nearby San Miguel Horcasitas to a well-heeled family, who, according to María Cordova, "often visited Tucson, as far back as the 1870s and 80s."[10]

Antonio and Telesfora's wedding took place in the port city of Guaymas in 1887, presumably to accommodate guests from Northern California who traveled by sea to attend the event. At that time, individuals from the elite classes who moved between Northern California and the Baja Peninsula preferred to travel via the Pacific Ocean rather than by land, as it was considered safer. As a display of their wealth, the Forte family imported a heavy silk gown with flowered inlays from Spain for the wedding (see Figure 1.2). They had it shipped to Álamos, the then capital of Sonora, and from there, transported to San Miguel Horcasitas. More than fifty years later, a photograph of Telesfora wearing the gown on her wedding day appeared in the *Tucson Citizen*. The 1952 "Arizona Album" feature revolved around her, portraying her as a symbol of elegance and regional history.[11]

The Navarrete Family Chooses Mobility

Antonio Angulo Navarrete and Telesfora arrived in Tucson around 1911, accompanied by their children, including María. It is likely that they

FIGURE 1.2 Telesfora Forte Navarrete on her wedding day. Featured in Albert Buehman's "Arizona Album," *Citizen*, May 27, 1955, 6. This image is a reproduction from the newspaper and is used with permission from © USA TODAY NETWORK via Imagn Images.

crossed the border to insulate themselves from the disturbances caused by the Mexican Revolution, although no family member ever discussed this monumental event. Local newspapers from that time indicate that the Southern Pacific Railroad was in need of labor and may have recruited Antonio because of his skills and experience. This need for labor coincided with a strike by Mexican railroad workers in January 1911, suggesting that the Navarretes' decision to relocate was also influenced by economic opportunities in the United States.[12] They were only one of the numerous families who left Mexico to move north during this time looking for work and stability.

Although the Navarrete family arrived in Tucson nearly fifty years after the Gadsden Purchase, their migration patterns offer a unique perspective on transnational movement in the nineteenth and early twentieth centuries. María's father's work on the railroad increased his mobility and allowed him to navigate the region with relative ease. Additionally, her maternal and paternal families were notably mobile, crisscrossing Sonora to visit relatives and forming attachments to various locations. This ongoing back-and-forth travel reflects a less rigid conception of borders, showing how the Navarrete family experienced the region as a fluid and interconnected space. As Gloria Anzaldúa writes, "Borders are set up to define the places that are safe and unsafe, to distinguish *us* from *them*."[13] In María Cordova's stories, which will be examined more fully in the next chapter, the boundaries between Sonora, Mexico, and Tucson often blur, folding time and place into a more integrated regional experience shaped by mobility, privilege, and her gendered perspective.

The perspectives of people from different class backgrounds on what "nation" meant to them at the turn of the century remain relatively unexplored. Around 1926, Mexican anthropologist Manuel Gamio interviewed more than one hundred immigrants about their experiences crossing the border and living in the United States, including a few from Tucson.

Because these men came from lower socioeconomic backgrounds and were used to construct "a sort of generalized Mexican immigrant," the interviews revealed little about how they understood the relationship between the two nations.[14] The interview questions reinforced a binary view of the U.S. and Mexico, framing the U.S. as the other side or "*el otro lado*." This approach erased the historical, cultural, and social connections that many migrants maintained across the border, promoting instead the idea that each nation was a distinct and self-contained reality. That framework differs from the way María Cordova and her family experienced the region.

At the same time, the arrival of people from south of the border during the same period changed the demographics of Tucson. According to anthropologist Thomas Sheridan, "During the first decade of the twentieth century, Tucson's foreign-born Hispanic population increased by only 270 individuals, or 12.4 percent. Between 1910 and 1920, however, the number of Hispanics born outside the U.S. rose from 2,441 to 4,261, a growth of nearly 75 percent. The Revolution clearly swelled Tucson's Mexican community."[15] Unlike these legions of migrants, some of whom we can rightfully refer to as refugees, as an adult, María's economic privilege afforded her the confidence to openly retain and express her cultural identity in ways that may have been more difficult for many working-class migrants.[16]

Tía Cuca (Refugio Dias)

Despite being two generations older, Refugio Dias, who was Telesfora Fort's aunt, became a pivotal figure in María Cordova's life. María and her great-great-aunt developed a lasting closeness, and María often referred to her affectionately as Tía Cuca, a diminutive form of Refugio. Born in 1855, Refugio was also from San Miguel de Horcasitas.[17] In English-speaking contexts, the name Refugio might be perceived as male, but it is deeply rooted in Mexican religious and cultural traditions. Names like Refugio, Socorro, and Rosario are traditionally unisex in Spanish-speaking cultures and have strong ties to Catholicism. Refugio is derived from "María del Refugio," meaning "Mary of Refuge," one of the titles of the Virgin Mary.

By 1877, Refugio Días was living in Tucson. Whether she moved there with her family remains unclear, but at least one brother and one sister also eventually settled in the city.[18] At the time, enough binational residents, connected by family and history to Sonora, lived in Tucson to support a Spanish-language newspaper, *Las Dos Repúblicas*. The paper's title reflected the unity and continuity of the binational territory. Two years later, another newspaper, *El Fronterizo*, emerged, further highlighting borderlands news and experiences.[19]

Manuel Carrillo

In 1877, a justice of the peace in the Territory of Arizona married Refugio Díaz and Manuel Carrillo. Little is known about their life together, but in the 1970s, preservationists researching the couple located a marriage certificate documenting the union, which had taken place in Tucson.[20] A decade earlier, in 1960, María Cordova sent a letter to the Tucson mayor and city council claiming that she owned the land that once included the old presidio and much of central Tucson. This claim, which will be discussed further in Chapter 3, was based on the 1877 marriage.[21]

María Cordova claimed that Manuel Carrillo had inherited a Spanish land grant from his father and held extensive property in Tucson prior to the Gadsden Purchase. According to her version of events, Carrillo's holdings included all the presidio and most of what would later become central Tucson. She also credited him with not only owning but building the original and oldest rooms of what would eventually become her home, later known as La Casa Cordova.

María's version of history had the potential to disrupt established property ownership, and despite preservationists' efforts in the 1970s, they were unable to uncover any documentation regarding Manuel Carrillo. After the marriage record was located, one preservationist wrote, "What you have turned up [the marriage certificate] is very interesting and only makes the mystery of the Cordova claim all the stranger. María Cordova was related to Refugio and not Manuel Carrillo, as the family claims."[22]

This statement in itself reflects the narrow and patriarchal influences from which preservationists conceptualized the chain of property ownership. Yes, María was related to Refugio, not Manuel Carrillo, but that distinction overlooks a key legal fact: Arizona Territory followed community property law. This meant that after their marriage, Refugio legally owned half of Manuel's assets, unless a prenuptial agreement had been drafted beforehand, which was highly unlikely in 1877.[23]

Preservationists also sought to establish a kinship link between Manuel and Leopoldo Carrillo, the most well-known and at one time wealthiest Carrillo in Tucson's history books. After all, they shared a last name. Born in 1836, Leopoldo moved to Tucson from his native Sonora around

1863. He became an entrepreneur and would go on to own more than a hundred properties and build the city's first two-story office building.[24] Preservationists searched through probate records of Carrillo family members to see if any connection could be made to Manuel. Despite their efforts, they failed to confirm any linkages with Leopoldo.[25]

While María Cordova's legal claims raised important questions about property and inheritance in the late nineteenth century, *Storied Property* is not an attempt to resolve those claims. It is a historical examination of the forces that shaped them. Preservationists in the 1970s, preoccupied with this issue, spent years toiling over documents and records and even conducted interviews concerning Refugio's connection to Manuel.[26] They were unable to track down a birth or death certificate, or any trace of Manuel's life beyond his marriage to Refugio.

Preservationists also looked at census records, but Manuel does not appear in the 1860, 1870, or 1880 reports. City directories were also examined, and all the research they conducted led researchers to surmise, "The conclusion can be reached that Carrillo arrived in Tucson after 1870 and died before 1880. There is no record of a will or probate of his estate."[27]

Research methods have advanced since then, and a more recent digital newspaper search revealed that Refugio and Manuel divorced in 1885.[28] This recent finding was unexpected and raises new questions about their relationship and the property agreements made at the time of their divorce. Under Arizona Territory's community property law, all property acquired during the marriage would have been jointly owned. Upon the divorce, Refugio was legally entitled to retain half of those shared assets and possibly more if such terms were agreed upon. That she maintained a higher standard of living than most women at the time suggests she may have negotiated favorable terms or retained access to significant property or resources.

Manuel Carrillo remains missing from all known and searchable records, even in an era of expanded online databases. There is no evidence indicating that Manuel married again, had children, acquired property, served on a jury, or voted. This is unusual and raises several questions. Did he leave Arizona and abandon the marriage? Did his absence lead to the divorce, or did he die soon afterward as preservationists assumed? If no will existed, Refugio could have retained or claimed additional property, especially if there were no children or direct heirs on Manuel's side.

Arizona Territory in the 1880s did not have comprehensive or centralized recordkeeping. Land transfers, wills, and property divisions were often informal or never documented. If Manuel died outside Arizona without a will and left no heirs, Refugio may have simply remained in possession. In the absence of a legal challenge or an heir to contest the estate, there was no need to initiate probate proceedings, which would explain the lack of official records. Decades later, María Cordova recognized the silences and contradictions in these records. The chapters that follow explore how she used absences in the record as evidence. Rather than relying on the archive to validate her claims, she worked with what was missing to construct her stories.

Refugio Rambaud: Owner of Three Houses on North Meyer Avenue

The official record offers little insight into what became of Manuel Carrillo, but Refugio's life continued. She resumed using her maiden name and, sometime afterward, met Severin Rambaud, a French-born businessman who was then regarded as an eligible and well-established member of Tucson's growing merchant class. Rambaud operated a French bakery and had invested in both real estate and cattle ranching. In 1884, he purchased a house at the corner of North Meyer Avenue and Washington Street. He likely regarded Refugio as a suitable partner for someone of his social and economic standing (see Figure 1.3).

When they married in 1892, they made their home at 203 North Meyer Avenue. A distant relative later recalled it as a "well furnished, comfortable house filled with books . . . The living room was in the northeast corner with a window facing Washington . . . There were lots of flowers and trees, but no walled patio. There was a front porch on Meyer Street and a picket fence south along Meyer. Mr. Rambaud kept his horses in a

FIGURE 1.3 Refugio and Severin Rambaud. Undated photograph. Courtesy of the TMA Research Library.

corral in the back of the house."[29] They had no children of their own but spent the next twenty-six years together.[30]

Severin died in 1918 and left half of his property and income to Refugio. The other half was left to his niece and sisters in France. He bequeathed twelve properties to Refugio. After his death, she began selling off some of his assets and properties. A few years later, she built a new house for herself on an empty lot between the home she had shared with Severin and the house they had purchased after their marriage at 173 North Meyer Avenue, which would later become known as La Casa Cordova (see Figure 1.4).[31]

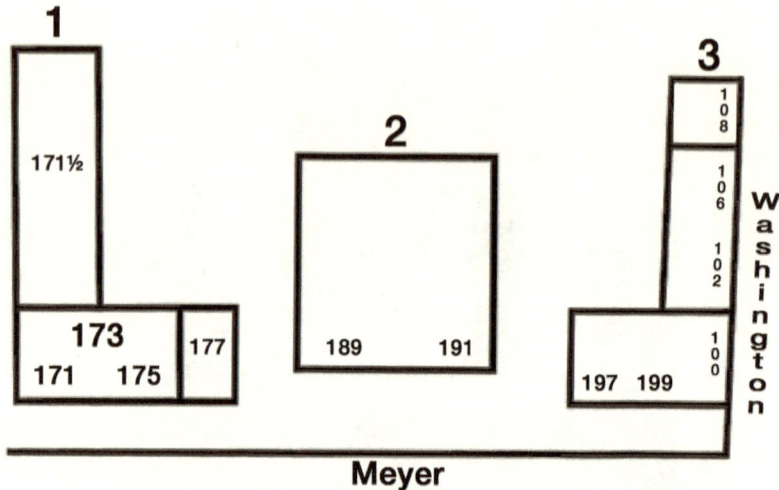

FIGURE 1.4 (1) María Cordova's home at 171–177 North Meyer Avenue. Now known as La Casa Cordova. (2) The house Refugio Rambaud built for herself no longer stands. It was condemned and demolished during urban renewal, but there is no paper trail indicating when the decision was made, what justified it, or whether it was the City of Tucson or the Tucson Museum of Art that authorized it. (3) The addresses associated with this building have changed over time. When Severin and Refugio lived in the larger house facing Meyer Avenue, the address was 203 North Meyer, and they rented the apartments on Washington Street. The city later amended the addresses and listed the property as 197–199 North Meyer Avenue. Through additions, the structure evolved into an L-shaped form. The Tucson Museum of Art, entrusted with the structure after 1972, designated it the Romero House, with the current address 102 W. Washington Street. For simplicity, this book refers to it as the house or apartments on the corner of Meyer and Washington. Address information was drawn from the 1947 Sanborn Fire Insurance Map, Block 183.

Deciding to move forward and supervise the construction of a new home for herself speaks to Refugio's enterprising spirit. Even in her sixties, she wanted something new and different. Still, Refugio seemed to live an active life and enjoyed being surrounded by flowers and trees. Her home was well-furnished and described as "wealthy" by some. She was also said to have "lots of books." A seamstress made her clothing, and she owned "beautiful jewelry." Refugio "loved to dress up" and would rent "a covered carriage drawn by two horses for special outings."[32]

It is important to note that although Severin left her several properties, she chose to remain on a block she knew and felt connected to. She built her house at 189 North Meyer Avenue, just south of the one she had shared with Severin. Astute in business, Refugio constructed two units. She lived in one for the rest of her life and earned rental income from the adjoining unit, as well as from her property at the corner of Washington and Meyer Avenue and from the house at 173 North Meyer Avenue. She rented the houses as apartments and also leased some of them to businesses. Photographs of the house Refugio built are rare. The cover image of this book offers a glimpse. It is the house to the right of what is now known as La Casa Cordova.

Family Ties and Neighbors

In 1923, Refugio suffered a great loss when her niece, Telesfora, died. Telesfora was only around fifty, and her death certificate indicates that she had battled cancer for at least two years. Telesfora's daughter, María, was with her at the time of death and is listed as the informant on the certificate. Initially, Telesfora's race or color was recorded as "Latin," but this was later crossed out and amended to read "Mexican."[33]

Unfortunately for Refugio, her goddaughter and niece María, whom she felt close to, left Tucson to marry. In 1924, María Navarrete married Raul H. Cordova in Phoenix on Christmas Eve.[34] They had five children: Raul Jr., Alfred, María Dolores, Arturo, and Fernando.

By 1931, having been widowed by the loss of his wife Telesfora, Antonio Navarrete, María's father, moved into one of Refugio's apartments

FIGURE 1.5 Severin and Refugio Rambaud lived in the larger house facing Meyer Avenue, formerly addressed as 197–199 North Meyer. They rented out the apartments on Washington Street. After 1972, the Tucson Museum of Art took responsibility for the structure and designated the entire L-shaped building the Romero House. The address is now 102 West Washington Street. La Casa Cordova is located to the left on Meyer Avenue in this 2025 photograph. Courtesy of Mauro Trejo.

at 108 West Washington Street (see Figure 1.5). That also meant he and Refugio remained in contact and now lived as neighbors, within walking distance of each other. We get a glimpse into their lives and what was on their minds in 1931 through the recollections of Arturo W. Jacobs, a member of a long-established Tucsonense family. That year, Jacobs visited Antonio's apartment to provide notary services. According to Jacobs, Navarrete was ill and wanted it to be known "that he was born in California and was an American citizen and that while working on the construction of the Nogales-Guaymas railroad several of his children were born in Mexico and that he wanted me to prepare an affidavit for him to sign to establish the American citizenship of his children." In the affidavit that Jacobs later filed in court, Antonio Navarrete swore that he was born in the city of Sonoma, California, in 1862.[35]

While attending to this issue with Antonio, Jacobs received word that Refugio, who lived in the brick house next door, was also in need of his services. He went to her house, where Refugio asked him to prepare a will because she wanted to "bequeath a house" to her *ahijada*, or goddaughter, María Cordova, who was living in Phoenix. Jacobs advised her that she needed more than a notary and suggested that she contact a lawyer.[36]

Antonio Navarrete passed away a year after notarizing his affidavit. He died in his apartment at 108 West Washington Street.[37] Refugio Rambaud also died a few years later, in 1934, in the house she had built. When she died, the *Citizen* published a brief article noting that after moving from Mexico, she had lived in Tucson for fifty-four years.[38] The other local paper, the *Arizona Daily Star*, also ran a short piece mentioning the pending funeral arrangements and reporting that she was 86 years old.[39] Refugio Rambaud's death certificate, however, listed her age as "about 79."[40] These discrepancies in her reported age foreshadowed later claims that she had lived to be over 100.

Passing on Property and Legacy

Not much about Refugio's funeral services appeared in the papers, but her passing gained attention due to the legal disputes surrounding her wills. Refugio left behind two: one dated twelve days before her death and another drawn up more than a year earlier, which named María Cordova as the beneficiary.[41] As a reminder, according to notary Arturo Jacobs, Refugio had expressed her wish to pass on her house to María three years before she died.

The earlier will was contested, leading to final legal arrangements negotiated by the family and their lawyers. As a result, the brick house at 189 North Meyer Avenue and the adjoining unit, where Refugio had lived, were left to her nephew Roberto Lopez. The house at 173 North Meyer Avenue, which would later become known as La Casa Cordova, was transferred to María Cordova's minor son, Arturo. Additionally, María inherited Refugio's personal belongings and the property at the corner of Washington Street and Meyer Avenue.[42]

After inheriting the two properties, María Cordova returned to Tucson with her children. On behalf of Arturo and as his guardian, she rented out the house at 173 North Meyer Avenue, which had long been

FIGURE 1.6 Advertisement for Arizona Zarape Restaurant, emphasizing its Mexican cuisine and location near City Hall. *Star,* February 2, 1940, 11.

subdivided into apartments, and moved into the house bequeathed to her at the corner of Washington Street and Meyer Avenue.⁴³ In 1939, she established a restaurant in that corner house, called the Arizona Zarape (see Figure 1.6).⁴⁴

In 1940, they moved into a section of 173 North Meyer Avenue, which María always claimed as her home. She leased out smaller rooms and eventually established another business there. As María Cordova embraced her new role as head of the household and manager of her properties, she also began formalizing a divorce from her husband, Raul. The two houses Refugio had entrusted to her became both her livelihood and a key part of her legacy. The rooms that would become known as La Casa Cordova were rented out to a photographer and to a series of bail bond offices, including Abe Salcido Bail Bonds. Well-known band leader Filiberto M. Quintero also operated a shoe-repair shop there until 1948.⁴⁵ The energy and effort María invested in maintaining, and even enhancing, the value of her house at 173 North Meyer Avenue were unmatched.

The film: *Arizona*

In 1940, as María Cordova and her family settled into their new home, Columbia Pictures was finalizing the production of their film *Arizona*. They were filming it just outside Tucson's city limits, at a studio designed to resemble what the filmmakers imagined to be the "rugged frontier town" of Tucson in 1860.[46] Most of the scenes in the film were set inside a replica of the presidio built on the movie set. To generate local excitement, Columbia teamed up with the *Star* for a "Pioneer Derby," a contest where winners would receive a signed book of the novel *Arizona* by Clarence Budington Kelland and tickets to the film's premiere.[47]

Characters in the film were fictional but loosely inspired by actual local figures. In order to be eligible to enter the derby, participants had to claim kinship with one of the characters in *Arizona*.[48] This mythmaking contest, much like the film itself, became a source of pride for longtime residents. But it also sidelined anyone who did not fit the version of Tucson's past that white settlers and Hollywood chose to celebrate.

This "Pioneer Derby" stands out because it documented the first time María Cordova stepped out into the public realm to talk about history. The unnamed reporter did not explain how they found or approached María, but it is clear they had a detailed conversation. She shared details about her family's deep roots in Tucson, but her story did not align with the contest's definition of a "pioneer." The *Star* declared she was ineligible for the derby because she was not related "to any of the venerable settlers of Tucson about to be immortalized" in the film.[49]

Arizona promoted a different vision of frontier identity, one centered on a new, fictional pioneer: Phoebe Titus. She served as an archetype of the white frontier woman who could outshoot, outsmart, and outlast the men around her. She was depicted as the only white woman in Tucson, boldly declaring her intention to stay, no matter the cost. At one point, she shames the men for doubting their resolve to remain in Tucson by asking, "You want to give what we built back to the Indians?" Filmmakers cast Phoebe Titus as a symbol of advancing civilization and the moral authority of Manifest Destiny.

As the only white woman in the Arizona Territory, Titus embodies the domestication of the frontier, the resistance against Indigenous presence, and the dual roles of fictionalized strength and nurturing, making her an idealized figure of the pioneer spirit. She saw Tucson as a place with tremendous growth potential, one that would always need more of everything: goods, cattle, and supplies. She dreamily reflected on the future, imagining the time when the railroad would bring in thousands more "real American" families.

People of color in the film are passive, existing primarily to serve the white characters. They are essential to the story as it establishes the legitimacy of the settlers' actions and reinforces the idea of bringing "civilization" to a land already inhabited by others. The filmmakers made it a point to highlight the Tohono O'odham as peaceful toward the white settlers and emphasize their hatred for the Apaches. Estevan Ochoa, one of the few named Mexican characters, appears fleetingly as part of a group of men who show up to listen and support the heroine. Ochoa is acknowledged as a capable freighter, efficiently running a hauling business with wagons pulled by large teams of mules, oxen, or horses, and as one who does not "gouge" his customers. But Phoebe Titus and the main merchant in the film, Solomon Warner, choose not to rely on him. Instead, they start their own freighting business, confident that the demand for goods and cattle in Tucson will continue to grow.

In contrast to Phoebe Titus's character, Cordova offered the *Star* another heroine: her great-aunt Refugio. She also shared information about a house that was not part of a fictionalized set but built before the Gadsden Purchase that still stood inside the original walls of the presidio.

Clearly, Cordova succeeded in getting a reporter to take note of her and had accomplished being seen as a figure worthy of recounting history. According to the paper, María recounted that Refugio had moved from Mexico and "became a beloved figure of early-day Tucson."[50] But the history she offered, and the heroine she introduced, were dismissed. It becomes apparent that Cordova felt the need to strengthen Refugio's story by anchoring it further back in time to match the mythic narratives circulating in the city and in the popular film. The contest rules and public emphasis on early white settlement had created a standard she felt compelled not just to meet but to exceed. To place Refugio inside the presidio in 1850, before the Gadsden Purchase and before the Civil War, Cordova claimed that Refugio, who died only six years earlier in 1934, had lived to be over one hundred years old.

Stretching the Timeline

This departure from fact had long been used as a tactic to assert that certain lives deserved to be recognized as historically significant. One such example was the case of Mariana Dias, which received extensive coverage and attention. In 1880, one of Tucson's leading white citizens, Samuel Hughes, and the Governor of Arizona Territory, A. P. K. Safford, interviewed Dias, who claimed to be over one hundred years old.[51] The life expectancy for someone born in the 1880s was around thirty-nine years, and even lower for someone born in Mexico.[52] For someone claiming to be born in the 1780s, such longevity would have seemed more than miraculous.

In addition to claiming to be 100 years old, Mariana Dias also stated that she had lived inside the presidio. She described life during the era of New Spain, noting that the surrounding fields were productive, meat was abundant, and most goods came from Sonora. Her account focused largely on Apache depredations and violence, which fit the type of narrative Hughes and Safford favored, where white settlement was portrayed as the force that brought order, protection, and progress to the region. Dias expressed gratitude for men like Hughes who, she said, kept Tucson safe. Hughes and Safford did not attempt to verify her age. They never asked when or where she was born, the names of her parents, or any of the basic questions that might have substantiated her claim. Instead, they offered the local paper only the parts of her account they found interesting. What appeared in print was not a direct transcription of her words.[53]

Mariana Dias's tactic of exaggerating her age functioned as a strategic maneuver by a Mexican woman seeking social leverage within an exclusionary white, male-dominated society. Her actions were a form of identity performance, in which she used her claimed longevity and presumed wisdom to influence those in power. Similarly, María Cordova employed a comparable strategy by asserting that Refugio Rambaud was over 100 years old. While these claims do not withstand historical scrutiny, such calculated moves allowed both women to be seen and heard within a system that was not built for them, a system that routinely dismissed or undervalued their voices and experiences.

A Family Business: Cordova Brothers Smoke Shop

The Cordovas continued to live at 173 North Meyer Avenue, and in 1951, María's sons established the Cordova Brothers Smoke Shop in the front south portion of their house, facing Meyer Avenue. It operated until 1971. While the extent of María's involvement in managing the business is not entirely clear, it is reasonable to assume she was the driving force behind it, and that she also played a central role in orchestrating the house's change of ownership the following year.

In 1952, the future Casa Cordova changed ownership once again. Arturo, now an adult, transferred the title of the house to his eldest brother, Raul, who was around 27 years old. By that time, Raul had served in the Navy during World War II and was attending college. His interest in law allowed him to oversee the legal aspects of the transfer. No funds were exchanged between the brothers. The Cordova Brothers Smoke Shop provided financial stability during this period, especially for Raul, who went on to attend law school.[54]

It is possible that Arturo's early ownership served as a legal placeholder, likely because as a child he could legally inherit under certain probate conditions. Given María's conservative values and close relationship with her eldest son, Raul, she may have always intended for him to take over the house once he was ready. Despite opportunities for career advancement, Raul remained closely tied to the family home and business. Rather than pursuing other paths, he stayed involved in the smoke shop and maintained his connection to his mother and the house he now legally owned.

Before the rise of convenience stores, smoke shops served as essential fixtures in many neighborhoods. These establishments specialized primarily in tobacco products such as cigarettes, cigars, and pipe tobacco. Unlike grocery stores, smoke shops did not stock a wide range of groceries but sometimes provided essential items like bread and milk. They kept longer hours, opening earlier and closing later than their grocery counterparts. The Cordova Brothers Smoke Shop was known for selling sodas, individually wrapped ice cream, and snacks, which allowed them to maintain quicker service. Chatting with María or other members of the Cordova family behind the counter added a personal touch. Additionally, it featured rotating racks of comic books and the local papers.

Today's urban planners would refer to this as placemaking. "Placemaking" describes practices where people use their homes, storefronts, and sidewalks to claim visibility and shape community life.[55] By operating a business out of their home, the Cordovas were anchoring themselves in the neighborhood's daily rhythm. That the entire family lived there only deepened their presence and visibility in the area (see Figure 1.7) This arrangement blurred the lines between family life and public interaction, creating a lived space that was active, familiar, and deeply rooted.

The Cordova Brothers Smoke Shop also played a practical role in how the family remained informed and connected. The small establishment was more than just a retail space. Its location near city hall, the police department, and other government offices made it a community hub where local news and gossip were actively exchanged. Police officers, lawyers, civic administrators, judges, individuals on their way to pay fines, those serving on jury duty, and elected officials all frequented the Cordova Brothers Smoke Shop. The shop's strategic location enhanced its role in facilitating the flow of information and keeping the Cordovas connected to political news and city developments. While managing customers and the cash register, María and her children listened to conversations and engaged in discussions with individuals who were knowledgeable about the city's future and plans. Working long hours expanded the Cordovas' connectivity as they formed relationships with influential city employees, police, and even judges. They may have

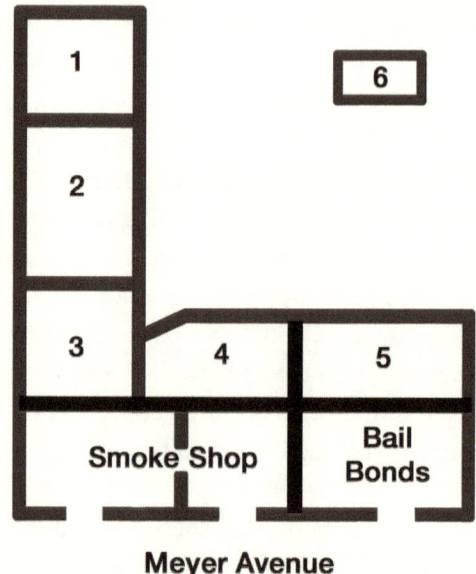

FIGURE 1.7 Layout of the Cordova residence in the mid-1950s shows how the family lived and worked at 173 North Meyer Avenue. Rooms 1 through 5 made up the Cordova living quarters. Room 1 stands out as the oldest, while rooms 4 and 5 were torn down by preservationists after 1972. Room 6, the detached structure, was used by the Cordovas as a storage room.

addressed them on a first-name basis and inquired about issues of interest, particularly those relating to their family properties and the changes they witnessed in their neighborhood.

Conclusion: Refusing the Background

When official histories, mainstream narratives, or Pioneer Derbies failed to acknowledge or validate the experiences and contributions of marginalized communities, it required people like María Cordova to seek alternative ways to ensure their stories were heard and remembered. Even in this instance, the *Star's* treatment of Cordova and Refugio Rambaud reveals the forces that relegated them to obscurity. Rather than including them in the pioneer fold, or even omitting them entirely, the *Star* reduced them to background figures, part of what the paper described as "the set."[56] In doing so, it cast their lives not as contributions to Tucson's history, but as decorative detail meant to enhance the architecture or environment. They were framed as supporting characters in someone else's story, present but peripheral, visible but stripped of significance.

In the years that followed Pioneer Derby, more journalists were drawn to Cordova's histories and found them compelling enough to print. From her perspective, enhancing her stories, such as claiming that Refugio lived to be over 100 years old, was part of a strategy to make her claims more relevant and capture attention. In contrast, events like the film *Arizona*, the Pioneer Derby, and other celebrations of white settlers relied on unchallenged embellishment. Those who crafted these narratives were hailed as resourceful and forward-thinking. Living within a settler colonial framework, Cordova could not openly name the dynamics at play, but she witnessed how the dominant culture manipulated stories to elevate its own past while silencing hers. In 1940, she felt the sting of her history being diminished and deliberately excluded. That experience shaped her approach to storytelling. Over time, she developed a more personal and intimate way of presenting her history.

CHAPTER 2

Location! Location! Location!

María Navarrete Cordova's historical accounts and personal reflections positioned her and her home at the heart of a broader geography that transcended the geopolitical boundaries separating the U.S. and Mexico, as well as those between Arizona and California. She envisioned a unified region, with her home at 173 North Meyer Avenue, located within the walls of the old presidio, serving as the focal point of this transborder landscape. She often found ways to leverage the symbolic location of her home and used her living room as a podium or stage to articulate the significance of her and her family's contributions to history, as journalists recorded and circulated her claims. Cordova lived in a house steeped in history, and she drew on this connection to remind others that she had been anointed to live there and to defend it.

The advantages of living in this prime historic location also made the Cordova properties vulnerable to the pressures of urban development. Living near downtown and City Hall generally benefited the Cordova Brothers Smoke Shop, ensuring a steady flow of foot traffic. Yet the growing demand for land to construct new high-rise buildings and parking lots in the old neighborhood placed their property in a precarious position, threatening the stability of María Cordova's home, business, and rental income.

Inside the Walls of the Old Presidio

Established in 1775, this presidio was not just a military outpost but a strategic installation that secured Spanish interests in the northern frontier.¹ The new settlers learned essential survival skills from the Tohono O'odham and other local tribes, adapting their practices to thrive in the challenging environment. As environmental and ethnographic historian Cynthia Radding reminds us, the arid lands of the Sonoran Desert were not barren and empty before the arrival of the Spanish. Indigenous peoples had long inhabited the region. Radding notes:

> Indigenous perceptions of their environment were rooted in the landscapes they had produced in the course of pursuing subsistence strategies, requiring access to a wide range of resources and ecological spaces. Their dwelling places in the floodplains, cultivated with rainfall or seasonal flooding, using techniques for channeling and draining water . . . [foraging] plants for medicines, food, building materials, and fibers, also provided the basis for creating historical memories . . .²

The Spanish positioned their presidio in Tucson to align with their own tactical interests, but did so by drawing directly on Indigenous knowledge about the land. The new presidio was intentionally situated on slightly elevated terrain near the Santa Cruz River to take advantage of natural defenses and agricultural activities. Archaeological evidence indicates that the Hohokam (ancestors of today's O'odham) had established a "large, sprawling village" and lived on the same site where the Spanish built their presidio in Tucson.³

While learning from the local Indians to survive in the desert, the Spanish settlers formed alliances with the Sobaipuri O'odham and Tohono O'odham to address conflicts with Apache bands. The first settlers, soldiers, their families, and missionaries formed a nascent agricultural community. The high adobe walls served as a defensive barrier (see Figure 2.1).⁴ While the presidio itself primarily functioned as a military structure, it played a supportive role in the broader colonial strategy by offering protection for missionaries who had arrived in the area as far back as 1698 and continued working in the region. This dual role underscored the Spanish Crown's broader colonial objectives to counter European rivals, secure trade routes, spread Christianity, and exploit local resources.⁵

FIGURE 2.1 Interpretive drawing of the Tucson presidio by Frank C. Lockwood and Donald W. Page. From *Tucson—The Old Pueblo* (Phoenix: The Manufacturing Stationers, Inc., 1930).

As the nineteenth century advanced, life in the presidio adapted to shifting colonial power dynamics. The early 1800s brought the decline of Spanish authority, and the Mexican War of Independence led to a realignment of governance. By the 1820s, Tucson fell under Mexican control, which meant new administrative and economic policies. This era also saw heightened tensions with Apache groups and funding reductions for the presidio.[6]

The transition to U.S. control following the Gadsden Purchase Treaty of 1853 brought accelerated change to Tucson. It is important to note that this shift in national sovereignty was marked by an unusually extended period of Mexican governance. December 30, 1853, marked the official land transfer according to the treaty. It was ratified a few months later, on June 8, 1854. Mexican troops, however, remained in Tucson for almost two more years, until 1856.[7]

Businesses and homes had begun to slowly spread beyond the presidio walls before the change in sovereignty. Mexicans had already started establishing homes, laying out streets, and creating new plazas that radiated mainly in a southern direction outward from the presidio. By the 1850s, Hilario Gallego, who was born inside the presidio, recalled that "... Theodore Ramirez had a store inside of the wall and there was also a saloon kept by Burruel Juan. He sold mescal only. The saloon and some stores were inside the wall. And there were a few stores on the outside."[8]

The U.S. military presence attracted more settlers, but around 1860, according to geographers, the town still retained its Sonoran character: "There is little evidence in the street pattern to suggest that [1860s] Tucson was anything but a rural Mexican village in spite of the early influx of Anglos."[9] Thus, it remained a largely rural town of mostly Mexicans living in houses clustered around the presidio and along the banks of the Santa Cruz River.

These settlement patterns are clearly evident in Tucson's first map, drawn at the direction of David Fergusson. It reveals Tucson's cultural continuity with Spanish colonial and Mexican influences through street names such as *Calle de la India Triste* (Street of the Sad Indian Woman) and *Calle de la Alegría* (Happiness Street). *El Camino Real* (Royal Road) spanned the west side of the former presidio and connected the once outlying fort with Sonora.[10] The Fergusson Map of 1862 (see Figure 2.2) also illustrates the new homes and businesses that had been established in a southward direction toward the La Plaza de La Mesilla and west toward the Santa Cruz River.

Interestingly, although Meyer Street was not yet laid out, two rooms resembling the layout of María Cordova's house at 173 North Meyer Avenue appear on the upper northeast corner of the 1862 Fergusson map. This detail confirms that the house's age extends back before 1862.

Charles Meyer and the Rewards of White Settler Privilege

Born in Germany, Charles H. Meyer arrived in Tucson in 1857, when 300 people lived in the presidio.[11] Despite speaking with a thick accent, the thirty-year-old Meyer was viewed as part of the white settler class. Thus, he was granted privileges and roles denied to Indians and most Mexicans. These racial distinctions were shaped by the logic of Manifest Destiny, which was underpinned by beliefs in the superiority of Anglo-Saxon and Northern European peoples. Immigrants from France and Germany, like Meyer, were perceived as racially close to the dominant white Anglo-American population.[12]

Meyer fully embraced his whiteness, as did others from the dominant culture. Despite his thick accent, other white settlers viewed him as

FIGURE 2.2 Close-up of a section from the 1862 Fergusson Map, available at the Arizona Historical Society, highlighting the structure preservationists contend is La Casa Cordova. An arrow has been added to number 80. In the 1970s, preservationists claimed that this early adobe structure was later built upon and incorporated into what became La Casa Cordova. This interpretation appears in Judith Hunt and Junior League of Tucson, *The Restoration of La Casa Cordova* (Tucson: Junior League of Tucson, Inc., 1978), 8. The 1862 map of Tucson by David Fergusson. (Courtesy Arizona Historical Society, Tucson).

attempting to assimilate linguistically and regarded his accent as a temporary barrier. In contrast, Mexicans, often of mixed Indigenous and European ancestry, were seen as clinging to their native Spanish language, which was interpreted as a refusal to assimilate. This is only one example of how white settlers' perceptions prevented most Mexicans from achieving a more privileged status. Geographer Laura Pulido describes white supremacy as "a set of attitudes, values, and practices emanating from the idea and practice that white people and Europe are of greater value than people and places deemed nonwhite and nonEuropean and are entitled to a great share of society's power and resources."[13] Meyer's ability to hold the position of Justice of the Peace without formal qualifications reflected the era's norms of favoring white settlers in positions of authority and allowed men like Meyer to institute the chain gang, where those accused of minor offenses were chained together and forced to perform hard labor, such as road construction and ditch digging.[14] This labor ultimately benefited those in power.

Local histories often portray Meyer as an enduring and quirky character, overlooking his role in shaping the mechanisms of settler colonialism. When dispensing justice, Bernice Cosulich, a journalist and historian, noted that "he had no legal training or knowledge, but plenty of 'horse sense.'" Regarding his professionalism, she added that "Judge Meyer was a social person, and pioneers have recalled that often he adjourned court to patronize a saloon, where he paid for the drinks with money just collected in fines."[15]

Claiming Streets, Claiming Authority

According to a newspaper account from 1890, Charles Meyer established Meyer Street just three years after his arrival in 1862. At that time, the paper described Tucson as a place where "law was a thing unknown, and almost the only government was 'everyman for himself.'" Such descriptions framed the city as a lawless frontier, justifying the strong-arm tactics used by men like Meyer and elevating them as necessary civic actors rather than opportunists. As is typical of settler narratives, men like Meyer were seen as clever. He "envisioned the need for such a thoroughfare," and he made it happen. Meyer laid out the street and "hired three Mexicans" to drive posts into the ground, declaring Meyer Street a public thoroughfare. A few, described by the paper as "squatters living in the vicinity," objected and built a fence across the street, blocking it and protecting their homes. However, "Meyer & Co.," who the paper did not bother to identify, but likely a powerful group aligned with the city's top law enforcer, quickly and "emphatically" removed the fence. Their strong-armed actions prevented any future attempts to obstruct the street. In time, it "became one of the principal thoroughfares of Tucson."[16]

Notably, the self-serving business motivation behind Meyer's actions is often overlooked in nostalgic remembrances of him, even though the street led directly to his drugstore a few blocks south on *Calle de la Alegría* (Congress). There are conflicting reports regarding when Meyer built the first drugstore in Tucson, leaving the question muddled as to whether the street or the building came first. Locals began referring to it as *La Botica*, but when his daughter took it over, she called it Fleishman's Drug Store. The store ultimately closed in 1935.[17]

Charles Meyer exploited his business acumen by strategically locating his drugstore facing *Calle de la Alegría*. He established his new business at what was quickly becoming the burgeoning hub of Tucson's evolving downtown. Congress Hall, built in 1868, stood across the street on the southwest corner from his drugstore, also facing *Calle de la Alegría*. This large saloon, which included gambling, was described as ". . . where the finest wines, liquors, and cigars were to be had."[18] It became the meeting place where new settlers strategized on facilitating Tucson's incorporation and securing priority access to federal funding that supported U.S. western expansion, including the Homestead Acts, railroad construction, military spending, telegraph expansion, irrigation projects, and land surveys.

Beyond reshaping Tucson's physical infrastructure and seeking recognition from Washington D.C., the new settlers prioritized renaming streets to mark their claim and assert their authority over the town. A 1923 news report titled "First Tucson Map Shows Mexicans Named Streets" referenced the earlier mentioned 1862 *Fergusson Map* to highlight how the new settlers changed street names shortly after their arrival. According to the newspaper, *Calle de la Alegría* was initially renamed Commercial Street for a brief period before being renamed again to Congress Street.[19] This latter change was intended to honor the numerous political rallies, mass meetings, and social functions held at Congress Hall. Subsequently, barbershops, cafes, hotels, additional saloons, and even the first public school were established on Congress Street, solidifying its status as the city's principal west-to-east commercial artery.

Meyer Street (Avenue): Tucson's Earliest Community Corridor

Despite its origins rooted in self-interest, Meyer Street also continued to evolve from north to south. It hosted new businesses and mixed-use establishments, commercial buildings that combined retail, office, and residential spaces, connecting the barrio south of Congress known as "La Calle" to downtown. Stone Avenue ran parallel to and east of Meyer. It also crossed downtown, but it was home to early car dealerships, banks, and hotels. Stone was intentionally designed to be a formal business corridor. The socioeconomic divides between the two streets became apparent, with Stone Avenue catering to wealthier clientele and Meyer Street providing household necessities and everyday services. Main Street also crossed but remained largely residential.

Although both Meyer and Stone evolved into vibrant thoroughfares, Meyer Street, in addition to fostering economic activity, welcomed working people who frequented the ethnically diverse cafes and small retail stores that dotted the street. Prior to the municipal buildings that stand today, City Hall housed the offices of the mayor, city manager, police chief, and also the jail. Its administrative offices, including those for paying parking tickets and water bills, were all located on North Meyer Street (see Figure 2.3).[20]

Looking back, Meyer Street stands as Tucson's earliest community corridor.[21] It crossed downtown, connecting neighborhoods to the north and south that shared many cultural similarities. Several service and commercial businesses emerged to satisfy the needs of barrio residents on South Meyer, including shoe repair shops, restaurants, *panaderías* (bakeries), grocery stores, many owned by Chinese Americans, tortilla factories, and meat markets. Jimmy's Chicken Shack also sponsored live jazz performances for African Americans.[22] On North Meyer, the El Rapido Tortilla Factory that opened in 1933 became known for selling the best tamales in the city and always attracted a devoted clientele.[23]

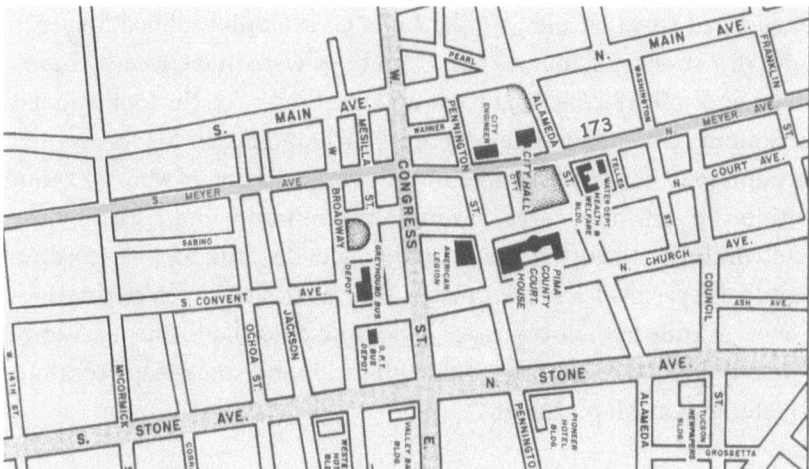

FIGURE 2.3 This pre-1965 map shows the Central Business District's main south-to-north streets. As shown, only three streets cross all the way through the area: Stone, Meyer, and Main. The author has highlighted Meyer Avenue and added "173" to North Meyer Avenue for reference.

Add to the list a beauty shop, Adobe House Jewelry and of course, the Cordova Brothers Smoke Shop.

Most of the homes and businesses that emerged on Meyer Street were built close to the street, ensuring it always remained rather narrow because there was no room to widen it. Meyer Street became a preferred route for locals who deliberately chose the more congested path because it held more interest and meaning. It attracted foot traffic and contributed significantly to the city's economic life. More than a commercial passageway, Meyer Street fostered cultural connections that spanned generations and supported Tucsonenses' social ties that extended beyond economic transactions. It also provided a route for those who lived in La Calle to venture north into a community much older than their own, where Tucson laid its roots.

The built environment also fueled the connection for barrio residents. Sonoran-style adobe architecture dominated Meyer Street on both sides of downtown. This visual continuity allowed residents to see that, as Tucson expanded, some cultural aspects remained constant. Adobe row house forms, characterized by flat roofs and lineal, unadorned street façades, similar to La Casa Cordova, lined Meyer in both directions. Of course, some buildings were influenced by newer styles and integrated gabled roofs and fire brick. Yet, the look and feel of Sonora remained visible on both North and South Meyer Avenue. Around 1970, urban renewal removed a large portion of Meyer Avenue within the downtown area, severing its continuity and creating dead ends on both its northern and southern ends. Still, for the Cordova family, Meyer held a special place. They consistently referred to it as Meyer Avenue in their correspondence and official documents. *Storied Property* follows their usage, although locals and some maps continue to refer to it as Meyer Street.

Invitation to the Inner Sanctum

Born in 1895, María Cordova grew up during a time when the delineation of public and private spaces for women was sharply defined. In Mexico, she learned that women's roles and behavior were shaped by strict conventions, particularly within the higher social classes where such customs were most ardently observed. Public spaces, including most workplaces, were typically reserved for men. Cordova took note of these gendered expectations and, in her later years in Tucson, invoked traditional customs to enhance her appeal to journalists and their readers. Despite her personal ambition and desire for visibility, she carefully portrayed herself as a dutiful domestic figure. Even as women's liberation made headlines in the United States, Cordova strategically managed her public persona to align with the gendered expectations of an earlier generation to mitigate perceptions that might portray her as a threat. When journalists met with her, they encountered a refined and knowledgeable transnational woman. This approach helped her secure an audience and a platform to express more radical ideas.

María Cordova often courted reporters and historians. She invited them into her home and offered a glimpse into her life and interior space. This act of welcoming outsiders allowed them to appreciate an environment she had carefully curated. She displayed paintings, historic photographs, a piano, and a collection of books. Cordova self-fashioned a transnational space that bridged an eventful family past with her present identity.²⁴ Inside her home, she became part of the ambiance. This careful presentation of both her home and herself allowed Cordova to push against the constraints of settler colonialism, even as she used its frameworks to subtly disrupt them.

Beginning in 1940, when she was featured in a story about the film *Arizona*, several newspaper articles about María Cordova appeared in the local press. None mentioned her speaking at public events. Instead, she chose to engage the public through print media. She often submitted letters and was a willing interviewee, choosing to tell her story only from within the walls of her home. She treated her history with care; like her home, it required safeguarding.

Although a section of her house served a commercial purpose, she only allowed special guests into her inner sanctum. When Cordova shared history with journalists and historians, it was one-on-one, as if sharing a secret. This type of exchange required reciprocity, and she gained confidants through these interactions. She formed a close relationship with renowned local photographer, politician, and former president of the Arizona Historical Society, Albert R. Buehman, that grew stronger over the years. He edited the "Arizona Album," a popular rectangular column that took up less than an eighth of a newspaper page but consistently drew attention for its black-and-white historical photograph paired with a brief narrative. Buehman's column ran regularly in the *Citizen*.

Albert R. Buehman

On October 18, 1951, Albert Buehman's column titled "Mary Navarrette Cordova" offered a compelling portrait of its subject. The accompanying photograph features an elegantly dressed Cordova sitting solemnly in the living room of her "101-year-old home" at 173 North Meyer Avenue. She is seated on a well-crafted wooden bench meant for two, with one side deliberately left empty, as if inviting readers to join her for a personal, one-on-one conversation (see Figure 2.4). Buehman refers to her as "one of Tucson's living historians," attributing to her a depth of knowledge that reaches back to the "early days of the Old Pueblo."²⁵

FIGURE 2.4 Referred to as Mary Navarette Cordova in the caption, María is pictured seated in her living room, as featured in Albert Buehman's "Arizona Album," *Citizen*, October 18, 1951. The Arizona Historical Society is in possession of a metal printing plate used to reproduce the image in the newspaper, but the original photograph is not preserved in local archives. This image is a reproduction from the newspaper and is used with permission from © USA TODAY NETWORK via Imagn Images.

In the "Arizona Album," María took the opportunity to share her personal connection to her house. She explained that she had inherited the home from her great aunt, Refugio, who had married Manuel Carrillo in 1877. According to María, Refugio—who later remarried—remained the heir to Manuel's property. Buehman never questioned this arrangement, possibly out of deference to María. He wrote, "Mrs. Refugio Díaz Carrillo Rambaud, whose first husband Manuel Carrillo inherited the property from his father and mother. They built the house [La Casa Cordova] in 1849."[26] This sequence of inheritances, spanning 101 years, may have seemed plausible to Buehman given Cordova's long-term residence in the house. This brief thread of information regarding Manuel Carrillo, barely part of the main story in 1951, would later take on greater significance in relation to the Cordova family.

Also in that short column, Buehman expressed admiration for an oil painting of the presidio that María had created, noting it was "based on her personal observations and on data given her by relatives now long dead." He described the painting as a "contribution" that offered insights, which he referred to as "new facts" regarding the old presidio wall and the location of a gate on its northeast corner. Reflecting on the barriers women of María's generation faced in pursuing art, curator Carolyn C. Robbins reminds us that "Earlier in the century, society often forced women to choose between living out their expected roles as wife, mother, and homemaker, or fulfilling their artistic impulses. Society either categorized women's artwork as a hobby or placed it in a submissive position with minor arts and crafts."[27]

Buehman ended his summary by noting that Cordova's children, including Raul, a Navy veteran, ran the Smoke Shop, and mentioned María's great-aunt Doña Cuca. The reference to Refugio Rambaud as "Cuca" suggests that Buehman had gained insider status, as only Cordova's close family members used that nickname.[28]

Buehman valued María's painting enough to convince the *Citizen* to feature it in another section of the paper. A rather lengthy article accompanied the image, informing readers that her ancestors had built the house she owned at 173 North Meyer Avenue, as well as another on the corner of Meyer and Washington. The reporter, Lew McCleneghan, described her as "well qualified" to paint the old presidio wall (see Figure 2.5). He noted that "Mrs. Cordova's knowledge is partly firsthand, partly from witnesses whose own knowledge was firsthand."[29]

María's painting offered a different viewpoint on the presidio, at least from McCleneghan's perspective, such as placing its gate on the north side, based on Refugio's frequent recounting. María also contributed new information about the wall's boundaries. The panoramic view included the main waterway, prominent mountains, hills, valleys, cultivated gardens and natural vegetation and corrals. The presidio takes up about twenty five percent of the canvas making it clear that María wanted to convey information about the presidio's location in relation to the

FIGURE 2.5 Photograph by Jack Sheaffer, December 16, 1960. María Cordova's painting of the Presidio, featured in Lew McCleneghan's article. The original painting or a color version has not been located by the author. University of Arizona Libraries Special Collections, Jack Sheaffer Photographic Collection, MS 435, Box 85, Folder 16034. Titled by the archive: "Painting of Old Pueblo as Walled Town by Mrs. Maria Cordova." Reproduced with permission of Special Collections, University of Arizona Libraries.

landscape and its surrounding environment. At first glance the structures within the presidio walls look odd because they resemble older Moorish strongholds and the walls are rather low in relationship to the few towering structures that line the back wall.

Painting Her Way into the Record

One can only speculate as to why Cordova's painting inspired such admiration in Buehman and McCleneghan. It is evident that they were not only invested in championing her art and story but were also genuinely captivated by her. Was it how she welcomed them, making them feel at home in her historic house? Did her personal warmth and storytelling lead to a fuller appreciation of her work, or was the painting itself that impactful? Cordova provided them with an engaging narrative, but seeing the actual painting must have added a visual dimension that deepened and grounded her version of history.

Cordova's paintings did not find their place in museums, nor did they gain recognition for their style or colors. Instead, she actively worked to get journalists to appreciate her art, leading to her painting being featured in the newspapers (see Figure 2.6).[30] As an amateur painter who had taken lessons as a child and continued practicing her craft despite

FIGURE 2.6 María Cordova's paintings continued to draw public attention. In 1962, the *Arizona Daily Star* published a photograph of Girl Scouts from Troop 346 of Townsend Junior High participating in a Heritage Hike, with the caption: "How the Walled Presidio Looked." The girls stood in front of the Cordova Smoke Shop, holding María's painting of the original Presidio. According to the brief caption, the painting usually hung inside the shop, which undoubtedly maximized its visibility. *Star*, February 8, 1962, C-9. University of Arizona Libraries Special Collections, Jack Sheaffer Photographic Collection, MS 435, Box 103, Folder 18901. Photograph by Jack Sheaffer. Reproduced with permission of Special Collections, University of Arizona Libraries.

family responsibilities, each of her works conveyed a distinctive, yet understated, political purpose.

Painting also allowed María the opportunity to further impressions of herself as cultured and respectable. The solitary act of painting within her home conveyed a calm strength and elegance. She painted significant sites from her past and the people who had inspired her. In short, she painted her transborder world and brought these elements to life on canvas. Painting also offered María another way to control the narrative. She used her artistic talent as a form of storytelling.[31]

In the years that followed, Buehman dedicated a few more columns to María Cordova, and the newspaper continued to reprint them for over a decade. One notable piece, printed in 1952, was titled "Front of Home Was Part of Old City Wall." It featured a photograph of the house on the corner of Meyer and Washington Streets that María Cordova owned and rented out for income. This was the other property at 102 to 108 West Washington Street that Refugio Rambaud had bequeathed to her. Clearly influenced by María, the story provided more detail about the Carrillo family, who "own[ed] much of the land inside the old wall." It also described the house's front wall, which jutted out at an angle, as evidence that it had once been part of the original presidio wall. The claim that a portion of the original wall was embedded in the structure of her house further solidified Cordova's connection to the presidio.[32]

Cordova's assertions about the presidio wall, its appearance, and the location of its gates underscore a broader challenge that still faces contemporary researchers: no site plan or map showing the original layout or building arrangement within the fort has ever been located. Researchers have relied on historical documents, archival photographs, trench excavations, and ground-penetrating radar to identify the original walls (see Figure 2.7). As archaeologist J. Homer Thiel explains, "Today the walls are lost, buried in the heart of Tucson below streets, lawns, sidewalks, and buildings . . . We have no contemporary descriptions of the wall; instead, we rely on accounts preserved by people in the 1920s and 1930s and, as a result, we have many conflicting details."[33] The following map indicates the general location of the presidio walls, as agreed upon

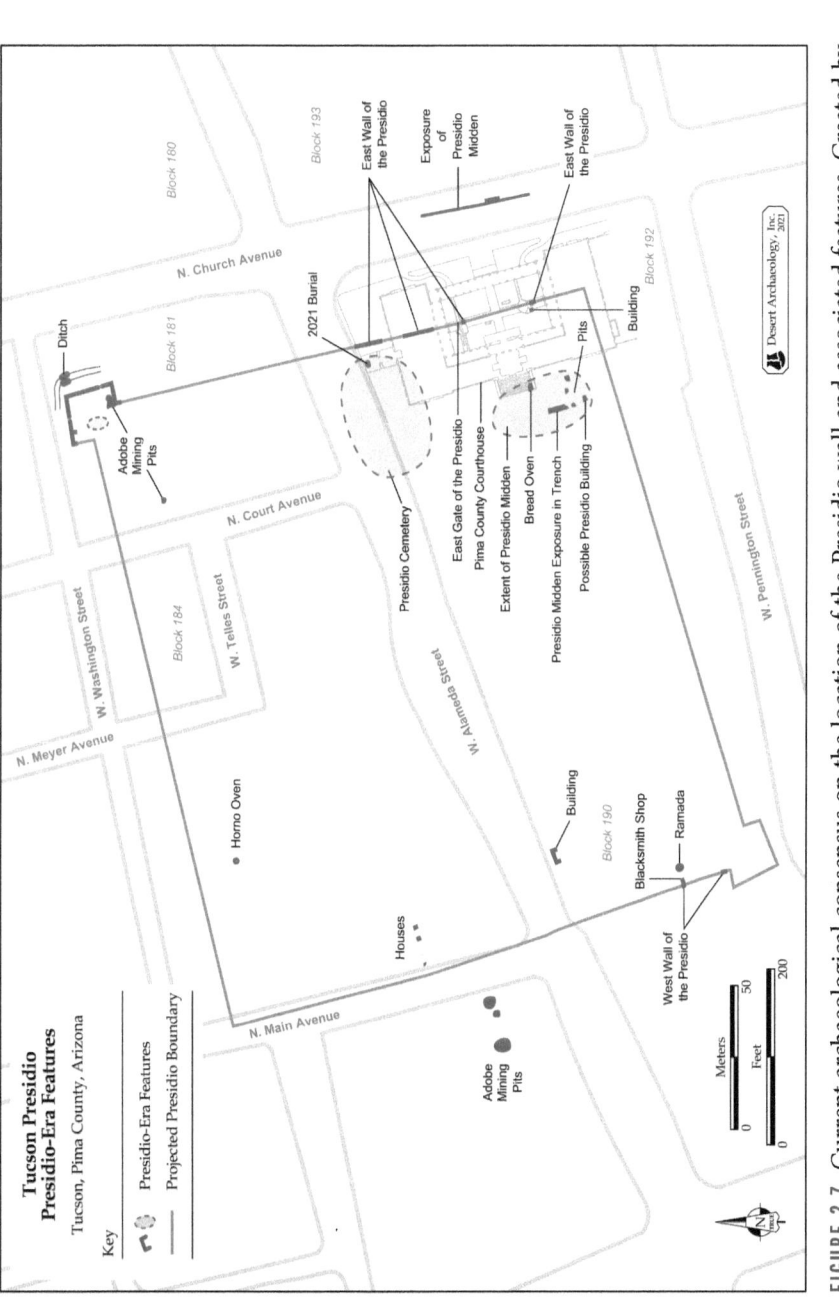

FIGURE 2.7 Current archaeological consensus on the location of the Presidio wall and associated features. Created by Catherine Gilman. Courtesy of Desert Archaeology, Inc.

by archaeologists, though the precise placement of a few sections remains unconfirmed.

Aiming Towards the Sky Near the Former Presidio

The Cordovas likely remained aware of ongoing city developments through conversations with customers in the smoke shop and reports in the local newspapers. Their home, near City Hall, was in a prime location and increasingly faced looming threats. In 1952, real estate investor Harry A. Sellers acquired the property across the street from María's home, just north of Washington.[34] The market located at the corner of Washington and Meyer, across from the apartments, had been a mainstay in the neighborhood for decades. Chinese American grocer Toy S. Don owned the Washington Market at 213 North Meyer Avenue.[35] Born in San Francisco, Don established and ran the store for more than thirty years until his death.[36]

After demolishing the market, Sellers likely diverted customers to the Cordova Brothers Smoke Shop. To move forward with development, he requested that the city rezone the property from residential to business.[37] In 1964, he sought zoning approval to construct what the newspaper referred to as a "high-rise" among the older structures in the area.[38] The aging sewer and electrical lines, along with the narrow streets, were spared the added strain, however, as Sellers' death brought those plans to a halt.[39] Today, the lot remains an empty parking lot.

An Early Warning: Federal Dollars and Private Agendas

In 1953, the Pima County Board of Supervisors, whose jurisdiction included Tucson, proposed a plan at the direction of the Chamber of Commerce to build a Civic Center that would have wiped out both Cordova properties and about eleven acres, or eight blocks, of the presidio neighborhood (see Figure 2.8).[40] The county intended to build a $3.2 million

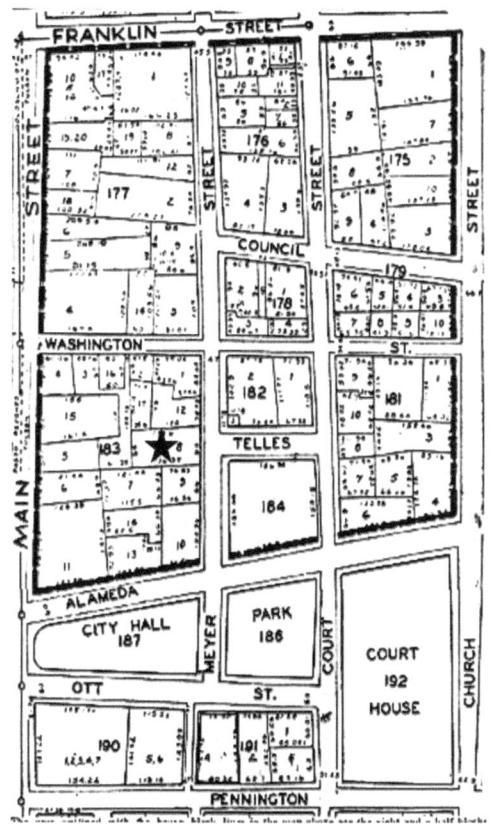

FIGURE 2.8 This map, featured in the newspaper, shows the eight-and-a-half blocks outlined with heavier black lines, marking the section north of City Hall that Pima County targeted for new county buildings. A star has been added to mark 173 North Meyer Avenue. "*$3.2 Million Pima County Office Center Proposed*," Star, January 30, 1953, 19.

complex of offices, a court annex, and a juvenile detention home. In the early stages, the Chamber considered acquiring federal aid to assist in building the structures. Real estate developer Roy Drachman sat at the helm of acquiring federal funding.[41]

Roy Drachman's stance is particularly telling, given that less than three years earlier he had opposed accepting federal funds for a public housing initiative. He formed and directed the Tucson Committee for Home Protection, which ran advertisements in newspapers to oppose the initiative. He warned, "When you accept federal assistance or handouts, you also accept federal dictation." At a housing debate, he declared that public housing was socialism and that "in Russia all cities have public housing and questioned 'whether we want that here.'"⁴² The initiative was soundly defeated, largely due to the campaign he led.⁴³

The influence of real estate and related business and professional groups, who pressed the pro-growth agenda that Drachman led, cannot be overstated. Real estate agents and financial institutions, along with their agents who underwrote mortgages, opposed public housing because they feared government competition and being left out of the revenue stream.⁴⁴ Roy Drachman may have fought against accepting federal funds for public housing, but when it came to seeking federal funds to destroy eleven acres in the presidio area, labeled as slum clearance in 1953, he shifted his stance. The contradiction did not seem to give him pause or present any ethical dilemma.

Revisiting this proposed project sheds light on the conservative political attitudes of the early 1950s. As stated, the Chamber of Commerce's committee initially proposed a county bond to secure voter approval for financing the project. However, a few days later, a Chamber committee introduced the possibility of a "federal aid angle" to build the civic center. This shift reflected the practice of conducting private negotiations or making significant decisions away from public scrutiny, a form of political maneuvering where powerful influences shaped city governance without a transparent process. Such practices blurred the lines between public authority and private interest, enabling developers to steer planning outcomes without transparency.

In 1953, it was Drachman who led the charge to obtain slum clearance monies from the federal government to build the Civic Center in the former presidio area. He insisted on investigating the matter because "If we can get two-thirds of the cost of the land from the federal government we certainly should make an effort to qualify."⁴⁵

Drachman's role in this episode of local urban development demonstrates the extent of his influence over both the Chamber of Commerce and the Pima County Board of Supervisors. His base of support continued to grow, and his decisions shaped much of Tucson's urban landscape. A *Citizen* assessment decades later underscores just how far-reaching that influence became. As Tucson entered the new millennium in 1999, a special feature in the *Citizen* asked, "Who were the most influential business people in changing the face of Tucson in the past 100 years?" Roy Drachman topped the list and was described as "quite simply, the most influential person who ever lived here."[46]

The two Cordova properties sat within the proposed eleven acres designated for the Civic Center. The former homes of Territorial Governor Levi Hughes, Edward Fish, Hiram Stevens, Samuel Hughes, and other early Tucson residents also remained on the site. At the time, the *Star* noted, "The buildings, of course, are not in their original condition. Many have been refurbished into Modern appearing structures, although still keeping their pioneer lines."[47]

Principles Over Projects: Republican Women Confront the Chamber

At the time, Republican Roy Drachman had not yet fully consolidated the power base he would later wield, and his push for federal aid faced resistance from within his own party. When the papers announced that the Chamber and Drachman were seeking federal aid for the Civic Center, it unleashed a formidable political obstacle: the Pima County Women's Republican Club. They mobilized the opposition, declaring, "It is time that the community upholds the Republican principle of paying its own way." The Club insisted that any plan for the Civic Center proceed only through the proposed bond issue.[48] At the subsequent county board meeting, a "rather large delegation of women" appeared to protest both the county's pursuit of federal aid and the Chamber of Commerce's plans. A few days later, the Chamber convened another meeting, this time exploring the possibility of constructing the Civic Center without federal support.[49]

And while the women's protest was certainly rooted in Republican principles of fiscal restraint, it was also driven by a desire to protect and preserve the presidio neighborhood. They did not consider the area as a slum. Stella Roca, a painter and founder of the Tucson Fine Arts Association voiced her objections and publicly challenged the use of the term "slum clearance" to describe the area.[50] At that time, the presidio neighborhood remained home to influential residents. One was Ellery Sedgwick, former owner of *The Atlantic Monthly*, who lived in the old Sam Hughes house on the corner of Main and Washington Streets. As a member of the East Coast elite, Sedgwick maintained connections to prominent literary and political figures, underscoring the area's continued relevance and appeal.[51]

The county ended up placing the fate of the Civic Center project in the hands of voters.[52] It is important to note, however, that exclusionary policies limited participation in bond elections. Arizona's voting rights were restricted to property owners, reflecting an idealization of citizenship that determined who was entitled to participate in these crucial decisions. This emphasis on property ownership had profound ramifications for residents later targeted by urban renewal, the majority of whom were renters.

Arizona law specified that only "persons who are real property tax payers [property owners], registered to vote, and who have lived in the state for one year, the county for six months, and in their ward for 30 days" could vote in bond initiatives. The statewide electorate amended the Arizona Constitution in 1930 to include this stipulation, rationalizing that municipal "bonds are liens" placed on property owners and that only they should decide the fate of those bonds.[53] This property ownership requirement became an economic restriction that effectively silenced renters and those who frequently moved, marginalizing their voices in decisions that would reshape their communities. It also reflected a broader legacy of settler colonialism, in which legal frameworks privileged property-owning citizens and excluded those most vulnerable to displacement. In Tucson, this meant that many of residents whose homes were targeted for removal had no voice in the decisions that sealed their fate.

The local Chamber of Commerce continued to endorse the Civic Center plan, while the *Citizen* voiced concerns over the hefty price tag and the potential loss of historic structures: "There are well-preserved structures along Main, Alameda, Washington, and Meyer streets which go back to the Old Pueblo days of the city wall a hundred years ago. . . .

It would be a shame if all these old buildings were sacrificed."[54] In July 1953, voters rejected Pima County's bond proposal by a margin of two to one. Although the bond initiative to build the Civic Center failed decisively, the idea did not fade. The prospect of receiving federal aid for slum clearance remained deeply appealing, especially to staunch Republican Roy P. Drachman.

The Encroachment of Luxury Development

Private development, too, posed a growing threat to older structures, including the Cordova properties, as investors increasingly turned their attention to downtown. In 1960, developer Lyle Palant announced that he had secured a 90,000-square-foot parcel, approximately two acres with plans to construct high-rise luxury apartments, a shopping plaza, and parking for close to 1,000 cars. The acquisition involved purchasing multiple small business offices and apartment buildings just two blocks from the Cordova properties.[55] In the numerous press reports, there was no mention of the area's historical significance or the impending demolition of older structures to make way for the new development.

Palant's plan to build skyscrapers downtown captivated the media and excited pro-development advocates. At twenty-three years old, he was portrayed as ambitious and someone who "liked to think big."[56] According to Palant, the proposed group of buildings would "become the nucleus of downtown Tucson." (Figure 2.9) The project required the city and county planning divisions to rezone the property and approve an exception to the city's 140-foot height limit, since the proposed structures were over 250 feet tall, or 28 stories.[57]

Although Palant's requests for rezoning and increased height limits posed challenges for newspapers to explain clearly, one publication captured the prevailing development mindset: "City planners have generally favored any construction program which would increase the assessed evaluation of property within the city limits."[58] This observation proved accurate. Palant successfully navigated the city's bureaucratic processes and secured both the rezoning and the height limit increase for his $16 mil-

PROPOSED FOR DOWNTOWN

This project, under consideration for downtown Tucson, would include a 15-story hotel (from left), a 30-story apartment unit in front of the hotel and a 20-story building which would house offices from the fifth floor up. Below the fifth floor, private clubs, restaurants and stores are planned. Grass in architect's drawing is on top of a three-story parking garage designed for 900 cars.

FIGURE 2.9 The proposed high-rise development would have blocked mountain views and overwhelmed nearby traditional buildings. As the newspaper caption explained: "This project, under consideration for downtown Tucson, would include a 15-story hotel (from left), a 30-story apartment unit in front of the hotel and a 20-story building which would house offices from the fifth floor up. Below the fifth floor, private clubs, restaurants and stores are planned. Grass in architect's drawing is on top of a three-story parking garage designed for 900 cars." *Citizen*, October 10, 1961, 17. This image is a reproduction from the newspaper and is used with permission from © USA TODAY NETWORK via Imagn Images.

lion project.[59] Fortunately for the residents and older homes nearby, the project unraveled before any buildings were constructed. Palant became embroiled in lawsuits, filed for bankruptcy, and was later convicted on four counts of felony fraud.[60] The large parcel remains vacant and is now used as a parking lot. It stands as a reminder of how city planners and politicians catered to the ambitions of an overconfident developer while disregarding both community well-being and historic structures.

Parking: Urban Renewal Prelude

Like the rest of the nation, car ownership in Tucson surged after World War II. By May 1950, the demand for vehicles had grown so rapidly that Arizona ran out of license plates.[61] The following year, the *Citizen* referred to car ownership as "mushrooming" and continually breaking records.[62] By 1958, over half of the U.S. population held driver's licenses, underscoring the growing dependency on automobiles. Calls for expanding the infrastructure, especially streets and highways, to accommodate the needs of the new car culture also dramatically increased.[63] The need for more parking spaces also evolved into a major urban planning challenge. This prompted the demolition of older homes to create parking lots and garages, particularly surrounding City Hall, where María Cordova lived.

As early as 1951, pro-growth advocate and real estate developer Roy P. Drachman voiced his frustrations in the newspaper about the lack of downtown parking. A champion of private-sector-led development, Drachman funded and directed his own private survey to show that the parking shortage was hurting downtown businesses. His goal was not to persuade city officials to create more public parking lots. Rather, he aimed to pressure them to cooperate with private developers like himself and allow them to take the lead in building them. Drachman pushed city officials to expedite the permit process, prioritize land clearance, and streamline procedures to accommodate more automobiles. As a real estate executive, Drachman stood to benefit financially from these transactions. The acquisition, sale, and development of properties generated significant profits. Ultimately, his efforts encouraged the construction of new buildings downtown and advanced his own business interests.⁶⁴ By 1953, the situation had escalated to the point where public lands, including the lawn on the north side of the Pima County courthouse, were converted into parking areas.⁶⁵ This action reflected a shift in urban priorities, where preserving communal spaces became secondary to accommodating cars.

As parking lots proliferated, historically significant buildings were often sacrificed in the name of urban development. A few landmarks located near María Cordova's properties, a former hotel, and the Parkview, a former opera house, were both demolished in the scramble to meet the growing demand for parking spaces.⁶⁶ As the decade progressed, the push for more lots increasingly took on a tone of inevitability. In 1962, two new parking areas near City Hall and close to the Cordovas were presented as modern civic improvements.⁶⁷ These developments remind us that downtown was already being transformed well before the official urban renewal program began.

In 1958, conservative *Star* editor William (Bill) Mathews expressed his approval of how the increase in parking availability had positively impacted downtown. He wrote, "Forthwith, numerous parking lots were developed to a point that despite the increasing population and suburban shopping centers, downtown Tucson has gone through a regeneration." He added, "Here in Tucson, we have seen urban renewal go ahead without any help from the federal government. It can continue to grow just as long as parking space is provided. Private enterprise can continue to do the job."⁶⁸ By taking this stance, Mathews hoped to discourage the push for federally funded urban renewal and steer the conversation toward local solutions driven by business interests. He would ultimately lose this battle, however.

Conclusion: The View from 173 North Meyer Avenue

As María Cordova observed city blocks being demolished for parking lots and ambitious developers near her home, she assuredly felt concern. Just as nineteenth-century residents of the presidio kept an eye out for intruders, the Cordovas remained vigilant about development. Given their proximity to City Hall, perhaps the Cordovas were even approached to sell their properties, although that is something we will never know. The demolition of historic buildings also symbolized a threat to their properties. María understood that the moment called for action and that new strategies were needed to protect her home and livelihood. But accommodating cars was not the only danger—the City of Tucson had established an urban renewal office in 1955. These were urgent times, and she responded accordingly.

CHAPTER 3

Rallying for Home
The Press, History, and the Courts

As urban development agendas targeted more properties around her, María Cordova came to see that her carefully maintained world was under threat. In 1960, from her desk, the woman who had long cultivated an image of refinement and respectability drafted a letter to the mayor and city council. The letter was anything but proper, as María Cordova threatened to upend property ownership in Tucson.

Raul, María's son who attended law school, took on a larger role in their battle to defend their home. As the formal owner of what would become known as La Casa Cordova, he filed a lawsuit to challenge the City and protect the property. María continued to use the media to draw attention to their struggle, but she soon discovered the limits of her advocacy. Making historical claims to the land was one thing; asserting actual ownership was another.

Settler Values, Racial Realities

As noted earlier, María and her family had benefited from settler colonialism, having "replaced" Indigenous people in Sonora. In the United States, Cordova expected her family's class standing would carry weight and elevate her position. In a society built on settler colonial values, landownership was the measure of success, and María had attained that. The rental income from her properties underwrote her livelihood. What she did not anticipate was a racial order that dismissed her class standing and cultural refinement, reducing her instead to a racialized outsider.

For María, the realities of her marginalized position in the U.S. became increasingly evident. As a transnational woman who spoke with a thick accent, María found that she was oftentimes treated as peripheral. The system of white supremacy that positioned her as an outsider is crucial to recognize, as it shaped how she responded to being cast in that role. But the way power operates is not always easy to pinpoint. White supremacy complemented and functioned within a broader structure of settler colonialism. As Patrick Wolfe reminds us, "settler colonialism is a structure, not an event."[1] María Cordova's actions must be seen within that structure, which organized power, land, and legitimacy in ways meant to constrain her.

Looking back, it is clear that María did not dismantle the structures that marginalized her, nor could she. Those systems were deeply embedded in law, policy, and cultural memory. Instead, she worked within the same systems that had marginalized her and other Mexican people in the United States. Hers is not a story of protest or community organizing but of using the mechanisms within the system such as newspaper columns, public storytelling and, later lawsuits to assert her family's place in history. Her focus remained on her own family's recognition, not on a broader call for inclusion of all marginalized Tucsonenses. Still, her efforts forced a recognition of the Tucsonense presence and contributions in public spaces that had long excluded them.

Weaving Another Thread into the Legacy

María Cordova continued to use Albert Buehman's "Arizona Album" to share her version of history and emphasize her family's distinctive lineage. In 1952, "The First Railroad in Sonora," featured a photograph of the first train that traveled from Mexico's interior and arrived in Nogales in the 1880s (see Figure 3.1). This moment signaled a major shift in regional connectivity, as it linked northern Mexico with the interior and integrated the transportation systems between Sonora and Arizona. María Cordova's father, Antonio Angulo Navarrete, was the cab engineer featured in the accompanying photo. In addition to being an engineer, the piece noted that Antonio helped build the line, acted as an interpreter, and contributed to surveying the route.[2]

FIGURE 3.1 Albert R. Buehman, ed., "Arizona Album: The First Railroad in Sonora—In 80s," *Arizona Album, Citizen,* June 24, 1964,16., 8. Used with permission from USA TODAY NETWORK via Imagn Images.

We can assume that the featured photograph came from María. At the end of the column, Buehman states that the information was "courtesy" of Cordova. Of particular interest is how María used this opportunity to introduce a new family connection. According to the article, her father "was born at Vallejo, Calif., at the home of his uncle, Gen. Mariano Guadalupe Vallejo, the last Mexican governor of California."[3] Highlighting her relation to Vallejo allowed María to remind journalists and readers that she came from a family that, in her transnational world, once wielded land, political power, and economic influence. This desire to assert continuity with that past echoes the kinds of relationships sociologist Thomas Faist describes. He explains, "Transnational communities characterize situations in which international movers and stayers are connected by dense and strong social and symbolic ties over time and across space to patterns of networks and circuits in two countries—based on solidarity."[4]

General Mariano Guadalupe Vallejo is recognized as a patriarch of Mexican California, known for his military power, vast landholdings, and hospitality. The 1849 Gold Rush was a pivotal moment rooted in Manifest Destiny, which fueled white settlers' sense of entitlement to expand westward. During this time, Vallejo served as the primary enforcer of Mexican laws in Sonoma, where he played a crucial role in managing Mexican sovereignty as U.S. settlers began challenging existing legal and cultural frameworks. He often welcomed white settlers and admired what he perceived as the U.S. system of democracy. As historian Alan Rosenus notes, "From the early 1840s on, his desire to make California a part of the U.S. became his most urgent political goal."[5] Despite being imprisoned by the Bear Flaggers, a group of U.S. settlers who revolted against Mexican rule in June 1846, Vallejo remained cooperative and optimistic about California's future as part of the United States.

María used the connection with Vallejo to draw parallels with her own effort to preserve her family's position and legacy across time and borders. She invoked Vallejo as a cautionary tale. Like Vallejo, who had served as a cultural bridge that welcomed white settlers and navigated the divide between Mexican and U.S. cultures, Cordova and her family, especially her father, helped link the two countries together through the railroad network. Though she did not possess Vallejo's power or status, invoking a connection to him in 1952 served as a call to action. Cordova sought to rally Tucsonans to her side, reminding them to support her efforts to protect her home and property from being taken, just as Vallejo had once lost his.

From Solo Effort to Partnership

María's son, Raul Navarrete Cordova, born in 1925, stands out because she selected him to carry her banner. Even as a child, María would remind him that she had entrusted him with the task of defending and protecting the interests of her and his immediate family. In front of cousins and others, she would say, "¡Éste! El va a ser abogado [This one! He is going to grow up to be an attorney.]."[6] As the first-born male child, and in keeping with patriarchal expectations, Raul must have felt pressure to fulfill his mother's legal and historical vision. He died in 1997, and we will never know how the weight of this role affected him. However, when forces in the 1960s threatened to uproot the Cordovas from their home, Raul stepped forward as both the family's legal expert and the extension of María's voice.

During World War II, as the nation sought heroes in 1945, María seized the opportunity to highlight her son Raul's courageous actions. At twenty years old, Raul had served in the U.S. Navy for three years, participating in numerous military campaigns across the Pacific. She contacted the local newspaper, and they published an "eyewitness account" of the battle Raul described in his letter the next day. The story was titled "Tucson Youth Had Part in Final Battle" and featured his photograph.[7] In 1945, fifty-year-old María had learned to use media networks and contacts to secure public recognition for Raul and deliver a story Tucsonans wanted during wartime.

After the war, Raul earned an undergraduate degree and attended law school. He became the Cordovas' public voice. María continued to engage in non-confrontational tactics rooted in a form of transborder femininity that valorized women who were private, reserved, and protective of their home. María's understanding of the legal sphere, predominantly controlled by men, shaped her approach to defending the Cordova property. Raul engaged in and challenged the legal system, while María continued to invite and share information with reporters in her *sala*, or living room. Although it may have appeared that she had relinquished power to him, she was quietly orchestrating efforts from the background where she believed she could exert the most influence.

Wielding History: Authority and the Land Grant

In February 1960, María wrote a letter to the Mayor and Council asking, "When was Tucson founded?" The *Star* found her request newsworthy and published a short column noting that she had encountered five conflicting dates for Tucson's Spanish founding, which she listed. The paper quoted her as urging action: "Under these circumstances, it is my desire that you take remedial measures regarding the dates of the establishment of Tucson."[8] For María, clarifying the city's founding date was not only about historical accuracy; it also positioned her as a knowledgeable and diligent researcher. It also evidenced María's decision to use history as a strategy to protect her home and her place in it.

A few days later, María sent a detailed letter to *The Star*, citing a line the paper had published regarding Tubac, claiming it as the oldest non-Indian town. She provided detailed sources that credit Tucson with that distinction. In her letter, she quoted a passage from page 387 of the book *Arizona*, which reads: "This fact is not generally known, but a Spanish land grant has been recently unearthed which bears the date of 1552, though the city was not founded until 1690." Always the polite cultural broker, María concluded her letter with, "My desire is that this information will be of benefit to you and your newspaper."[9] The letter reads like a short legal brief, so it is not a stretch to assume Raul played a significant role in drafting it. Even if he wrote all of it, Raul knew that his mother carried more clout than he did. She had established herself as a presence in Tucson, something Raul, despite his legal knowledge, could not claim.[10]

It was no accident that María brought up a long-forgotten land grant. The letter also indicates the depth of research that the Cordovas had engaged in. City Attorney Calvin Webster remarked that the city "first heard of this in 1960 [about a land grant], when Mrs. Cordova wrote a letter to the mayor and council and claimed land that she apparently feels still belongs to her and her family in and around the old Presidio."[11] The timing of Cordova raising land grant issues in the media aligned with the increasing perceived threats to their properties mentioned in the last chapter and in the next that focuses on urban renewal.

Also in 1960, reporter Don Robinson interviewed María Cordova and invited her to share more of her history. The interview took place in her living room, which he vividly described: "As you sit in one of the tomblike rooms of the old house at 173 N. Meyer St. you can almost hear the distant shouts of the mule skinners, the tramp of grumbling troops drilling on the nearby parade ground and the cries of children at play in the old Spanish Pueblo known as Tucson" (see Figure 3.2). Robinson seemed to enjoy being in her presence and described María speaking in a "voice that carried the gentle and refined dignity of a family that once ruled Baja California." Robinson also noted that although Raul was present, Raul never spoke.[12]

In that interview, María Cordova told Robinson that the house they were sitting in had been built by her great aunt Refugio Diaz's first hus-

FIGURE 3.2 Photograph of María Cordova taken during an interview with reporter Robinson. The original newspaper caption read, "Proud House, Proud Owner." Located in University of Arizona Libraries Special Collections, Jack Sheaffer Photographic Collection, MS 435, Box 85, Folder 16034. Photograph by Jack Sheaffer. Reproduced with permission of Special Collections, University of Arizona Libraries.

band, Manuel Carrillo. His father had owned a Spanish Land Grant. After Manuel died, Refugio became the legal owner. Cordova related that, "My aunt always told me she never sold any of the land under it. When the Americans came in 1853 [Gadsden Purchase], they told her it [the land grant] covered too much land for one person to own. That it would hold back the progress of Tucson if she did not give up most of it . . . and that she could keep the Presidio." Apparently, Refugio had possession of the "old title" (although it is unclear whether it was the Spanish title or the lease arrangements worked out with the new settlers) until she died, but according to María, "somehow the papers disappeared. If I can just find the papers."[13]

As mentioned in Chapter 1, a Territory of Arizona certificate recorded the 1877 marriage of Refugio Diaz and Manuel Carrillo. In her conversation with *Star* reporter Robinson, however, María claimed that Manuel was in Tucson in 1810 and that Refugio was negotiating with new settlers in 1864. These dates stretch plausibility, as Manuel would have been at least sixty-seven when he married Refugio. Yet this was the version of family history María chose to share. It also helps explain why she at times claimed Refugio lived to be over one hundred. After Manuel, Refugio married Severin Rambaud. Photographs suggest she appeared youthful in both demeanor and style. Little is known about Refugio, and that ambiguity worked in María's favor.

For the next few years, the Cordovas kept a low profile, likely because the late 1950s urban renewal plan faced strong opposition and was ultimately filed away in 1962. With redevelopment temporarily on hold, the *Citizen* featured María in another article in 1963, "150 Years Live Vividly in Memory of Pioneer." It included a close-up photograph of her, and true to her strategy, she once again invited the reporter inside her home. The reporter noted that "Reminiscing is easy for Mrs. Cordova, seated in her lofty-ceilinged territorial home . . ." María touched briefly on a number of topics, one of which was Refugio's marriage to Manuel Carrillo, ". . . who had inherited all the land encompassed by the city wall. This land was an original Spanish land grant, passed down by the Carrillo family. After my uncle [Manuel] died, much of it was leased." After discussing other topics, María returned to the issue of the land grant, again lamenting, "I wish I had the family records so I could tell you the exact dates and facts . . . It is important to tell the truth about historical happenings for the sake of one's children, so they will know the truth."[14]

Raul Navarrete Cordova's Battle

The influx of federal funds and the chance to reshape downtown were irresistible to city officials and the developers poised to profit from it. On February 1, 1965, a newly formalized urban renewal project expanded its boundaries to include a square block north of City Hall, where the Cordova family lived.[15] Reading about it and seeing a map with revised boundaries that now encompassed their neighborhood and home most certainly heightened the family's sense of being targeted.

Raul Cordova, as María had always expected him to do, began to speak out and take a stand against urban renewal. On February 4, 1965, he wrote a letter to the *Star* editor titled "Historical Heritage to Be Destroyed," expressing his anger. He criticized the paper's coverage of urban renewal, stating, "you forgot to mention that the Tucson City Council, with the proposed aid of our federal government, has decided to try to throw to the dump heap about one-eighth of the area that is the site of the former Tucson Presidio, with some of its old buildings still standing. That includes where I have my smoke shop, which we have preserved to the best of our ability since 1934." He also made it clear that he considered both the city and federal government to be the primary culprits behind the urban renewal efforts.[16]

Nine months after writing his letter, on November 4, 1965, Raul Navarrete Cordova took legal action. He filed the complaint himself, signing as the sole plaintiff since he alone held title to the property at 173 North Meyer Avenue. He paid $15.00 to ensure that both the U.S. government and City of Tucson attorneys were formally served.[17] For the first time, he gave a name to the land grant that María had previously referenced—the Tucson Presidio Title.

In his petition, Raul claimed ownership of the Tucson Presidio Title and challenged the legitimacy of the City of Tucson's acquisition process.

He argued that the U.S. Executive Department had exceeded its authority by violating the Gadsden Treaty and federal laws. The 1854 treaty between the U.S. and Mexico included provisions protecting land and property rights, which Cordova asserted had been ignored. In essence, he claimed the title had been improperly transferred or invalidated, and sought legal intervention to protect his claim.[18]

An article by reporter Dale Wittner, titled "Downtown Land Title Action Filed," about Raul's claim appeared on the front page of the *Citizen* a few days later. The larger, bolder headline at the top of the page, "Urban Renewal Plan Adopted," signaled what the *Citizen* considered the most important news of the day. It also confirmed a decision the Cordova family had come to expect. Wittner described María and her family's claim to the land as "the old walled presidio on which the Pima County Courthouse and City Hall now stand" (see Figure 3.3). It noted that the Cordova home was within the urban renewal area, and although the extent of the land claim was unclear, it reminded readers that "the old Mexican and Spanish land grants to families in this area often exceed 100 acres." Wittner also dismissively added, "Apparently the Cordova court action is simply a century late . . . The last U.S. approval of such a claim came in 1871."[19]

Wittner interviewed City Attorney Calvin Webster and confirmed that the city had indeed been served a summons to answer Raul's petition. Webster stated his intentions to take the matter seriously, "What's at stake here is apparently a good deal of land in the downtown area. We are not going to ignore the petition and lose by default." Wittner reached María by phone and asked her for a comment, but she refused. The most telling question he raised, and the one most urgent for the Cordovas, was, "What effect, if any, the petition might have on the urban renewal proposal was not known."[20]

The *Citizen* also cast doubt on Raul's legal skills, undermining the petition's credibility in the eyes of the public and reducing its perceived legitimacy. Wittner asked and reported, "whether an attorney had helped prepare the petition. No lawyer was named in the court document."[21] This may have influenced Raul Cordova's decision to speak to the *Citizen* the day after they ran the story. He shared that he did not intend to dis-

FIGURE 3.3 The boundaries of the Tucson Presidio Land Grant were never officially outlined. In an interview, Raúl Cordova described it as comprising approximately ten square miles, stretching from the University of Arizona to St. Mary's Hospital, and from 14th Street to Speedway Boulevard. The author created this map to reflect an approximate boundary, using information from a report by Dale Wittner, "Tucson Land Claim: Cordova Says He Seeks Only to Clear Home Title," *Tucson Citizen*, November 10, 1965, 3.

place or "inconvenience any innocent people (living on) the land now" but expected to be compensated for the land. He reiterated that "he seeks only to clear the title to his historic family home." In legal terms, a "clear title" refers to a property title that is free from any legal claims, disputes, or encumbrances, meaning the owner has full and undisputed rights to the property. Since Raul was already listed as the owner of the property at 173 North Meyer Avenue, his reference to seeking a "clear title" may have reflected a desire to secure ownership that could not be contested or overridden by eminent domain, the legal tool the city was using to remove residents as part of the urban renewal plan.[22]

The other local paper, the *Star*, also reported on the legal petition in the days following its filing. They noted that María had been reached for comment, but she refused. In lieu of a direct interview, they quoted a section from a 1960 feature by Don Robinson (mentioned a few pages earlier), in which María had brought up the land grant. They reiterated: "In 1874, Tucson Mayor Sidney R. DeLong acquired from the federal government a tract of land consisting of 1,280 acres, and according to

Mrs. Cordova, this is when the land grant conditions were violated." María had stated, "The presidio was included in the land he [DeLong] bought at the sale in Prescott . . . My aunt [Refugio] insisted she had never signed away her right to that part. She told me that in 1864 she had granted a 99-year lease to the county for the land on which the old courthouse was built."

As María noted, and as history confirms, Mayor DeLong applied for 1,280 acres from the U.S. government to formally establish Tucson as a village, and later a town. After Sidney W. Foreman completed a new survey and several amendments were made to the application, Tucson received notice on July 25, 1874, from the U.S. Land Office in Arizona that a formal deed or patent for the townsite had been granted (see Figure 3.4, reproduced and discussed in a subsequent chapter).[23] However, aside from the deeds recorded between 1862 and 1864 by William S. Oury, there appear to be no surviving property ownership or lease records for the presidio area prior to its incorporation as a town, or at least none that have surfaced in public archives to date.

Spanish and Mexican Land Titles

Historically and presently, Tucson has always belonged to Indigenous peoples whose deep-rooted connection to the land shaped their communities long before the arrival of settlers and nation-states. This relationship was first disrupted by Spanish and then Mexican colonial systems, and further complicated by U.S. territorial expansion. The Gadsden Purchase of 1853 introduced new legal mechanisms that enabled the takeover of the region, as white settlers redefined land ownership through property distribution and land titles. The same settler colonial processes that displaced Mexican residents also deepened Indigenous dispossession, culminating in the reservation system. At the heart of this new wave of displacement was the imposition of U.S. legal frameworks that invalidated existing Mexican property claims and shifted control of the land to incoming white settlers.

The absence of Spanish and Mexican land titles, combined with the complexities introduced by the U.S. legal framework and the autonomy granted to local authorities, has produced a fragmented and uncertain historical record. Land ownership in the Tucson area remained unclear and largely undocumented. This review of past scholarly conclusions about the lack of documentation surrounding Spanish and Mexican property titles raises more questions than answers. After the signing of the Gadsden Treaty, incoming white settlers were allowed to establish a local system of government. Although broadly outlined by federal authorities, local officials were left to handle land claims with little oversight, compounding the confusion. After reviewing colonial land-tenure issues dating back to the *Recopilación de Leyes de los Reynos de las Indias* in 1681, attorney John C. Lacy concluded that when the Gadsden Treaty was signed in 1853, "Still, no one had anything close to 'title' to any land around Tucson. The conferring of permanent titles for persons residing on the land and farming the fields would ultimately follow processes established under the public land laws of the United States."[24]

In the case of Tucson, the lack of written records outlining the full scope of Spanish and Mexican land grants raises the question of whether former presidio military commanders actively issued such grants or refrained from doing so altogether. Looking back to the inception of the presidio, anthropologist Henry F. Dobyns, author of *Spanish Colonial Tucson*, affirms its dual role as both a military installation and an institution "designed to foster civilization on imperial frontiers." In 1772, Spain's King Charles III issued the *New Regulations for Frontier Posts*, encouraging settlement near military installations. One directive stated, "I order the captains to distribute and assign lands and town lots to those that ask them, with the obligation that they cultivate them and that they keep horses, arms, and munitions for use in expeditions against enemies when necessity demands it and they are so ordered."[25]

The proclamation indicates that presidial commanders were not only encouraged to assign land but were authorized to do so. As historian Kieran McCarty reminds us, the presidial captain wielded unparalleled power: "Civilian settlers occupied lands and homes only by virtue of subordination in all things to the military activity of the presidio. The presidial captain was the only authority known to the populations, military and civilian alike. In legal cases involving civilians . . . the presidial commander was always the judge." This centralization underscores the importance of records pertaining to land distribution and legal rulings in the region.[26]

In the mid-1980s, noted expert on Southern Arizona and Sonoran history, anthropologist James E. Officer, outlined the complexities involved in researching Spanish and later Mexican documents. He lamented that, "many of the documents that might tell us more of the Arizona story have never been found or are distributed among so many different archives that chasing them down is almost a life's work."[27] He also confirmed that in 1856, when Mexican troops withdrew from Tucson following the U.S. acquisition of the territory under the Gadsden Purchase, "all of the civil, religious, and military documents pertaining to the Tucson presidio and its population were carried by the Mexican soldiers to Imuris, Sonora," which is located about forty miles south of the then-new international border. To underscore the neglect and mishandling of crucial records, Officer shared a story about the soldiers tasked to care for the documents: "Having no interest in the records and probably no place to store them, the soldiers sorted through the documents and separated out those written on paper that could serve for rolling cigarettes. Then, they burned the remainder."[28]

In the second half of the nineteenth century, Hubert Howe Bancroft, a prominent historian of the U.S. West, sought information to support his scholarship by collecting books, documents, and records. He also employed a team to copy and transcribe government and mission archives and conducted several oral histories.[29] The discovery of documents in 1879 at a church in Magdalena, Sonora, located about fifteen miles south of Imuris, however, directly contradicted the story of soldiers destroying the presidio's records.

In 1879, Alphonse Louis Pinart, a French linguist and researcher assisting Bancroft, was scouting for documents in Sonora. While there, Pinart learned of a collection of old papers stored in a room next to the dome of the church in Magdalena. The priest, however, refused him access, claiming the documents were "of no historical interest." Undeterred, Pinart waited for the priest to leave town and, with the help of a church worker, gained access to the collection. According to Officer, Pinart "found a great many documents of interest to himself and Bancroft, and he loaded them into his satchel." The original Tucson documents located by Pinart are still held at the Bancroft Library.[30] As Pinart sifted through the documents, and knowing that only so many would fit in his bag, he favored those related to military operations. This led Officer to describe Pinart's find as "among the choicest items available to the scholar interested in the military history of southern Arizona during the Mexican years."[31] Pinart's discovery indicates that Tucson's presidial records were dispersed and relocated to other places for safekeeping, and that Imuris may not have been their final destination.

One Man's Testimony

Most historians, including Officer, believe that when Mexican forces withdrew from the Tucson presidio in 1856, they took the official records to Imuris. Francisco S. León, a cavalryman in the Mexican army, likely accompanied the other soldiers and the cargo being shipped. Evacuating the presidio may have required several trips. León and his family eventually settled in Imuris before returning to Tucson. While the exact timing of his return remains unclear, an 1859 land transaction record suggests he returned to Tucson with the intent to stay. He purchased a large lot at what would become the corner of present-day Main and Pennington streets, where he opened a store. He also owned a farm near the Santa Cruz River.[32]

Following the treaties of Guadalupe Hidalgo and the Gadsden Purchase, the U.S. government publicly pledged to honor the land titles of Mexican residents, but locating records and resolving competing claims proved increasingly difficult. In 1882, Francisco S. León was called to testify before the U.S. Court of Private Land Claims about Spanish and later Mexican land ownership in southern Arizona. Fluent in English, León became the primary source for claims that the presidio records ended up in Imuris. Every other reference to Imuris as the records' destination is secondary and relies on León's testimony or indirect accounts rather than firsthand knowledge. Although he testified under oath, the brevity of his statement is striking. When asked about the missing records of the Mexican Justice of the Peace in Tucson, León said, "They had been taken to Imuris, in the District of Magdalena, Sonora, and thereafter I do not know what became of them."[33]

This brief exchange reveals a missed opportunity. Those involved in the land court proceedings had access to someone with first-hand knowledge of the presidial records, yet they failed to ask the follow-up questions that could have clarified critical historical claims: How were the records transported? Did they fill two or three wagons? Were the documents wrapped and organized, and who was responsible for loading them and ensuring their safe return to Mexico? Were any of the documents recorded or cataloged before being transported? Furthermore, it's important to note that Imuris was not a presidio, so where exactly were the items stored upon arrival? Were they left at a church or a government building? If so, which one?

Moreover, the brevity of León's response raises concerns. He did not return to Tucson immediately, and while stationed in Imuris, he was likely in a position to witness or learn what became of the cargo he had traveled with. Given his role, he also would have known which military office or individual had been tasked with overseeing the documents.

By 1879, when he testified, León was among the few Tucsonenses whose financial wealth increased dramatically after the arrival of the Anglos. He had developed close relationships with key figures like William S. Oury (discussed in the following section), cementing his position within the new power structure.[34] León served on the town council and three terms as what today would be considered an Arizona Senator, underscoring how he cooperated with and adapted to the new political and social systems. By the time he died in 1891, León owned 300 acres of property.[35] León's role in the case of the missing archives reveals how gaps in the historical record, whether accidental or strategic, allowed new settlers and their allies to dismiss earlier systems of recordkeeping and assert their own authority.

William S. Oury

After the Gadsden Purchase, the incorporation of the new territories into the U.S. proceeded quickly. Arizona was originally a part of Doña Ana County in the New Mexico Territory. The Butterfield Overland Stage Company began operations in 1858, running between St. Louis and San Francisco, with stops in El Paso, Tucson, and other locations.[36] This service reduced Tucson's isolation, connecting it to the broader national network by providing regular mail, supplies, and bringing more white settlers to the area. That Tucson that had hosted fewer than 400 Mexicans in 1820 had become a distant memory by 1860, when the census recorded a population of over 900 residents.[37] Sheridan describes it as "Sonoran Tucson, after all, was a community with a past, not a raw frontier town. And although territorial Tucson was beginning to take its place, the transition was by no means complete. In a sense, Tucson in 1860 was a dual, almost schizophrenic, settlement, one divided between Mexican families rooted in the land and aggressive young male Anglo immigrants seeking fame and fortune on the Apache frontier. This demographic duality in large measure determined Tucson's destiny for the next twenty years."[38]

A "colorful" white settler who significantly influenced early U.S. property transactions and played a pivotal role in shaping land deals, William S. Oury settled in Tucson in 1856 to seek his fortune. An ardent expansionist, Oury repeatedly placed his life at risk to ensure the dispossession of Mexican territories. Born in Virginia around 1811, he arrived in Texas in time to play a role in the Alamo and fought at the final and decisive battle of the Texas Revolution in San Jacinto. He later joined the Texas Rangers and served as a soldier in the U.S.-Mexican War. Through his military service, Oury contributed to the efforts that led to the annexation of Mexican territories.[39]

Along the way, Oury married Inez García, a Mexicana from Durango, Chihuahua, and moved to California during the Gold Rush. He arrived in Tucson in 1856 and decided to stay, as his biographer notes, because Oury saw it as ". . . a free place where a man could stretch out and make his own way without the hand of authority to molest him. He could grow up with this land, and become a part of it, and so decided to stay."[40]

The outbreak of the Civil War led to the withdrawal of U.S. troops from Tucson, who were needed elsewhere. After they left, on March 18, 1861, a group of sixty-eight prominent Anglo settlers, including William S. Oury, held a meeting and declared their allegiance to the Confederacy. In fact, this group of secessionists claimed the power not merely to voice support for a cause but to assert control over the region's political future. They claimed sovereign authority, or the legitimate and independent power to govern as if they were a recognized government. They declared allegiance to a foreign nation (the Confederacy) and selected Oury's brother, Granville, to represent the territory as a delegate to the Confederate Congress, signaling their defection from the Union.[41]

In February 1862, when Confederate troops arrived and occupied Tucson, southern sympathizers celebrated. As expected, Oury was "as elated and noisy as any other" and "dance[d] a jig."[42] However, this moment of triumph was short-lived, as Union forces returned to Tucson a few months later in May 1862 and declared martial law. Union Brigadier General James H. Carleton moved quickly to punish the rebel sympathizers for treason. Among others, William and his brother Granville were convicted of treason. The brothers' properties were both confiscated and sold at auction.[43]

With property ownership in disarray, Carleton transferred authority over Tucson to Major David Fergusson on July 21, 1862, who then moved to address the issue. On August 5, 1862, Major Fergusson ordered the citizens of Tucson to document their properties, relying in large part on the honor system to begin the process. Historian Sue Smith describes how Tucson's earlier settlement patterns made issuing and recording deeds more challenging. She observed: "Adding to the confusion, the prevalent method of acquiring land [was] by moving onto a vacant plot, erecting an adobe house, and establishing ownership by the fact of possession."[44] Fergusson also commissioned the first survey and map of Tucson (a reproduction is included in Chapter 2), known as the Fergusson map. In an unexpected but telling turn, he appointed William S. Oury as registrar and recorder, placing him in charge of recording the properties.[45]

Fergusson's appointment of Oury is difficult to reconcile. Instead of seeking to resolve property matters, Fergusson's main goal seemed to be unifying a town controlled by Confederate sympathizers. Oury's appointment testifies to his local influence. It also suggests that Fergusson recognized the region's social and political structure, where a small group of powerful white settlers exercised considerable control over a population largely composed of Tucsonenses and Indigenous peoples. To view the appointment as merely politically pragmatic is to ignore how invested those in power tend to be in defending the status quo. At a time when the Union was taking punitive actions against Confederate sympathizers, Fergusson chose to overlook the moral implications of Oury's role in the secessionist movement, especially considering he had been found guilty of treason. Instead, Fergusson's appointment reinforced the prevailing power structures, further entrenching the dominance of a small group of white settlers.

Oury spent the next several months recording the properties, marking what, in the absence of earlier records, appears to be the first formal documentation of properties in Tucson. However, his task was soon interrupted by a significant new development. Arizona had originally been established as part of the New Mexico Territory, but on February 24, 1863, President Abraham Lincoln established the Territory of Arizona. He appointed John N. Goodwin as its first Governor. The next year, Governor Goodwin formally incorporated Tucson as a town by proclamation and appointed William S. Oury as its first Mayor.[46]

Oury would go on to be elected Sheriff and hold key positions, further consolidating his political influence in the region. In April 1871, he led the Camp Grant Massacre, where an Apache village was surrounded at dawn, and nearly 150 men, women, and children were murdered in their sleep.[47] Despite this violent legacy, Oury's political patronage in Tucson remained strong. When one of the most transformative events in the city's history occurred in 1880, the arrival of the railroad, it was William S. Oury who was chosen to give the keynote speech. This underscored how those who reaped the greatest rewards of settler colonialism, including a select group of Tucsonenses, consistently rewarded Oury for steering the city's agenda in alignment with the prevailing ideals of "progress": the displacement of Indigenous peoples, the appropriation of land, and the consolidation of settler control, regardless of the human and moral cost.

William S. Oury's recording of titles is preserved at the Arizona Historical Society. In referencing an 1863 example, attorney John Lacy noted how little legal formality governed the transactions. For example, Solomon Warner acknowledged that he did not have legal title to a parcel of land he sold to Samuel O. Wise. Lacy adds context to these exchanges by pointing out, "These 'titles' must have seemed relatively secure" not only because money was exchanged for the properties, but also because "the purchasers had little fear of some future claimant exercising his or her rights under the preemption laws [the legal right of a previous occupant or owner to reclaim the land]."[48] Some Tucsonenses also acquired land and took advantage of the loose documentation practices that characterized the period.

Although the surviving records offer some insight, the full nature of these early deed transactions remains unclear. Many of the exchanges were likely part of informal favors or reciprocal arrangements that benefited both the sellers and those in positions of power, particularly given Oury's role in overseeing land records. Because Oury had lost his property when convicted of treason, he managed to purchase five properties for himself, all near the old presidio. His brother Granville also secured two properties. Oury even recorded deeds for white settlers who were absent from the territory. Charles H. Meyer's property was also formally documented, not because he purchased it, but because it had been "taken up and improved in 1862."[49] Oury also took the opportunity to record a mining claim for himself.

In 1875, the federal government intervened again, allowing Mexicans with U.S. citizenship under the treaty to claim land if they had occupied it for twenty years. Some white settlers, such as Samuel H. Drachman, claimed land despite not meeting the residency requirement. Meanwhile, a handful of Mexicans who managed to navigate the complicated process were able to secure title to land, particularly in the agricultural fields near the river and Sentinel Peak.[50]

Claiming land and the formalization of property deeds advanced with the Federal Townsite Act of 1867, which required Tucson's incorporation as a village to secure property and establish local government. In 1872, when Sidney W. Foreman plotted a town plan that introduced an orthogonal grid layout with distinctive 90-degree corners and straight lines, it marked a departure from the Spanish and Mexican street models, which often ran at angles in response to natural barriers or geography (see Figure 3.4). It cleared the way for the sale of township lots, and some, like Charles O. Brown, purchased eight of them.[51] By 1877, Tucson had incorporated, and the regulations, rooted in U.S. legal frameworks and customs, favored white settlers and the generations that followed. In the 1960s, the Cordovas were challenging embedded cultural and institutional connections that had enabled white settlers to capitalize on the opportunities provided by a land distribution system built on deception and greed.

An Unfruitful Lawsuit

It is no surprise that *Raul Navarrete Cordova v. United States of America and the City of Tucson* was dismissed. Raul appeared at four hearings alone and faced six different motions he was required to respond to and prepare for.[52] Among other arguments, the City of Tucson invoked the Doctrine of Adverse Possession to claim ownership of the land. It asserted, "The defendant, City of Tucson, in its development as a thriving metropolis, has completed every legal prerequisite necessary for adverse possession, should the plaintiff or his predecessors have or ever had legal claim of right."[53] In essence, the City argued that its long-standing occupation and development had fulfilled the legal requirements of continuous and open possession. Even if the Cordovas had once held a claim, their rights were now invalid due to the City's extended use of the land.

Raul was up against formidable opposition, battling a well-resourced municipality and the full power of the U.S. government, entities designed

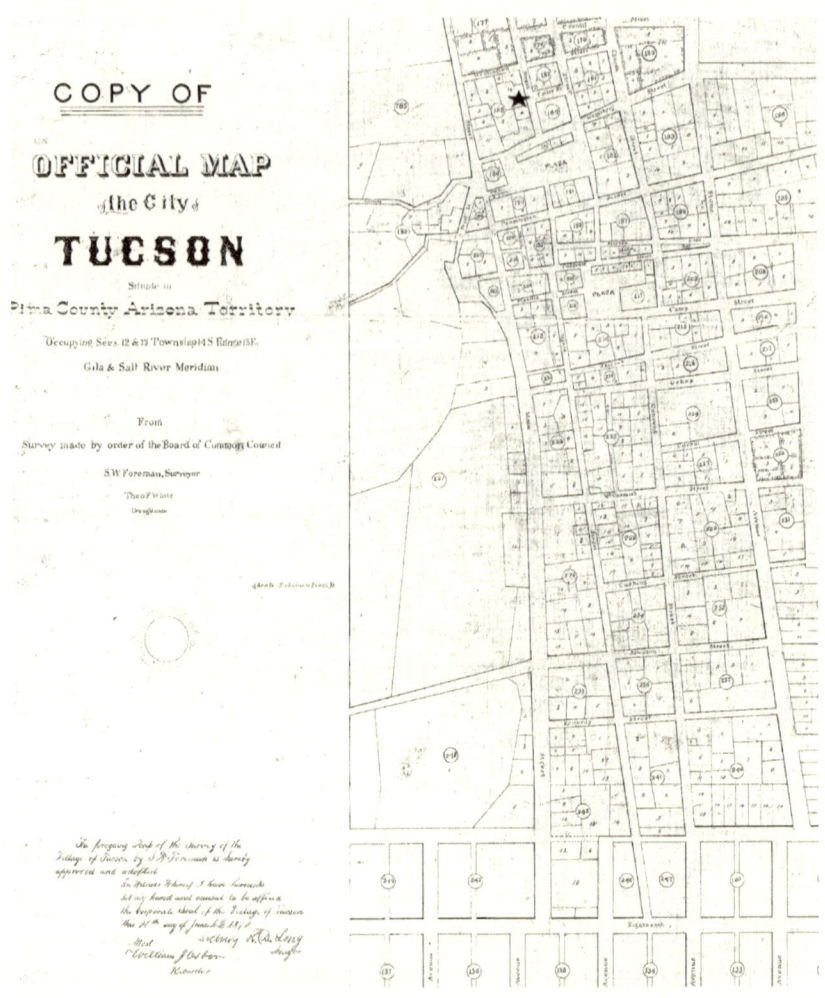

FIGURE 3.4 This faint reproduction of the 1872 Foreman map reflects the imposition of a rectilinear grid system, with orthogonal street layouts and evenly divided property parcels as the city expanded. Though difficult to read, this cropped view still marks a key shift in land planning. A star has been added to indicate the location of 173 North Meyer Avenue. Located in, and reproduced with permission from, the University of Arizona Libraries Special Collections.

to maintain control and order. Despite his efforts, as an individual up against a team of lawyers, he struggled to keep up. The U.S. Attorney continued to demand more evidence: "Petitioner Raul Navarrete Cordova does not set out the land claimed, the time, the basis for which petitioner . . . claims title, but what document, if during his lifetime, both by what document if before his lifetime, and what claim of title."[54] The U.S. also made it clear that lawsuits against the federal government required its consent to proceed. As a sovereign, it claimed immunity from any lawsuit unless it had consented both to be sued and to allow the court to hear the case.[55] Raul Cordova's case was dismissed on November 1, 1966.[56]

At this point, there is no way to prove the existence of the Presidio Land Title that the Cordovas claimed. Although Refugio once had a copy, the family often stated that the land grant had been recorded in Mexico and believed it would eventually be located in an archive there. Raul searched extensively in Mexican libraries and archives trying to find it. But the passage of time has made it increasingly unlikely that documentation will be found. Still, the question arises: what if the story, or parts of it, were constructed as a strategic response to dispossession? Even if the legitimacy of the land claim is uncertain, the lawsuit stands as a powerful example of resisting settler colonialism by using its own legal system to challenge property narratives.

Raul Cordova's legal action marked a pivotal moment in Tucson's history and in the battle over property rights. And without María Cordova claiming its historical value, there would be no Casa Cordova. The ingenuity required to craft a legal argument rooted in historical precedent, such as the Gadsden Purchase, to contest urban renewal a century later and protect the Cordova home deserves recognition, not only for its legal implications but as a testament to a family's commitment to retain their home and assert their humanity.

This legal battle ended in dismissal, but the Cordovas continued to fight for their property. María Cordova kept painting and invited reporters into her home to share her family's story. However, a more forceful legal challenge lay ahead, one in which the City of Tucson would become the plaintiff, seeking to remove the Cordovas from their home. María Cordova's words, "I wish I had the family records so I could tell you the exact dates and facts . . . It is important to tell the truth about historical happenings for the sake of one's children, so they will know the truth," still resonate in the historical record. While we may never fully know the truth of all she referenced, or may even choose to dismiss her claims, the truths we do know, particularly the reality of María Cordova losing her home, are documented. And they are devastating.

CHAPTER 4

Caught in the Crosshairs
A Bullseye on the Cordovas

In 1959, the City of Tucson premiered an exhibit titled "Target: Improve Tucson through Urban Renewal" at 324 W. Franklin Street. The Tucson Fine Arts Association (TFAA), which operated the building, hosted the exhibit located less than three blocks away from the Cordovas. Today, the site is known as Kingan Gardens, a venue that hosts many weddings and celebrations.[1]

Before acquiring this location, the arts group never had a permanent home and had been housed in other temporary locations. Founded in 1924, the TFAA's members included socialites with an interest in the city's cultural and aesthetic development, usually those from the wealthier classes. Large donors with national and international connections made it possible to display works by prominent artists such as Diego Rivera, Jackson Pollock, Eliane de Kooning, Pablo Picasso, and Andy Warhol, among others.[2]

In the early 1960s, the group changed its name to the Tucson Art Center (TAC) (see Figure 4.1). Ten years later, they managed to acquire the land and built a new multistoried, modernist art center. The group changed its name once again to reflect the expanded facility, which included several smaller structures, and is now known as the Tucson Museum of Art and Historic Block (TMA), located at 140 North Main Avenue.[3]

Selecting this location in the city's most historic neighborhood to premiere the urban renewal exhibit in 1959 made political sense because city officials needed the backing of the cultural elite to support their plan. It is likely that María Cordova and her family walked through the "Target" exhibit. Up to that point, the events the Cordovas had witnessed had prompted them to stay informed about redevelopment plans. Their

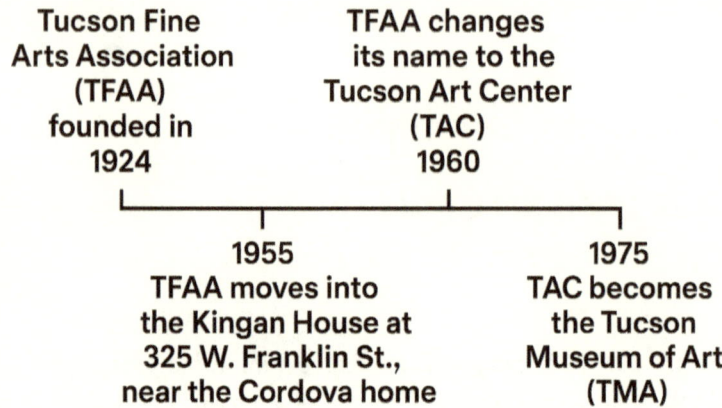

FIGURE 4.1 Timeline showing the institutional evolution of what is currently the Tucson Museum of Art (TMA).

suspicions and defensiveness notwithstanding, they could not have anticipated the devastation that awaited them a decade later.

The TAC, which hosted the exhibit, along with the City of Tucson, would play pivotal roles in the sweeping changes that reshaped the area once home to the former presidio. At the behest of the TAC, the City of Tucson issued and enforced directives to build the arts group a new, expansive, and multistoried modern art center. Both entities formed an alliance and moved forward with a plan that also targeted the Cordova properties, all the while overlooking that the Cordovas still lived, and wished to continue living, in their home. Raul Cordova filed a lawsuit on November 4, 1965, to claim the Tucson Presidio Title. Some of the alliances and developments described in this chapter help explain why he did so in response to the accelerating urban renewal plans, with the TAC playing a central role in ensuring that the Cordova properties were targeted.

Old Pueblo District Project

Urban renewal projects had already been funded through the U.S. Housing Act of 1949, but the federal government broadened its support with the Urban Renewal Act of 1954. This new initiative promised to cover two-thirds of the net cost for slum clearance projects in cities.[4] Eager to capitalize on this opportunity, states across the nation, including Arizona, moved quickly to apply for the funds. In response, Republican Governor John Howard Pyle signed an emergency clause that had been introduced and promptly moved through the state House. This clause granted cities across Arizona the authority to establish housing codes for slum clearance, to define the power to acquire property through eminent domain, and develop general plans to secure federal funds.[5] Urban renewal in Tucson began with an initial 1958 plan that was eventually set aside in favor of a new proposal, which local voters approved on March 1, 1966.[6]

In the latter part of the 1950s, then Mayor Don Hummel spearheaded an early plan known as the Old Pueblo District (see Figure 4.2). To qualify for available federal funds, Hummel, City Manager Porter W. Homer, and his staff began designing a plan. On July 17, 1958, the city council approved a resolution that officially designated Hummel's proposed district as a "slum" area.[7] Since no building or neighborhood wanted to be labeled as such, the designation provoked disagreement. To address this, the mayor clarified that "the designation was not intended to cast a bad light on the buildings in the area," explaining that identifying the area as a "slum" was a requirement for securing federal funds. Hummel also added that "many of the buildings in the proposed district are not slum dwellings."[8] Notably, the Cordova properties and the former presidio neighborhood were excluded from this early phase of urban renewal.

Like urban renewal projects across the nation, the Old Pueblo District disproportionately targeted communities of color and ignored the social and historical significance of the neighborhoods it affected. This initial project focused on nearly 400 acres south of downtown, an area bounded by Stone Avenue to the east, Congress Street to the north, the freeway to the west, and 22nd Street to the south. Mexican and Mexican American residents made up 74% of the target area's population, while African Americans accounted for 19%.[9]

The city's first urban renewal effort stands out as more considerate in its treatment of those displaced than the version ultimately implemented

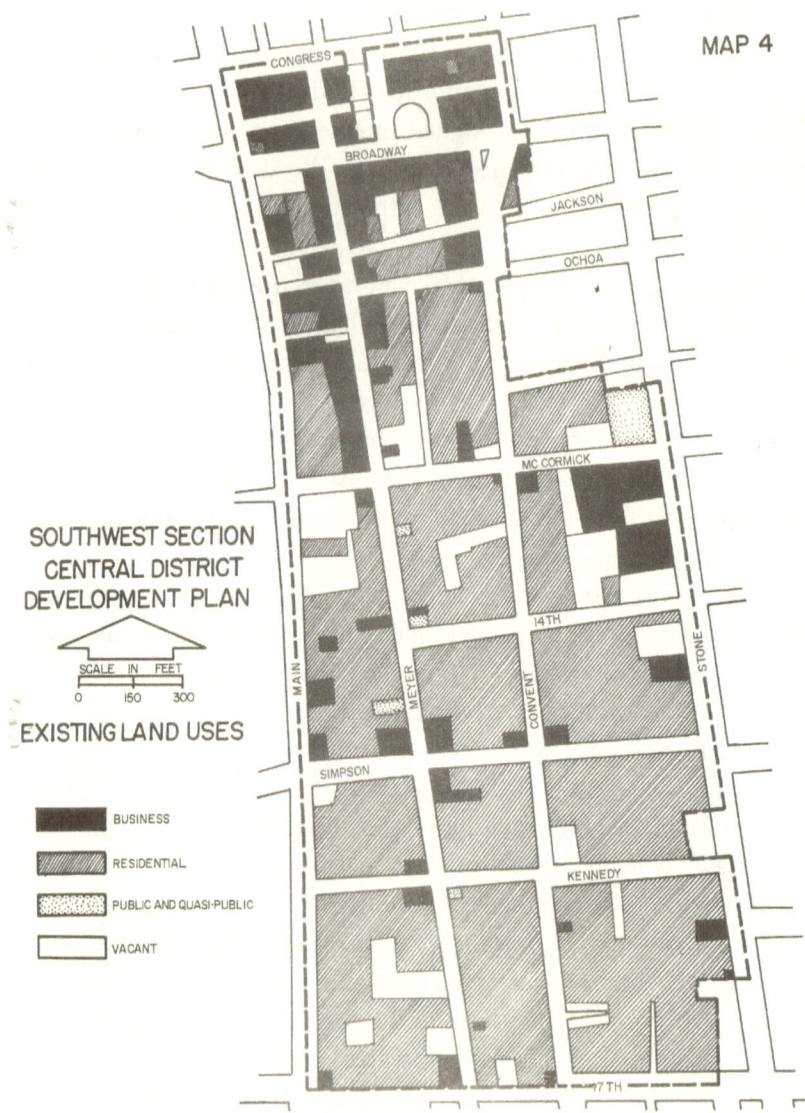

FIGURE 4.2 As indicated in this map from Mayor Don Hummel's 392-acre urban renewal plan, a significant portion of the area was designated for residential use. From *Redevelopment Plan: Southwestern Section Central District Development Plan (Old Pueblo Project, Ariz. R-6)* (Tucson: City of Tucson, March 22, 1962).

eight years later. City Manager Homer and his staff began by personally visiting homes in the proposed urban renewal district and gathering information directly from the residents. They interviewed families about their income and, if relocation became necessary, inquired how much they could afford to pay for housing. According to the *Citizen*, "The purpose of the study is to give city officials detailed information of the relocation problems they must solve before any clearance work can be done in the project area."[10] In total, the urban renewal staff interviewed 1,310 families to gather data to shape their plan. Since most of those interviewed preferred to stay close to downtown, the city moved forward to make that a possible option.[11]

Homer developed a strategy that prioritized both geographical preferences and affordable homeownership. This approach is best captured in the *Citizen*'s opening line, which reported, "Many families living in Tucson's proposed urban renewal slum clearance area may wind up owning brand new homes not far from where they live now." Homer detailed how these objectives could be achieved through "the extremely lenient initial investment and monthly payments for new, low-cost homes that can be built under special Federal Housing Administration (FHA) provisions."[12] Even before this announcement in the newspaper, City Manager Homer had already sent a request to the FHA to build 500 housing units. The plan called on private builders to construct the houses, which would be sold for around $7,000 to displaced families eligible for forty-year FHA mortgages. Down payments would be as low as $200, including closing costs.[13]

This vision of building new housing subdivisions for those displaced from their homes was pathbreaking and prioritized community welfare. The inclusion of low down payments and long-term FHA financing set this initiative apart from typical housing programs, which often excluded lower-income families from homeownership. This goal prompted reporter Peter Starrett to marvel, "it will be not only unique, but something of a miracle. Tucson may be the only city in the U.S. where renewal families are relocated in such a complete way." That city officials were invested in offering residents long-term stability and a pathway toward homeownership indicates a concern beyond physical redevelopment and an intent to improve the quality of life for displaced residents. This approach reflected a somewhat progressive view in a city obsessed with urban growth, where realtors and pro-development interests held significant sway over local politics and continue to do so today. It also serves as an overlooked instance of virtuous city leadership. However, as is often the case, these intentions were later tested by the realities of implementation and by opposition that made housing for historically marginalized communities difficult to achieve.

The City Manager also considered those from lower income brackets who could not qualify for FHA mortgages, promising public housing funded by both local and federal resources. According to the plan, public housing would be "rented to families on the basis of what they can afford to pay—not what the living unit is worth." It is important to note that urban renewal laws did not mandate the relocation of displaced residents; the city chose to take on the moral responsibility of doing so. At the time, Tucson had one public housing complex with 160 units, La Reforma, located south of downtown. Due to high demand, there was a waiting list for available residences.[14]

Mayor Hummel understood that public support for his plans was critical. At this point, he and his administration focused only on housing and urban renewal. Plans for a new civic convention center had been brought up but were not central to the discussions.[15] The program eventually required voter approval, and Hummel expected the strongest and most vocal opposition from those against accepting federal funds and public housing, groups that were, in many cases, one and the same. Attempting to quell the growing concerns over public housing, the Mayor began to temper his ambitious plans, stating, "there will be little or no need for additional public housing . . . and there is sufficient turnover in La Reforma low-income project to take care of some in the blighted area who are not able to buy homes."[16] To gain more traction for his program, the Mayor over the years whittled down the project area to seventy-six acres.[17]

Amid accusations of improper city purchases and other controversies, Hummel's term ended at the close of 1961. The changing of the guard came with the election of Republican Lew Davis as Mayor. A realtor who had named his firm after himself, Davis had also established several subdivisions. In 1960, he helped found Stewart Title and Trust of

Tucson, a primary source of home mortgages. He held the position of president of the title company when he ran for Mayor.[18] Following Davis's election, City Manager Porter Homer felt pressed to resign, and on May 7, 1962, city officials effectively shelved Hummel and Homer's urban renewal plan, distancing themselves from any of its provisions or promises.[19] However, the prospect of federal funds, which could be used to modernize downtown and attract tourists by making it more "American," remained too enticing for Mayor Davis and his boosters to file away and forget.

While elected officials publicly distanced themselves from the earlier urban renewal plan, private institutions and civic leaders quietly began positioning themselves for the next iteration. Among them was the TAC, which had its own ambitions for expansion. As discussions about redefining downtown resumed behind the scenes, the TAC made a strategic hire that would ensure they had a voice in Tucson's redevelopment efforts.

The Art of Influence: Frank Sanguinetti and the Tucson Art Center (TAC)

In July 1964, the TAC hired Frank Sanguinetti to lead the organization.[20] Born in 1917 into wealth in Yuma, Arizona, where his family operated a chain of department stores, Sanguinetti earned a bachelor's degree in economics and later a graduate degree in art history from the University of Arizona. He is described as a devoted supporter of the arts who loved ballet, opera, and the symphony, "believing art, regardless of the form it took, was essential to living the good life. But his passion, his great love, were the visual arts."[21] In addition to organizing the TAC, its collections, and exhibits, Sanguinetti used his connections and business acumen to elevate the institution and promote a larger role for the arts, both locally and nationally.

He had lived in Tucson since 1960 and used that time to establish connections with city leaders and influential power brokers, positioning himself to influence upcoming decisions. Moreover, Sanguinetti knew the person who could make things happen: Roy Drachman, who would become the driving force behind Tucson's urban renewal efforts. The two had served together on the board of directors of Arizona Savings and Loan Association, a professional relationship that predated or overlapped with their roles in determining what got built during urban renewal (see Figure 4.3). Their shared position on this financial board placed them squarely within Tucson's elite economic and political networks. Their financial strategies and visions for urban development were closely aligned, and both stood to benefit from reshaping the city to serve tourism, real estate, and institutional expansion.

The most consequential conversations about urban development and programs like renewal often took place in spaces such as gallery openings, luncheons, celebratory dinners, and on the golf course. These informal settings allowed the privileged, Sanguinetti, Drachman, and others, to advise one another, coordinate, and move plans forward without public scrutiny. Reporters would sometimes refer to "City Hall

FIGURE 4.3 Advertisement listing the board of directors of Arizona Savings and Loan Association, including Roy P. Drachman and E. F. Sanguinetti, published in *Star,* January 30, 1953, 14.

observers," unnamed sources who offered insight into the direction city officials were moving. These observers understood the dynamic well. Important conversations took place offstage, not in public venues but in private ones. "City Hall observers," more often than not, knew who was really running the show.

Pueblo Center Redevelopment Project

In what the *Star* referred to as a "180-Degree Turn" in its headline on December 1, 1964, Tucson embraced urban renewal once again. Mayor Davis had changed his stance and was now eager to accept federal aid for a new urban renewal project. The initial proposal that he and the city council endorsed covered seventy-six acres and included a convention center. At that point, the boundaries of the plan remained unclear, or as city officials put it, "informal," but it focused exclusively on the area south of downtown.[22]

Urban renewal also made the front page of the *Citizen*, Tucson's other major newspaper. Reporter Steve Emerine picked up on officials' reluctance to define clear boundaries and suggested they were withholding information. Regarding the new plan, Emerine wrote: "The fact that the mayor and council declined to establish definite boundaries for the 'study' area gave strength to the belief by City Hall observers that the council is weighing the possibility of including land north of City Hall."[23] A year later, when city officials announced new boundaries that included a section north of City Hall, the "City Hall observers" who informed Emerine were proven correct. The conversations that took place offstage did not, in themselves, threaten the Cordovas. It was the decisions they influenced, such as redrawing the boundaries to include their home, that posed the real danger.

Mayor Davis appointed Roy Drachman to chair the committee tasked with developing the new urban renewal program, which would later be called the Pueblo Center Redevelopment Project.[24] The committee, which Drachman led, was named the Committee on Municipal Blight (COMB), an acronym intentionally selected to spell out "comb." The *Cit-*

izen reported that "Davis [Mayor] and the council indicated that they like the abbreviation since they plan to go over the South Meyer and Covent Avenue slum area 'with a fine-tooth comb to get rid of blight.'"[25] Drachman, along with the pro-development, pro-tourism business team he assembled, put forth a plan that was far less considerate than the one proposed in the 1950s. No provisions were included to build new housing for those displaced.

The first step in applying for federal funding required city officials to define the boundaries of the urban renewal project area. They offered a glimpse of their new boundaries on February 1, 1965. The headline of the front page of the *Citizen* read, "Urban Renewal Area, Plan OK'd." In a little over a year, the project area had increased from seventy-six to close to eighty acres. City officials emphasized that the project area was not final and that the boundaries might still need to be adjusted, suggesting that behind-the-scenes negotiations, not public input, were driving the shifts. It included 263 buildings, and the city manager estimated that it would displace 1,170 residents who lived in the project area. The map outlining the proposed project area now included a square block north of City Hall where the Cordova family lived (see Figure 4.4).[26]

This expansion signaled not only a shift in boundaries but an overall broadening of the urban renewal program. These changes occurred six months after the TAC hired Frank Sanguinetti as its executive director. On behalf of the arts group, Sanguinetti pushed for inclusion in the city's urban renewal plan with the goal of building a new art center complex north of City Hall.

The Historic Block

Historic preservation quickly emerged as a strategic tool in advancing the urban renewal plan. At one meeting, a developer warned what city officials already knew: opposition to urban renewal could escalate for "political and philosophical reasons," and that opponents "may try to raise a protest over historic buildings in order to defeat the whole program."[27] Four months after announcing that they were moving forward

FIGURE 4.4 "Structures in Project Area Study," in Roy P. Drachman and Vincent L. Lung, *The Pueblo Center Redevelopment Project: Report Presented to the Central City Council of the Urban Land Institute, April 23, 1965*, by Roy Drachman, Chairman, Citizens Committee on Municipal Blight, and Vincent L. Lung, Assistant City Manager and Coordinator of Community Development (Tucson: City of Tucson, 1965). The redevelopment area covered nearly eighty acres and included around 290 structures. Arrow added to indicate the location of the Cordova home at 173 North Meyer Avenue.

on an updated urban renewal plan, the city formally established a Committee for Historical Sites. In the early stages of shaping this new urban renewal initiative, the Historical Sites Committee became a subcommittee of COMB. Chaired by Isabel Fathauer, a prominent civic leader who also served as president of the Pima County Republican Women, the Symphony Society Women's Association, and several charitable boards, the committee was tasked with making recommendations and justifying to consultants and city officials which structures merited preservation.[28]

After an initial assessment and tour of the area, in May 1965, the Historic Sites Committee issued a list of six "must save" houses located within the urban renewal area. Except for what was then called the John C. Frémont House (now known as the Sosa-Carrillo House), located south of downtown, the others were situated within the boundaries of the former presidio. During a tour of the area, Fathauer remarked, "the area even when intermingled with modern architecture would 'lend charm and romance to our city.'"[29] Like many preservationists of the era, Fathauer viewed historical buildings as aesthetic or nostalgic assets, rather than as lived-in homes with social and political significance. Fathauer did not advocate full preservation but instead favored selective retention based on architectural credentials and visual appeal, even as two hundred older Sonoran-influenced adobe row houses south of downtown were slated for demolition. Her stance ultimately reinforced the broader urban renewal agenda, which prioritized demolition and redevelopment over the preservation of existing communities.

All four houses on the "must save" list north of City Hall were over a century old and located within the same square block. Rather than focusing on individual buildings, the Historic Sites Committee recommended that urban renewal officials consider preserving the entire block. This approach acknowledged the architectural and historical cohesion of the area. As a result, the four "must save" structures began to be referred to collectively as "The Historic Block" (see Figure 4.5). Both of the Cordova properties made the list. According to the Sites Committee, "The Houses were built around 1850 and are practically unaltered." The Fish and Stevens homes, located west of the Cordova properties and built in the 1860s, were described as "good examples of early territorial

FIGURE 4.5 Historic Block outlined in white to show its location in relation to the urban renewal projects completed just south of downtown, the largest being the Tucson Community Center around 1971. Used with permission from the Arizona Historical Society.

architecture in good repair."[30] The committee's report also noted that the Cordova, Fish, and Stevens buildings were "still in use," but offered no guidance on who would remain or what would happen to the residents. It simply proposed that these buildings, as they put it, be "pardoned" from demolition.[31]

E.N. Fish: A House with Presidio Foundations in the Historic Block

Born in Massachusetts in 1827, Edward Nye (E.N.) Fish moved west during the California Gold Rush. He arrived in Tucson in 1865 and used the associations he had established in San Francisco to freight goods into the region, founding E.N. Fish & Co. He prospered by selling hay, grain, and other supplies to ranches, mines, and military posts during the Apache Wars. Fish also served on local governing bodies, including the Pima County Board of Supervisors and the Tucson City Council, and invested in mining and cattle ranching. By 1870, his wealth had reached $148,000.[32]

Fish began building his house in 1868, and it still stands at the southwest corner of Main Avenue and Alameda Street.[33] Before the house existed, this location marked the main entrance to the presidio, the gate that opened westward toward the Santa Cruz River and surrounding agricultural fields. When the presidio was dismantled, sections of its western wall were incorporated into the Fish residence, and adobe bricks from the original fort were used to construct the Sonoran-style row house with its characteristic thick walls. The land was acquired during the 1862 period when William Sanders Oury began documenting claims. At that time, another white settler with a checkered past, Mark Aldrich, claimed ownership of the property. He described it as including the "La Guardia," or former guardhouse or barracks, and sold it to Fish for $3,000 in 1868.[34] Although the Fish property marked a critical site in the former presidio with an important function, it is unaccounted for in historical records, as no Mexican or Spanish deeds or previous owners before Aldrich are included in the property's deed transactions.

Hiram Stevens House: Power and Historical Amnesia in the Historic Block

Hiram Stevens arrived in Tucson in 1854. He ran a trading post and hardware store and made a considerable amount of money selling beef and hay to military troops engaged in the wars against the Apaches. Stevens later served as a Territorial delegate to the U.S. Congress, as well as on the Pima County Board of Supervisors and as a tax assessor. He also participated in the 1871 Camp Grant Massacre, a pre-dawn attack that killed over one hundred Apaches, most of them women and children.[35]

Hiram Stevens purchased the property at 130 North Main Avenue in 1865.[36] The exact date of when he started building his home remains unclear. As with the Fish House, no Mexican or Spanish deeds or previous owners appear in the property's chain of title before the Oury Property Records of 1862. That year, U.S. Marshal Milton B. Duffield acquired the land next to Stevens and built a one-room house. In 1873, Stevens purchased Duffield's property and connected the two structures with a corridor, which is why the residence is sometimes referred to as the Stevens-Duffield House. Stevens continued to expand the home and was known for entertaining extensively there.[37]

In describing Stevens, literary scholar Frank C. Lockwood wrote that "he was one of the richest men in the territory. He did things in a big, breezy, western way and possessed both the vices and the good qualities of the typical pioneer. He was a man of nerve, was free from boasting, was a crack shot."[38] Lockwood may have known more than he chose to reveal, particularly in his choice of words. "A crack shot" hints at a darker side to Stevens' character. In 1893, after attempting to murder his wife, Petra Santa Cruz Stevens, by shooting her in the head, a hair comb deflected the shot, and Petra survived. Hiram Stevens then killed himself. She lived in the house until 1916.[39]

Close Neighbors, Worlds Apart

By the time the urban renewal "Target" exhibit opened a few blocks away in 1959, no descendants of either the E. N. Fish, Hiram Stevens or Milton B. Duffield families remained in their former homes. Seasonal resident Hoagland Gates of Maryland had purchased both properties around 1935. Born into a privileged New York family, Gates had built his wealth by acquiring and expanding a 197-acre dairy, Broadlands Farm, in New Jersey. He made most of his money shipping his prize-winning Jersey cattle to the western U.S. by railroad.[40] Gates renovated both houses and converted them into apartments, and he and his wife, Margaret Mackey Gates, lived in one of the units during the winter months.[41]

In the late nineteenth century, living in the Historic Block carried social clout. The decision by Fish and Stevens to build their homes just north of City Hall suggests the area was considered a prestigious location. Directly to the north sat Snob Hollow, a neighborhood known for its upper-class residents and older mansions. By the 1960s, the area remained a draw for affluent residents, particularly those connected to Tucson's art circles. The TAC, which had found a home on Franklin Street just a few blocks away, reflected this upscale shift. Its modest structure became a cultural hub that helped reenergize the surrounding area.

One of the newer residents drawn to the Historic Block was TAC director Frank Sanguinetti, who lived in an apartment in the former E.N. Fish House on Main Street, just behind María Cordova and the Cordova Brothers Smoke Shop.[42] He often entertained and held events in his home and clearly appreciated the area's ambiance and history. Sanguinetti formed a personal connection to the Historic Block, and it is difficult to imagine he never exchanged words with someone in the Cordova family or failed to read about them in the newspaper. Given his interest in art, it is worth wondering whether he ever asked María to show him her paintings.

Turning Public Attention into a Campaign

The announcement that the block north of City Hall would be included in the urban renewal project did not shock the Cordovas. Sanguinetti and the TAC's push for a new art center had already received newspaper coverage. Perhaps seeing how readily the city moved to appease and accommodate the TAC's designs by redrawing the boundaries for such a defining project galvanized the Cordovas. Days after learning that the urban renewal boundaries had been adjusted to include the Cordova properties, Raul Cordova wrote an angry letter to the *Star* editor titled "Historical Heritage to Be Destroyed."[43]

The next month, in March 1965, Raul wrote another letter to the *Star*'s editor with a different tone and intent. He criticized the "shortsightedness" of those responsible for urban renewal. Regarding the preservation of historic buildings, he wrote, "However, for us the job remains, which is the preservation of the historical buildings and the documents pertaining to them. This we shall proceed to do to the utmost of our resources."[44] His mention of "documents" suggested that Raul believed these materials, perhaps property deeds, historical records, or evidence of the Cordova family's longstanding connection to the property, were key to demonstrating the historical value of the buildings and securing their protection. To him, it also seemed that "preservation" meant not only maintaining and updating structures, but ensuring that the people who lived there could remain in their homes. Raul's perspective, though unconventional, reflected a more holistic view of preservation, one that encompassed both the physical space and the people within it. Less than eight months after writing this letter, Raul Cordova filed his lawsuit claiming legal ownership of the original Presidio lands, including much of downtown Tucson.

For the Cordovas, the Historic Sites Committee's May 1965 decision to add their home to the "must save" list during urban renewal likely brought relief. The designation validated María Cordova's longstanding efforts to draw attention to her historic home, and as an added plus, the committee's announcement attracted new interest from journalists eager to document its story.

The *Citizen* published another installment of Albert R. Buehman's "Arizona Album," titled "Home Once Inside Presidio." The article highlighted key historical details about the house at 173 North Meyer Avenue. It related that it had been built around 1850 with 24-inch-thick adobe walls, wooden and saguaro cactus beams, and a layered roof of thatch, wet adobe, and dry dirt. It omitted that Raul Cordova was the legal owner and instead stated that the house had been inherited by María Cordova through her great-aunt, Refugio Díaz Carrillo Rambaud, "whose first husband, Manuel Carrillo, was the son of the man who built the house." The piece also reminded readers that in 1965, the structure housed the Cordova Brothers Smoke Shop.[45]

It is also important to note that, as the city deliberated over which historic houses to preserve during urban renewal, María reached a deeply

FIGURE 4.6 This is a rare photo of one of María's paintings of the home on the corner of Meyer Avenue and Washington Street that was displayed at her exhibition at the Arizona State Museum. She allowed them to display seven of her paintings, although photos were only taken of two. These are included as supporting materials in the Arizona State Museum's, "Restricted Loan Agreement with Mrs. Navarrete Cordova," Invoice 1066, dated April 28, 1965, signed by Museum Director Raymond Thompson. A copy of the document is in the author's possession.

personal milestone: the Arizona State Museum unveiled a small collection of her paintings (see Figure 4.6). The exhibit, commemorating Cinco de Mayo, ran from May 2 to 16, 1965. According to a reviewer, María "put her memories on canvas . . . In typical Mexican folk style, in vivid Mexican colors" According to reports, Cordova's paintings included local scenes, a spring where people once washed clothes, El Tiradito Wishing Shrine, and depictions of Tucson in the past.[46]

A month after her show, *Citizen* reporter Eric Cavaliero wrote a piece aimed at rousing support for Cordova and preserving her house. True to her style, María invited Cavaliero to sit in her living room. She deliberately positioned herself across from the reporter, who described interviewing María as she sat "under a photograph of her great-aunt and her mustachioed great-uncle." Instead of reporting that they had engaged in a historical discussion, Cavaliero referred to it as "reminiscing." He wrote that Refugio Rambaud lived to be 100 years old and ". . . loved the street [Meyer Avenue] where she spent much of her long life." She married Severin Rambaud from France, and according to María, a French Catholic bishop attended a 1908 soirée the couple hosted at 173 North Meyer Avenue. The gathering marked the fortieth year the Rambauds had lived in the house. In keeping with their higher class standing, they served guests fine wines and cheeses.[47] This perspective is worth noting, given how later preservationists would choose to curate the home. In María's version, shared with Cavaliero and others, she described those who had previously lived in the adobe house as living in "luxury."

María Cordova's voice resonated throughout Cavaliero's article, which concluded: "Mrs. Rambaud died in 1924. But she would be gratified to know that her greatniece [sic], now Mrs. María Navarrete Cordova, still lives on Meyer Avenue. And, that she makes her home in a 117-year-old house whose two-foot-thick adobe walls, and high ceilings of saguaro ribs and timbers attest to its territorial vintage." Cordova also offered a lesson in geography, noting that people once referred to the house she lived in on Meyer Avenue and the one she owned to the north as "the two L's" because of their shape.[48]

Using descriptions typical of pioneer narratives that she knew would attract attention, and inserting dates that filled gaps rather than aligned with archival evidence, María set a familiar stage for her aunt Refugio's arrival in Tucson around 1840. She portrayed it as a time when "the harsh frontier had not been tamed." Adding to the hardship, Refugio's brother, María recounted, "was hanged by Indians on a mesquite tree which stood on the site of the present San Agustín Cathedral" on Stone Avenue. According to María, a year after Refugio arrived, she married Manuel Carrillo, who had built the house at 173 North Meyer Avenue in 1848. He raised cattle and, according to Cordova, had inherited large amounts of property from his father. She described it as "all the land encompassed by the city wall [or presidio]." Upon Carrillo's death, María claimed, the property transferred to his widow, Refugio. The title to the vast property holdings, Cordova said, had been "lost" sometime after her aunt's death.[49]

Near the end of Cavaliero's interview, Raul Cordova entered the room, not by coincidence but with purpose, carrying a "fistful" of English and Spanish documents. Cavaliero reported that one document in particular dealt with "claims to lots or parcels of land in the village of Tucson." Raul declared, "Here's proof that these claims were registered." This dramatic presentation of evidence and chain of property transfers concluded with the unresolved issue of the missing title, to which Raul added, "I have a feeling that the title may turn up in the archives down in Mexico."[50] These claims would become the foundation of the Presidio Land Grant lawsuit he filed seven months later, in November 1965.[51]

In June 1965, the *Citizen* dedicated an entire page to the Cordova properties and their connection to the former presidio. The feature included a photograph of María Cordova pointing to a painting, accompanied by an authoritative headline: "Here's How It Looked" (see Figure 4.7). In the image, Cordova wears a black dress and a slight smile, looking directly at the camera, her arm raised, finger pointing decisively at what she identified as the presidio's entrance. She clearly embraced the opportunity to present herself as knowledgeable about the presidio and its history. The canvas is strikingly large, about six feet wide and more than four feet tall. According to the caption, Cordova based her rendering on her own memories and on information she had gathered from her great-aunt, Mrs. Severin Rambaud.[52]

Tucson Art Center: Selective Preservation and Strategic Gain

By the early 1960s, the TAC had entered a period of growth and expansion. Since its founding in 1924, women formed the backbone of the organization, sustaining its daily operations and programming.[53] However, men consistently held the top positions, such as presidents of the board of directors and as paid executive directors.

FIGURE 4.7 A rare glimpse of a happy María Cordova, positioning herself as both artist and authority, linking her family's legacy to the city's Spanish colonial past. With the caption, "Here's How It Looked," below this photo in Eric Cavaliero, "The Old Lady Had a Story to Tell," *Tucson Citizen,* June 26, 1965, 21. Photo by Mark Godfrey. Used with permission from USA TODAY NETWORK via Imagn Images.

Edward H. Nelson exemplified the TAC's broader outlook in the early 1960s and helped steer its priorities. He was a vocal advocate of urban renewal from the outset.[54] Nelson served as TAC's Vice President in 1959, and in 1960, when he became president, he co-chaired the Civic Center group that prepared a report for Mayor Hummel and the city council.[55] A few years later, Nelson became an active member of the Citizens' Committee on Urban Renewal (CURE), a group deliberately named to reflect their belief in "curing" the city's social ills. CURE promoted a convention center as a strategy to revitalize downtown, attract tourists, and stimulate economic development. Nelson argued that such a facility was essential because "it is a place where singers, athletes, Boy Scouts, square dance people, and others can come." He also asserted that tourists and potential investors would "have a bad impression of the city if he sees slums so close to the downtown businesses."[56] Nelson was one of the many associated with the TAC who welcomed and selected Frank Sanguinetti to piece together a plan that would result in building them a new, larger art center complex.

In July 1965, on behalf of the TAC, Sanguinetti wrote to the mayor and city council seeking formal inclusion in the city's proposed urban renewal plans. This request did not come as a surprise to top city officials or to those on influential committees like COMB and the Historic Sites Committee. Undoubtedly, the networks and relationships cultivated by the TAC, not just by Sanguinetti, enabled the group to shape decision-making within city government. The deal Sanguinetti proposed involved the city gifting the land to the TAC in the former presidio area to construct a new multilevel gallery, in exchange for preserving the historic buildings in the Historic Block. As reported by the *Citizen*, the TAC made it clear that "the needs of this program would require the entire block." The Art Center proposed repurposing the historic buildings as public museums and galleries to enhance the new art center that would be built on the land not occupied by the preserved structures. The TAC described this as an "extraordinary opportunity."[57]

The TAC publicly stated their intentions to raise about a half-million dollars to aid in the older homes' restoration, and of course, to build their new 25,000-square-foot art gallery that included gardens and sculptures. Sanguinetti opined that "Such an area would be a way of enriching the community life and would provide a historical, psychological and cultural focus around which the whole city might pulse." In keeping with their aims and to stress their role in historic preservation, the director added that "In any case the block should be set aside as a historic prize, linked to early Tucson. There are a few buildings within the block which should be preserved and that could be used to relate some of Tucson's early character."[58]

The TAC's selective embrace of preservation served multiple purposes. By focusing attention on saving the Historic Block, an area closely tied to elites and the arts community, the organization framed itself as a steward of local heritage. This rhetorical investment in preservation lent cultural legitimacy to the group's goals. At the same time, the TAC fully supported urban renewal plans that called for the demolition of over eighty acres, including more than 200 Sonoran-influenced adobe row houses south of City Hall. The TAC crafted a version of urban renewal as balanced and civic-minded because it worked for them, even as it displaced working-class residents and erased entire neighborhoods.

Sanguinetti began to articulate that he envisioned the historic houses in the Historic Block to serve as "attractions" and spaces for craft exhibits, art displays, and a Latin American Folk Art Museum.[59] As plans crystallized further, he described converting a particular house into a "typical dwelling of the period of the Mexican occupation, complete with characteristic exterior paintings and interior furnishings." While he never explicitly identified which building in the Historic Block he intended to transform, the implication was unmistakable. Sanguinetti and the TAC had targeted the Cordova home.

By late 1965, the Cordovas realized that, while their house would not be demolished, city leaders and the TAC had no intention of allowing them to stay. On November 4, 1965, Raul Cordova filed a lawsuit asserting that his family owned much of downtown. Even without key land grant documents, he moved forward. The lawsuit became their only means to challenge the authority of the TAC and the city. After the filing, journalists stopped knocking on María Cordova's door. Nothing about her had changed, nor had her stories, but once the family took their claim to court, she was no longer seen as quaint or harmless.

CHAPTER 5

A House Preserved, A Home Lost

On March 1, 1966, the voters of Tucson approved the Pueblo Center Redevelopment Project, which targeted the most densely populated 80 acres in Arizona. Although Mexican Americans dominated the renewal area demographically, most of the city's Asian and African American residents also lived there. The state's first major urban renewal project included plans to build several government buildings, a modern retail complex, and its showpiece, the Tucson Community Center, a new performance arena and community-conference facility.

With the passage of the vote, the Pueblo Center Redevelopment Project became an official city mandate, setting into motion the forced displacement of hundreds of families and the demolition of entire neighborhoods.[1] The project area included the Historic Block north of City Hall, where both Cordova properties stood. Urban renewal brought the unstoppable force of eminent domain to María Cordova's doorstep. Despite her defiance, the city's legal machinery and the political influence of the Tucson Art Center (TAC) proved too formidable to resist.

Art, Image, and the Politics of Inclusion

In public discussions the issue of saving the houses in the Historic Block became linked with building a new art center.[2] During TAC Director Frank Sanguinetti's tenure, membership soared to more than 1,500 members.[3] He focused on fundraising because his plans grew more ambitious, and doing so convinced city leaders that they were partnering with a group that not only had "ideas" but also the ability to secure the necessary fiscal backing to make them happen. In a matter of months, the cost of the new art center rose to 1.5 million dollars, and Sanguinetti began referring to it as a "museum."[4]

The Cordovas' lawsuit, though it received limited media coverage, likely pressured Sanguinetti and the TAC to adopt a more culturally sensitive approach in their plans for the new art center. The Cordova legal challenge, combined with rising public awareness of widespread displacement affecting Tucsonenses, may have contributed to this shift. In response, Sanguinetti promised the new museum "would house a major collection of Spanish colonial art, which would be the only such collection in the United States," along with a permanent collection of pre-Columbian, contemporary, and Latin American art.[5] The TAC's actions revealed a clear disconnect between those from privileged backgrounds, who were eager to bring Latin American art to the city, and the struggles of the very communities whose history they claimed to honor.

Sanguinetti and the TAC's actions reflected the gap between cultural efforts to promote Tucson as a center of artistic refinement and the difficult realities faced by those most affected by urban renewal. The emphasis on Latin American, Spanish colonial, and pre-Columbian art sanitized and idealized Tucsonenses' connection to those histories. By focusing on art that aligned with those aesthetic values, the TAC reinforced power dynamics that excluded the lived experiences of Tucsonenses, both in the present and recent past, further entrenching their marginalization. These attitudes overlooked the large-scale displacement of Mexican and Mexican American communities on the other side of downtown, where families were packing up their belongings and awaiting the demolition of their homes at the same time Sanguinetti was announcing the TAC's plans to establish a large collection of Hispanic art.

The TAC's goals highlighted the power of museums and galleries to provide cultural enrichment and serve the public good. However, they failed to confront, let alone consider, the broader social injustices embedded in the implementation of urban renewal, including the Cordovas' desire to remain in their home.

Fallout and Fractures Among Elites

City plans also included the idea of building a new planetarium. Early conversations suggested placing it near City Hall. In November 1966, architects and a citizens' committee proposed locating the new planetarium next to the proposed Art Center. At that point, no contract or lease had been drafted or signed by city officials with the TAC. A few weeks after the city unveiled the planetarium proposal, Sanguinetti resigned his position as TAC director and moved to Utah. The *Citizen* lamented the potential derailment of the project, stating that "the preservation of historical sites must not be allowed to falter. The challenge to leadership becomes greater than ever."[6]

There are a few plausible reasons for the director's departure. The prospect of sharing a prime location with a planetarium may have raised concerns about public attention and funding, potentially diverting resources away from the museum. Additionally, Sanguinetti's commitment to preserving the Historic Block and maintaining the cultural integrity of the area may have led him to view the planetarium as a futuristic intrusion, one that would disrupt the measured atmosphere of the historic homes surrounding the Art Center. Ultimately, as his departure suggests, Sanguinetti may have felt undermined by those in power at City Hall who failed to support his vision.

The courts dismissed Raul Cordova's land grant case around the same time Sanguinetti moved to Utah. His departure underscores how differently he and the Cordovas were connected to the area. Sanguinetti lived in an apartment that had once been part of the former Fish home.[7] He viewed the historic district as a space for revitalization and redevelopment. He was not rooted in the home or the block in the way Cordovas were. For him, the area represented an opportunity for transformation, a project to be shaped into something new. His and other privileged residents' support for preservation, while rooted in an appreciation for the aesthetic value of historic buildings, failed to recognize the complex, intergenerational ties that families like the Cordovas had to their homes and to the land that once housed the presidio. Sanguinetti dismissed residents whose attachments interfered with what he considered progress, viewing the Cordovas and others as obstacles to development and disregarding the depth of their connections to place. As urban policy specialist Mindy Fullilove summarized, "urban renewal was a synonym for "progress." Progress meant new technologies, new jobs, and—here is where urban renewal comes in—new uses for the land. Those who sought to maintain the old city stood in the way of progress, and progress was a magic word back then."[8]

Sanguinetti's departure, however, signaled to city officials that they had pushed too far. The TAC, as elites often do, expected city leaders to accommodate their desires. Allowing a city subcommittee to propose placing a planetarium near the new art center, which may have led to Sanguinetti's resignation, was taken as a slight. With access to deep pockets and wealthy donors, the TAC had options. In the years that followed, its inner leadership seemed to play a game of cat and mouse meant to teach city officials a lesson. The TAC had the means to take its business and art center elsewhere. In the meantime, even though the Cordova properties and the rest of the Historic Block remained at the center of these tensions, both city leaders and the TAC chose to selectively overlook them, treating their displacement as an inevitable consequence of progress.

Legal Authority and Dispossession: Resolution No. 6874

As required by the U.S. Department of Housing and Urban Development, the city needed to adopt an official policy in the form of a resolution to move its $15 million Pueblo Center Redevelopment Project (No. Ariz. R-8) forward. By early April 1967, according to the *Citizen*, the city still needed to acquire 221 properties. To advance the project, urban renewal officials drafted Resolution No. 6874 and presented it to the mayor and council for approval. It authorized the City Manager to acquire properties and to "institute condemnation proceedings." It also ordered that "all City officers and employees be, and they hereby are, authorized and directed to do all things necessary or desirable to carry out the provisions of this resolution."[9]

```
                    ADOPTED BY THE
                    MAYOR AND COUNCIL
                       4-3-67
     RESOLUTION NO. 6874

RELATING TO URBAN RENEWAL; FINDING THAT THE PUEBLO CENTER
REDEVELOPMENT PROJECT NO. ARIZ. R-8 IS A SLUM
AREA AND THAT REDEVELOPMENT THEREOF IS NECESSARY
IN THE PUBLIC INTEREST; AUTHORIZING AND DIRECT-
ING THE CITY MANAGER TO NEGOTIATE FOR AND THE
CITY ATTORNEY TO CONDEMN, WHERE NECESSARY, ALL
PARCELS OF REAL PROPERTY AND IMPROVEMENTS THERE-
ON WITHIN THE PUEBLO CENTER REDEVELOPMENT PROJECT
NO. ARIZ. R-8, FOR PURPOSES OF SLUM CLEARANCE AND
REDEVELOPMENT.

     BE IT RESOLVED BY THE MAYOR AND COUNCIL OF THE CITY
OF TUCSON, ARIZONA, AS FOLLOWS:
     SECTION 1. That all those certain parcels of real
property, as such is defined in Section 13-1471-13, Arizona
Revised Statutes, 1956, as amended, within the area and ne-
cessary to the completion of the Pueblo Center Redevelop-
ment Project No. Ariz. R-8 which is hereby found to be a
slum area within the City of Tucson, the legal description
of which project area is a matter of public record on file
in the office of the City Clerk of the City of Tucson,
Arizona, be acquired by the City of Tucson, a municipal
corporation, for the purposes of eliminating slum conditions,
removing structures therefrom, improving the sites thereof,
and disposing of said parcels of real property for redevelop-
ment incidental to the foregoing, which redevelopment of
said slum area is necessary in the interest of the public
health, safety, morals or welfare of the residents of the
```

FIGURE 5.1 First page of the City of Tucson's Resolution 6874. The full document was obtained through a request to the City Clerk's Office, City of Tucson

The resolution was unanimously passed, adopted, and approved by Mayor Lew Davis and the city council at their April 3, 1967, meeting (see Figure 5.1). According to newspaper accounts, there was no debate, suggesting that no council member questioned or sought clarification on any of the five sections that made up the two-page resolution.[10] It became the city's official land acquisition policy and went into effect immediately.

Resolution No. 6874 authorized the Pueblo Center Redevelopment Project to declare the targeted area a slum in need of clearance and redevelopment. The resolution *did not define* what constituted a slum, nor did it provide specific criteria such as structural conditions, poverty levels, or public health concerns, to justify the designation. Instead, it broadly stated that redevelopment was necessary for the public interest, health, safety, morals, and welfare of residents.[11]

This lack of a clear definition of what qualified as a slum allowed city officials to apply the label "slum" to any area they wished to redevelop, regardless of actual conditions. By framing the project as essential for public well-being, the resolution granted the city broad authority to seize private property, whether through negotiation or condemnation under eminent domain. The document focused on securing land and funding for the project but included no objective standards to justify forcing people out of their homes or businesses.[12]

A month after passing the resolution, Chief Urban Renewal Director Don Laidlaw and his assistant, Phil Whitmore, held a press conference to announce that Tucson had "the fastest urban renewal project in the West." They reported that demolition in the project area had already begun, stating, "Today, 65 of the 294 old and usually vermin-infested buildings that stood in the area have been swept away by the federal bulldozer."[13] By describing the buildings this way, Laidlaw and Whitmore dehumanized not only the structures but also the people who lived in them. They framed displacement as both inevitable and necessary by portraying the area as filthy and outdated, celebrating its destruction, and treating speed and scale as signs of civic achievement. While urban renewal officials celebrated demolition, the TAC quietly regrouped.

Wrangling for a New Art Center

It took about ten months for the TAC to hire a new director, Edward Lawson. His first public statement reminded Tucsonans that other cities like New York, Denver, and even Phoenix supported their art museums, and that Tucson's "will be a major tourist attraction."[14] His goals did not deviate much from his predecessor, and Lawson promised he "would like to see the museum develop a Spanish Colonial art collection unlike any existing in the world."[15]

In November 1967, the year closed with a record turnout in the mayoral election. James "Jim" Corbett, a Democrat, was elected and tasked with implementing urban renewal. His victory also ensured that Democrats controlled City Hall for the next two years. The city's commitment to urban renewal remained unchanged, highlighting that both Democrats and Republicans advanced the same agenda.

The city kicked off 1968 by demolishing the eighty-eight-year-old, two-story Lionel and Barron Jacobs mansion, located north of City Hall and about fifty feet south of the Cordova home (see Figure 5.2). Referred to as a "showplace," it stood at the corner of North Meyer and West Alameda Street. It was one of the largest and last remaining two-story adobe structures in the city. The mansion featured ten-foot-high decorative doors and a forty-foot dining room. At one time, thriving gardens flanked both the east and west sides. Even the newspapers recognized that the demolition signaled the city's eagerness to clear space for the

FIGURE 5.2 Demolition of the Jacobs Mansion during the first week of January 1968. The photo was taken from a vantage point near the Cordova home, looking toward the site. University of Arizona Libraries Special Collections, Jack Sheaffer Photographic Collection, MS 435, Box 212, Folder 343. Photograph by Jack Sheaffer. Reproduced with permission of Special Collections, University of Arizona Libraries.

new art center. One article noted that the "88-year-old structure had to come down to make way for progress. The site has been designated for the new Tucson Art Center."[16]

As Mayor Corbett moved to appease the TAC, it is important to recognize that the dominant culture's view of progress, rooted in dynamics reminiscent of settler colonialism, framed both buildings and people as expendable for a so-called greater good, a good defined by those in power. Coverage in both local newspapers regarding the Jacobs mansion reflected this consensus. The *Star* headline read, "Revered City Landmark Will Yield to Progress," signaling that even the most cherished structures were expected to give way to the city's new urban vision. Similarly, the *Citizen* featured a photograph of the former mansion's demolition, with the new City Hall looming in the background, accompanied by a caption stating, "The city is dumping the remains of the once-grand Victorian home into a fill."[17]

Although the new mayor had demonstrated loyalty to the TAC agenda by making room for their proposed art center, the relationship soured in early 1968. TAC board president Patricia Ann Murphey Groom sent a letter to the city's newspapers and to Mayor Corbett outlining the problems involved in locating the new art center downtown. It seemed more feasible, Groom asserted, for the TAC to build the center at Randolph Park (now called Reid Park), located more than four miles from the Historic Block. She also reminded the mayor, "It was hoped that the Art Center could acquire [Historic Block] . . . either through an outright gift, or through a leasing arrangement with a small fee. The acquisition of this block has not, to date, been resolved."[18]

Apparently, U.S. Department of Housing and Urban Development (HUD) regulations were making it more difficult to transfer the property to the TAC. Groom explained that the TAC had raised money for construction of the new building, but not for acquiring the land. "If, however, we must also raise money for the purchase of the land, our task will be virtually impossible," she warned. Reporters tracked down Chief Urban Renewal Officer Don Laidlaw for comment, since plans and alliances years in the making were now at risk. Laidlaw had not received a copy of Groom's letter, but in typical City Hall observer fashion, he admitted that he had "heard rumors that something of the sort was afoot."[19]

The *Citizen*, clearly alarmed, outlined what was at stake: "Should the Art Center decide to seek the Randolph Park site, a host of problems would be raised. The city would be left without a buyer for the block and hopes of restoring the 100-year-old buildings there could be ended."[20]

While the *Citizen*'s concerns were real, they may have been overblown. Since city officials already owned Randolph Park, they refused to accommodate the TAC's request for a site there. As a counter move, the TAC sent another letter to the mayor and council. This time, they disclosed that the organization had been gifted a generous parcel of land in the Catalina Foothills. They described it as "appreciably superior" to locating in the Historic Block. The *Citizen* assessed the situation and concluded, "Any possibility that the new Tucson Art Center will be located in the city's urban renewal area is apparently dead."[21] In that same letter, however, the TAC also offered to meet and continue discussions with city officials. Although the location of the new art center remained uncertain, the city continued moving forward with its broader urban renewal agenda. That same summer, it escalated efforts to acquire land in the Historic Block, including the Cordova property.

City of Tucson v. Raul Navarrete Cordova and María Cordova

On July 31, 1968, the City of Tucson filed a condemnation complaint (*City of Tucson v. Raul Navarrete Cordova et al.* Civil 108818) to seize what is now known as La Casa Cordova at 173 North Meyer Avenue. Raul Cordova held legal title to the property, and the city justified the condemnation by invoking Resolution No. 6874, which authorized the acquisition of private property for public use. The city argued that the resolution had already established its legal authority to take the land, leaving compensation as the only issue to be decided.[22]

The city also requested that the court order the defendants to present any claims, meaning the Cordovas had to formally assert any legal rights or objections. This included the right to challenge the city's justification for condemnation, dispute the valuation, or assert ownership stakes. If the defendants failed to present claims, they could lose any right to contest the condemnation or seek compensation before the land was permanently transferred to the city.

Similar condemnation complaints were sent to all property owners targeted for removal within the Pueblo Center Redevelopment Project area. Exhibit A was the resolution. Exhibit B was a map outlining the urban renewal area and its boundaries. Exhibit C was individualized and included a description of the specific property by lot and block numbers, along with its location.

On Monday, August 19, 1968, at 11:35 a.m., on a day that reached 93 degrees, Raul was served the condemnation complaint at his Smoke Shop. María Cordova, the owner of the property at the corner of Meyer Avenue and Washington Street, was also served a condemnation complaint (*City of Tucson v. María Cordova et al.* Civil 108822), dated July 31, 1968.[23] Initially, the cases were litigated separately, but in October, they were consolidated into one.

Despite the significance of the moment, as urban renewal officials moved to evict a long-established family from the Historic Block, the action was not considered newsworthy. The eviction notices, though public records, went unreported (see Figure 5.3). A search through the newspapers revealed that none of the local publications covered the Cordovas throughout the entire year of 1968. By then, María and her family had become an inconvenience. They represented the old, established community that did not fit into the city's vision for the future. The media shifted its focus away from those being displaced, like the Cordovas, and instead focused on progress, revitalization, and the ongoing negotiations between the city and the TAC.

Wrestling for a TAC site

As Mayor Corbett continued trying to smooth over tensions with the TAC, internal divisions within the organization began to surface publicly.[24] Thirty-five members circulated petitions urging the board of

FIGURE 5.3 Cropped image of an exhibition panel at La Casa Cordova, Tucson Museum of Art, featuring María Cordova and her adult children standing in front of 173 North Meyer Avenue. María appears much older in this photo, which may be the last known image of her. No date available.

directors to hold more open meetings and expand discussions. Those quoted in the newspaper made clear their preference for a downtown location, while the site in the Catalina Foothills remained, in their words, a "deep, dark secret."[25]

Adding to the drama, in April 1969, TAC director Edward Lawson resigned. He openly stated, "Maybe Tucson is not ready for a new art museum," and claimed that "city officials are not interested in art and culture."[26] Lawson's remarks were addressed at the next city council meeting, where one councilperson dismissed them as an attempt to deflect from internal divisions within the TAC board, adding that "some of them want to build an exclusive hideaway in the Catalina Foothills." The councilperson went on to say he was "sick and tired of trying to help these people, then getting hit over the head for my efforts." In response, Mayor Corbett reassured the public that the mayor and council remained committed to what he called "cultural progress."[27]

In May 1969, the TAC and city officials agreed on an entirely new site. Both parties now preferred to build the new art center closer to the city's community center (TCC) complex, which was under construction on the south side of downtown. The TAC favored a location on the west side of Main Street, across from the TCC, because it offered more space. Limited parking in the Historic Block had also raised concerns. The new site relieved the TAC of any responsibility for restoring the homes in the Historic Block.[28]

The TAC moved on to select an architect to design their new building at this site. Top business leaders formed the TAC committee that reviewed the candidates. They sat through eleven presentations and unanimously chose William Wilde. Unlike his competitors, Wilde did not arrive with blueprints or drawings. He only needed to outline his vision to get the assignment. He proposed a 70,000-square-foot structure that would "create a new environment for the men of today and blend with the forms of yesterday which still surround us. This is the best way in which we can pay the deepest homage to our heritage."[29]

Since the TAC had decided against building on the Historic Block, city officials began exploring options for the historic properties. They did not mention the Cordova properties but raised the idea of using the Fish and Stevens property as the official mayor's residence.[30] In these discussions, the Fish and Stevens adobe structures were referred to as "mansions" and "stately old homes," terms that were never applied to the Cordova properties. Despite architectural similarities, the Fish and Stevens homes were set apart by their association with white settlers, revealing the racial and cultural biases that shaped how value was assigned to historic buildings (see Figure 5.4).

The Cordovas in Plain Site

Meanwhile, the Cordovas continued to appeal the eminent domain case in court. Despite Raul's legal training, they retained attorney James M. Murphy, who had more than twenty years of experience. He had established his own firm and, over time, brought in new partners to form Murphy, Vinson and Hazlett. Before taking on the Cordova case, Murphy had served as president of both the State Bar Association and the Arizona Historical Society.[31]

The condemnation proceedings moved slowly, and the Cordovas showed no willingness to negotiate. The Plaintiff's Pre-Trial Memorandum filed on September 15, 1969, indicates that they were intentionally

A House Preserved, A Home Lost 129

Mayoral Mansion?

The century-old Fish-Stevens home on Alameda Street across from city hall in the background might someday be a mansion for the mayor of Tucson. Councilman Conrad Joyner made the suggestion during a discussion of a use for the block of land just north of city hall, rejected as a site for a Tucson Art Center museum in favor of a location south of city hall. The old home with its three-foot thick walls is one of several historic buildings on the block. (Sheaffer photo by Harry Lewis)

FIGURE 5.4 "Mayoral Mansion?" Newspaper clipping from the *Arizona Daily Star*, May 21, 1969, page 21. Original caption (excerpt): "The century-old Fish-Stevens home on Alameda Street, across from City Hall in the background, might someday be a mansion for the mayor of Tucson." Used with permission © Harry Lewis—USA TODAY NETWORK via Imagn Images.

slowing down the legal process.[32] The document states that the defendants had not yet answered the city's interrogatories, meaning the Cordovas had failed to respond to key legal questions required before trial. This lack of reply suggests an effort to delay proceedings in their eminent domain case to prolong their occupancy and monitor how the city's unresolved deal with the TAC would unfold.

While the case moved through the courts, the Cordova family followed newspaper reports that outlined plans for their properties and the Historic Block. From their home at 173 North Meyer Avenue, they witnessed firsthand the slow but steady preparations to take over the area. Their outlook likely depended on the confidence they had in their legal fight. At times, they may have believed they were exempt from the city's plans. At other times, they may have felt they were simply buying time before the inevitable.

María and her family also had to endure the growing number of people coming to see the Historic Block after it was featured in the newspapers. While some visitors stopped by the Smoke Shop to buy snacks and refreshments, perhaps helping the business, the home tours arranged by elites eager to showcase the charm of the Historic Block must have stung the Cordovas.

In 1965, the influential Catalina Junior Women's Club staged home tours to raise funds for historic preservation. Dressed in late nineteenth-century costumes, club members wandered through the Historic Block, serving as guides to "give Tucsonans a glimpse into the Old Pueblo's past." That year, Frank Sanguinetti opened his home and served refreshments.[33] In the years that followed, tour organizers included the older homes of well-heeled residents, allowing them to showcase their

FIGURE 5.5 "Archaeological excavations led by Jim Ayres of the University of Arizona, ca. 1968." Courtesy of the TMA Research Library. These digs took place just steps from María Cordova's home, scattered across the Historic Block. While still living there, she and her family were forced to witness institutions treating their surroundings as artifacts.

chandeliers, antiques, and objects collected in the Orient alongside the thick adobe walls characteristic of Sonoran-era structures. The Cordovas were never mentioned during these tours, but by 1971, their property appeared on a map published in the *Star*. Although the family did not participate, organizers encouraged visitors to study the exterior of 173 North Meyer Avenue.[34]

Throughout urban renewal, the Cordovas remained in plain sight. Appraisers, surveyors, urban renewal officials with clipboards, preservationists, and home tour participants could not ignore that the family still lived there. The Smoke Shop remained open until November 1971. At the time, the perimeter wall now surrounding La Casa Cordova had not yet been constructed, leaving the backyard fully exposed. From the street, it was easy to see into the yard. Family members tended to plants, sat outside, or parked their cars in the rear. Until late 1972, the property remained an active residential space. It was obvious that the Cordova home was still occupied, but most observers lacked the capacity or empathy to truly see it.

TAC Targets Historic Block . . . Again

In the midst of working out architectural details for the site south of downtown, an anonymous donor offered the TAC $500,000 worth of real estate in the nearby Catalina Foothills. The gift was contingent on building the complex in the Historic Block. The TAC moved swiftly to meet the donor's request.[35] Once a deal was reached, the organization planned to sell the donated property and raise an additional $1 million to build the new museum-art center.[36]

The large donation also caused city officials to act quickly to negotiate an agreement with the TAC that summer. The mayor and council met in a special study session with TAC representatives to discuss a site and decided once again to "set aside" the Historic Block for the new museum.[37] Two weeks later the TAC presented city officials their building and restoration plans and the two reached an "tentative" agreement. The Mayor and Council entered into a 99-year lease agreement with the TAC in exchange for one dollar a year for the Historic Block. The City agreed to allocate $60,000 a year for interior and exterior maintenance, because according to the Vice Mayor, Conrad Joyner, "it was in the city's best interest to see that property in 'what is becoming one of the finest civic centers in the country' be kept up properly." City officials also agreed to construct a pedestrian bridge over Alameda Street intended to link the museum and Historic Block to a new city-county underground parking garage.[38]

City officials gave the TAC several requirements, including a three-year window to begin construction of the art complex. The city also assigned responsibility for restoring historic sites, specifically the Fish and Stevens Houses and one of the Cordova houses, though they did not specify which Cordova house. Under the terms set by HUD, which managed the urban renewal program, the TAC had five years from the lease signing to complete the task of restoring the buildings. The Mayor and Council adopted the resolution on July 13, 1970, but it remained tentative because the city was negotiating and making promises about property it did not yet own.[39] The Cordova properties were still tied up in court. Because the city had overreached, it was forced to formalize a new agreement in 1973, only after the legal issues were resolved.[40]

Cordovas' Fight Against Eminent Domain

While the City and TAC were making plans based on property they did not yet control, María and Raul Cordova were still fighting to hold onto it. On May 21, 1971, their legal team filed a Defendant's Memorandum challenging the City's use of eminent domain. The document laid out a case against procedural violations, arbitrary decision-making, and contradictions in the city's legal justification.

The city had already acknowledged that the Cordova properties were not slum properties. Yet it still sought to condemn them using laws intended for slum clearance. The defense exposed contradictions in the city's justification, arguing that its actions failed to meet the legal requirements for eminent domain. Their memorandum outlined five key points:

- **The Cordova properties were not slum properties.** *The city had already acknowledged that the Cordova properties were not slum properties and recognized their historical significance yet still attempted to take them under a slum clearance ordinance.*
- **The city's stated use was questionable.** *If condemned, the properties would not be redeveloped but would instead be transferred to the TAC in their existing condition, raising questions about whether eminent domain was legally justified.*
- **Unequal treatment of the Cordova properties.** *The Historic Block was the only area in the slum clearance program that was not razed, suggesting inconsistency in how the city applied its redevelopment plans.*
- **Violations of Arizona's eminent domain laws.** *The city planned to transfer the Cordova properties for little or no cost, violating Arizona Revised Statutes 36-1480, which required fair market value and public bidding for condemned properties.*
- **Failure to provide a clear justification.** *The city relied on vague claims of public benefit rather than specifying an actual use, contradicting Arizona Supreme Court precedent that required a concrete reason for taking private property.*

By highlighting these legal contradictions, the Cordovas' defense undermined the city's justification for condemnation and portrayed the condemnation as an abuse of power rather than a legitimate act of urban renewal.[41]

On May 25, 1971, the Superior Court of Arizona, Pima County, ruled in favor of the City of Tucson. The decision upheld the city's claim that it had the legal authority to take the Cordova properties through eminent domain as part of its urban renewal project. The ruling confirmed that the properties would be condemned, marking a significant loss for the family. At the same time, the city stated that the Cordova properties were intended for transfer to the TAC.

With this ruling, the only remaining legal question was how much compensation the Cordovas would receive, not whether the city could take their properties. The court determined that Raul Cordova would receive $82,500 for 173 North Meyer Avenue, and that María Cordova would receive $52,750 for her property at the corner of Meyer Avenue and Washington Street. The city issued these payments, and the Cordovas had no choice but to accept the court-determined amounts, even as they prepared to challenge the ruling.

The Cordovas responded by filing a Notice of Appeal on July 19, 1971, taking their case to the Arizona Court of Appeals, Division Two.[42] They refused to accept the court's decision as final and fought to overturn it. Although they had been forced to accept financial compensation for their properties, they continued to challenge the condemnation itself, pressing forward with the hope of reversing the ruling.

On July 23, 1971, the City of Tucson shifted gears and introduced a new legal maneuver by filing a Designation of Additional Portions of Record in response to the Cordova appeal. The city sought to expand the official record to be reviewed by the Arizona Court of Appeals, ensuring that more of the legal proceedings, including documents supporting the city's position, were included. One of the most significant aspects of this filing was the city's change in stance regarding the fate of the Cordova properties. Initially, the city had stated that the properties would be deeded to the TAC, a move that could have raised legal challenges under Arizona's redevelopment laws. The Cordovas had already pointed out that condemned properties needed to be transferred at fair market value rather than gifted. In this filing, however, the city corrected its previous statement and clarified that it would retain ownership of the properties and lease them instead. By making this change, the city avoided potential legal challenges the Cordovas might have raised against the condemnation in court.[43]

Although depositions are standard in eminent domain cases, the city's approach raised questions. Miller, Pitt & Feldman, the law firm representing the City of Tucson, required both María Cordova and Raul to be deposed. Their depositions were scheduled individually on August 18, 1971, at the firm's offices, ensuring the city controlled the setting and reinforcing the power imbalance in the case. At 75 years old, María was compelled to testify, underscoring the city's determination to justify its condemnation efforts. Were city attorneys seeking to wear her down emotionally and legally, or was the deposition a tactic to push the Cordovas toward settlement? Whatever the intent, the depositions held at Miller, Pitt & Feldman's offices never made it into the public record.[44]

Less than three months after the deposition, the *Star* ran a story titled, "'Holdout' Determined to Resist City." The paper had asked urban renewal official Phillip B. Whitmore if the Cordova's appeal threatened the art center's future. He responded by saying the "holdout [Raul] will cause 'no delay in building the center' if the city can get possession of the property by February." The paper followed up by asking Raul to respond to Whitmore's comments and Raul announced that if he lost the current appeal, which would not be decided until at least February, he would "carry the case to the Arizona Supreme Court." The reporter ended the article by warning: "But more immediately, if Raul Cordova carries his appeal of condemnation of his property to the state's highest court, the Cordovas will remain in their old house into the spring and the Art Center will just have to wait for the property."[45]

Despite the ongoing condemnation case and the condescending label of "holdout" slapped on Raul, the *Star* article revealed that he still held hope in his Spanish land grant claim. Raul had traveled extensively in Mexico conducting research, so much so that he had recently closed the Smoke Shop. The other businesses operating in the building, such as Salcido Bail Bonds, were also preparing to vacate. Raul reiterated that he saw a strong correlation between his house and the land grant, but when pressed for details, he did not reveal whether his research had unearthed any new evidence.[46]

In the article, Raul expressed anger over the low compensation he received for his home. The total payout was around $132,341.00. If their attorney billed by the hour, legal fees could have added up significantly over the years, potentially reaching tens of thousands of dollars. In a worst-case scenario, if the attorney charged a thirty percent contingency fee, approximately $39,702 would have been deducted from the $132,341 check issued to their legal team. That would have left the Cordovas with roughly $92,639 for both properties—equivalent to about $770,000 in 2025 dollars when adjusted for inflation.[47]

While the payout may seem substantial, it was far from life-changing, especially considering the Cordova family lost not only their home, but also their businesses and rental income. By that point, with the Smoke Shop closed and other revenue sources gone, the Cordovas were living off the city's compensation. How the family divided those funds remains a private matter, particularly as litigation continued. Searching for new opportunities after the loss, the brothers eventually established a curio shop in Nogales, Arizona, though it is unclear how soon after the payout this occurred.[48] At some point, only María and her daughter remained in the house. They stayed for eight months after all legal appeals had been exhausted.[49]

Another Threat to the Cordova Home: Demolition

Shortly after the story of the "holdouts" appeared in the papers, the *Citizen* ran a piece headlined "Two Old Bedrooms Spark Furor." The article had nothing to do with the eviction of an elderly woman and her family who still lived in the home. Since the city and the TAC had agreed that the Historic Block would house the new art center and museum, architect William Wilde began designing a new structure on the land the city had cleared for it. The "furor" stemmed from Wilde's proposed design, which called for the demolition of two back bedrooms of the Cordova home. According to preservationists and as María had claimed for decades, these rooms dated back to before the Gadsden Purchase.

Wilde flatly refused to amend his plans. Moving the structure just fifteen feet south, closer to Alameda Street, as suggested by preservationists, was, in his view, out of the question. "That would mean redesigning the entire building," he snapped, "and you just might have to get yourself another architect." He refused to consider compromises or revisions. City urban renewal officials backed him and pointed to a supposed breakdown in communication. They argued that the contract with the TAC did not specify which Cordova property warranted restoration and insisted that planners had always intended, though they had no documents or meeting minutes to support the claim, that only the front part of the Cordova home would be preserved. Isabel Fathauer, active in Tucson's Committee for Historical Sites, was furious. She warned that many donors "are going to renege on their pledges (donations made toward the construction of the new center) because of this plan. And they're big pledges."[50]

To pressure city officials to protect the entire structure, groups like the Arizona Historical Society consulted state and national preservation experts. They determined that the most effective way to protect the Cordova home was to nominate it for the National Register of Historic Places.[51] Preservationists understood that HUD could withhold urban renewal funds if the property received federal recognition, as guidelines prohibited alterations to designated historic sites. By securing this designation, they aimed to use federal regulations as leverage against the TAC's plans to demolish the two back rooms of the Cordova home.[52] At the same time, María Cordova remained in the house, even as decisions about its future were made without her.

Cordovas Lose Their Appeal

Amid the mounting controversy over the Cordova home, Division Two of the Arizona Court of Appeals upheld a Superior Court order approving the condemnation of both Cordova properties. As debate over the home's fate intensified, both major city newspapers covered the ruling. The *Citizen* ran the headline "Cordova House Condemnation OK."[53] Although this marked another legal blow, the Cordovas responded by filing a new appeal, continuing their fight against condemnation.

On March 13, 1972, they filed a motion asking the Court of Appeals to reconsider its decision. The city opposed the motion, and the court denied it. The Cordovas then filed a petition asking the Arizona Supreme Court to review the case. That petition was denied on April 25. Three days later, on April 28, 1972, the Court of Appeals issued its "Mandate," finalizing its ruling in favor of the City of Tucson.[54]

With no further options for appeal, the lower court's decision stood, granting the City of Tucson full legal authority to "condemn" the Cordova properties. This marked the legal end of the Cordovas' challenge and left them with no remaining recourse in the courts. Despite their sustained efforts, the legal process unfolded entirely in favor of urban renewal, reinforcing the city's power to decide the fate of both the properties and the people who lived there.

National Register of Places

As the courts prepared their final rulings, preservationists pushed ahead to list the Cordova home on the National Register of Historic Places. They were not deterred by their lack of access to the inside of the house and did not have the Cordova family's cooperation. Robert Fink, the Historic Sites Preservation Officer for the Arizona State Parks Board, signed the nomination form, though other preservationists assisted him. It was dated April 18, 1972. The form incorrectly listed María Cordova as the property owner, even though legal ownership was public record then, as it is now. Verifying ownership is one of the most basic steps when preparing any legal form involving real property, especially something as prominent as a National Register nomination. That the form named María instead of Raul, who held legal title, may have been an oversight, but it also signals a willingness to move forward with the preservation effort without verifying fundamental facts.[55]

The nomination's description includes an ominous "NOTE" in the description, acknowledging that "because of pending legal difficulties between the City of Tucson and the Cordova family, the historical surveyors and others have been denied access to the interior of the house." Fink did not clarify what those "legal difficulties" involved. In the context of widespread urban renewal, this kind of phrasing functioned as coded language that hinted at legal conflict without acknowledging the displacement. Fink knew the house was still occupied, and in the status box, he checked "occupied." Still, that detail did not influence the rest of the nomination. Focused on the task at hand, Fink optimistically added, "When this situation improves and an inspection of the house's interior is permitted, this report will be amended accordingly."

Fink provided visual descriptions of the structure, such as the fired adobe blocks that formed the walls, which were twenty-four inches thick. The report noted that "in typical Mexican town house style, the doors open directly to the street and walk." The "Statement of Significance" referenced "a tangled and uncertain deed history" but largely relied on María Cordova's version of history. Fink added that the rear section of the house "may be the oldest surviving structure in Tucson," dating back to 1848, and "also the City's oldest continuously occupied residence."[56] These claims were not substantiated by any scientific testing, such as dendrochronological analysis of the wooden structural beams.

Fink also confidently stated that the City would acquire the house "pending court settlements" and proceed with leasing the property to a local historic preservation group. At that point, all conversations and court filings indicated that the City intended to transfer the property to the TAC. His phrasing, referring vaguely to a "local preservation group," suggests an awareness of behind-the-scenes negotiations that were not yet formalized in public documents.[57]

The actions taken by Fink and other preservationists make it clear that they saw value in the structure, not in the people who lived in it. Within this framework, residents were viewed as temporary or even as obstacles to a cleaner narrative or a more usable past. For preservationists of that era, once a site was framed as historic, the inhabitants became expendable. The presence of María and her family, defiant and still fighting in court, complicated matters. It was easier for them to describe bricks and beams than to confront displacement, contradiction, or the politics of urban renewal. That is why they pushed forward with the nomination, even without access. The story they were constructing did not need the Cordovas. In fact, it worked better without them.

Preservationists, as will be discussed in the following chapter, turned a lived-in home into a historical prop, often for the benefit of outsiders. And they did so quietly, under the guise of "honoring history."

The emphasis on aesthetics came through in Fink's closing statement: "National Register listing was requested on the basis of the house's value to the City of Tucson as an architectural entity which has survived from the period when Tucson and all Arizona south of the Gila River were once part of Mexico." He concluded the nomination by citing a crucial threat: the oldest section of the house was at risk from "private construction." The final sentence conveyed a clear sense of urgency, asserting that "Register listing would lend the necessary recognition and prestige to ensure that the site was not permanently impaired."[58]

After Fink had submitted his application, and the threat of demolition of two back rooms did not subside, Raul Cordova agreed to let a team of architects, anthropologists, and members of the Arizona State Parks Board enter the home to augment their application to the National Register. This was the first time Raul allowed such an inspection.[59] Despite María Cordova's decades of advocacy, credentialed experts and outsiders now walked through her home and had the final say over the home's historical significance.

Twenty days after submitting the application, the Arizona State Parks Board provided photographs to document the building's architectural features and interior (see Figure 5.6). These images offered a rare but limited glimpse into María Cordova's lived-in space. Paintings still hung on the walls, with one prominently displayed above the fireplace, likely a piece María had painted herself. Yet parts of the house appeared stark or empty, suggesting that the family had already begun the process of moving out.

Despite preservationists' concerns and their intervention through the National Register nomination, the TAC and their architect still refused to revise their plans, which called for demolishing the back rooms of the Cordova home. Dennis McCarthy from the Arizona State Parks Board, who had also helped draft the nomination, scheduled a meeting with the TAC board. He warned them of what was at stake and stressed that if they and their architect did not adjust the proposed design for the art center, Tucson could risk losing access to future historic preservation grants.[60]

On May 5, the Cordova home made front-page news. U.S. Representative Morris K. Udall announced that the house had been officially listed on the National Register of Historic Places.[61] With this federal recognition in place, the TAC and architect William Wilde had little choice but

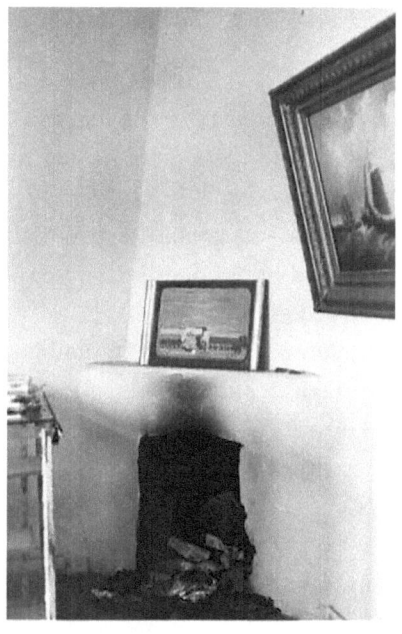

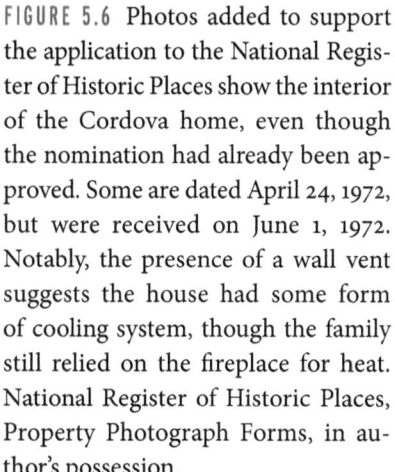

FIGURE 5.6 Photos added to support the application to the National Register of Historic Places show the interior of the Cordova home, even though the nomination had already been approved. Some are dated April 24, 1972, but were received on June 1, 1972. Notably, the presence of a wall vent suggests the house had some form of cooling system, though the family still relied on the fireplace for heat. National Register of Historic Places, Property Photograph Forms, in author's possession.

to amend their plans, shifting the future art center-museum two feet to leave the Cordova house intact.[62] It was also a clear demonstration of the growing clout and influence of preservationists, who had successfully used the National Register designation as leverage to protect the property.[63]

Fading from the Official Record

At some point, only María and her daughter remained in the house. A mutual friend introduced María Luisa Tena, who will be discussed in the following chapter, to María Cordova after the home had been officially declared a historic site. Tena recalled that María was unable to get out of bed, which was moved into the room that had once housed the Smoke Shop. María's daughter, María Dolores, served as her caretaker.[64]

A request from city records did not yield an eviction notice following the Court of Appeals decision in April 1972. Whether the absence of such a document reflects an informal or drawn-out process remains unclear. If the city encountered public pressure, logistical delays, or legal obstacles in carrying out the final steps of condemnation, those circumstances were not documented. What is clear is that María Cordova did not leave her house easily. She resisted in ways that have not been fully recorded. While legal battles determined ownership on paper, the act of physically removing people from their homes was often more complicated, shaped by personal resistance, city enforcement practices, and the realities of relocation.

María Cordova left her historic home at 173 North Meyer Avenue perhaps as late as the start of 1973.[65] The storied property no longer belonged to her or her family. The city's payout may have offered the family temporary financial relief, but large sums of money often bring complications. Whether due to financial strain or declining health, her final years were spent in a nursing home. Two years after leaving her home on Meyer Avenue, María passed away on January 3, 1975. She left behind an adobe structure that carried the weight of her presence, her claims to history, and the contested meaning of what would be known as La Casa Cordova.

CHAPTER 6

La Casa Cordova
A Storied Property, Restored to Forget

By late 1975, only a handful of older structures within the Pueblo Center Redevelopment Project had survived. City officials and urban renewal proponents considered the nearly 270 demolished buildings dispensable.[1] The few that endured did so because preservationists intervened, persuading city leaders to support their efforts and transfer ownership or long-term leases of selected properties to quasi-governmental agencies. The Tucson Art Center (TAC) granted the Junior League of Tucson full control over La Casa Cordova: how it would be restored, what it would be named, which version of the past to emphasize, and how that history would be presented to the public.

The Junior League of Tucson, not the city or the TAC, had the most influence over the restoration of La Casa Cordova. In the 1970s, this group of civic-minded elite women raised funds, gathered research, and oversaw the transformation of the Cordova home into a staged version of a mid-nineteenth-century Mexican residence. The home became a period museum, rooted in aesthetics but disconnected from the woman who had lived there just months earlier.

Revisiting the house's restoration, however well-intentioned, reveals who was allowed to shape public memory and who was left out of it. All pasts are imagined, some more than others, and the statement "the past is a foreign country" often applies.[2] Here, the past was not only foreign, it was *curated* as such and reflected the values of those with the power to stage it. In 1975, the restoration was complete, but it was carried out in a manner that encouraged forgetting. A few years later, however, María Luisa Tena, another binational woman like María Cordova, stepped into the house and built a Nacimiento that grew over time and brought new meaning, energy, and people back to La Casa Cordova.

The Tucson Art Center becomes the Tucson Museum of Art

María Cordova left her home sometime in 1973. The circumstances of her departure remain unknown, and the press took no notice. The only evidence about her leaving comes from Junior League reports. There is no dispute that the group knew she wanted to stay and that the Cordovas had contested eminent domain. On October 5, 1972, one report stated, "We are now waiting to gain access into the Cordova Houses. The Smoke Shop should be empty in 2 weeks time as Mrs. Cordova is ill and being moved temporarily."[3] In reference to acquiring access to the house, another Junior League document states, "First because the Cordova family was suing the city and then because Mrs. Cordova was too old and sick to allow visitors in her home. Finally, just before this Christmas (Dec. 72) the old lady was moved to a more comfortable home and the house was vacant and available for our inspection."[4] In *A History of La Casa Cordova*, Bettina Lyons extends the timeline of María's departure, writing that "Maria Cordova continued to live in the house until 1973, when she was moved by her family to a nursing home."[5] This framing softens the reality of her removal by casting it as a family decision rather than a forced displacement and subtly shifts attention away from the city's role in pushing her out.

In January 1973, while María Cordova may still have been living in her home, the Tucson Art Center unveiled an architectural model of what the new 36,000-square-foot art center would look like. They had raised $1.2 million in donations and still needed more to cover construction and maintenance costs, but everyone involved remained optimistic. The older buildings in the Historic Block influenced the design of the new facility, and at the unveiling, the TAC board voted to rename the institution the Tucson Museum of Art (TMA).[6] Although the city had yet to formalize the land transfer to build the new art center or any of the Historic Block properties, the TMA board, the Junior

FIGURE 6.1 Cropped section of a "1974 aerial view by Fred Wehman," courtesy of the TMA Research Library. This photo captures the construction of the new art center. The arrow points to 173 North Meyer Avenue. Note the widening of Alameda Street and how North Meyer Avenue is now dead-ended.

League, and other stakeholders treated it as a done deal. Their insider relationships and institutional influence made an updated, official lease seem like a mere formality, and construction of the new TMA moved forward.

In October, the city council approved another 99-year lease for the TMA in exchange for one dollar a year.[7] The following month, in November 1973, the TMA held a groundbreaking ceremony. Helen Murphy, honored with a silver hard hat for the occasion, was chosen to turn the first shovel of dirt. When plans surfaced to build the new art center elsewhere, she and her husband had been the anonymous donors who contributed $500,000 to ensure the building would rise in the Historic Block. The *Citizen* described the large number of attendees as a "throng" and called the event "the realization of a dream shared by many" (see Figure 6.1).[8]

Leading the Cordova Restoration

More than two years before the museum celebrated its groundbreaking with fanfare, another effort in the Historic Block was already underway. As early as April 14, 1971, Junior League representatives had started meeting with the art center board to "discuss areas in which the J.L. could develop a project. One of these areas was historic preservation."[9] This behind-the-scenes planning for the restoration of La Casa Cordova began at the same time that María and Raul Cordova, along with their legal team, were actively challenging the City's attempt to condemn their property. The Cordovas' Defendant's Memorandum, filed on May 21, 1971, makes clear that they were fighting to remain in their home, arguing in court that the City's use of eminent domain was both unjustified and unlawful.[10] The Junior League was undeterred. They moved forward, setting up meetings with preservationists, historians, anthropologists, and other experts, forming alliances and establishing informal agreements.

Since more than 200 homes south of downtown had already been torn down, the Junior League's efforts made it appear that something positive was happening amid what many Tucsonans considered progress. By moving quickly to restore La Casa Cordova, the Junior League claimed the moral high ground and positioned their project as a cultural gain rather than as part of a larger story of loss and bulldozers. Speed was not just about logistics. It was about control, optics, and shaping public memory while the dust of urban renewal still hung in the air. By advancing swiftly, the Junior League helped bury María Cordova's story by replacing her presence with a new narrative for the house. Most people did not even know she had been evicted. Her departure became an obscure footnote.

In April 1973, about four months after María Cordova left her home, the Junior League made its first public statement confirming that it would assist the TMA by taking the lead on restoring the house. The League not only claimed credit for initiating the project but also took full responsibility for its planning and fundraising. In their announcement, the group declared that, once completed, "it will be the only Mexican museum in the state." Bettina Lyons, appointed chair of the project, announced that the Junior League would allocate $50,000 of its own funds, which would be approximately $355,000 in 2025 dollars, to restore the

Cordova home. This was a substantial commitment. Ten months later, the Junior League secured a $15,000 grant from the Arizona State Parks Commission to support the project.[11]

The Junior League pledged to be "as faithful as possible to Mexican territorial culture," announcing that rooms added after 1900 would be removed and that wood floors in the older section of the house would be replaced with packed earth to restore the original dirt flooring. They also secured commitments from the Arizona Historical Society and San Xavier del Bac Mission to contribute "authentic articles of the Mexican period" for display.[12]

The Junior League's announcement emphasized the structure's architectural value, highlighting that the home predated the Gadsden Purchase. The League cited an expert who claimed the building "exhibits practically every architectural feature of early territorial Tucson, including handsewn mesquite door lintels, corner fireplaces, and adobe walls." When the restoration was complete, the plan was to turn management over to the TMA, which would operate it as a museum.[13]

Before taking on the Cordova project, Lyons had already led another major restoration effort. For four years, the League had collaborated with the Arizona Historical Society to fund and coordinate the restoration of the Fort Lowell Museum, a military post located about eight miles from downtown that had been active from 1873 to 1891. In November 1963, at a public ceremony, Lyons, representing the Junior League, formally handed over operations to the Historical Society along with the regimental flags of the old Fort Lowell troops.[14] At just thirty-five, she directed what was considered one of the most important historic restoration projects of that time. While many factors contributed to Lyons's leadership role, her standing within the Junior League was central to her credibility and influence. This earlier success made her the obvious choice to lead the Cordova house restoration less than a decade later.

Junior League

Like other chapters across the country during the mid-twentieth century, the Junior League of Tucson treated historic preservation as a form of civic service.[15] They raised funds, coordinated volunteers, and exercised influence over nearly every aspect of the project. Like the national organization, the Junior League in Tucson allowed only the most elite women entry into their group. In *Women of the Upper Class*, Susan Ostrander explains, "They had help running the households and paid household help and therefore have more time to dedicate to their volunteer work. This is the importance of the volunteer work done by upper-class women to the class structure. It upholds the upper class; it legitimates the class; it deflects challenges to its power; it constructs a class network that is inaccessible to people from other classes."[16]

The Junior League implemented a strict vetting process for membership. They were able to weed out those with more radical leanings, from the lower class, and different ethnicities through a variety of organizational mechanisms. Two sponsors needed to vouch for potential new members to ensure compatibility with Junior League goals. Local member Helen Brooks recalled, "one had to have friends among the actives who would 'put you up' as they used to say."[17] Thus, sponsorship served as the first round of the vetting process and ensured that women younger than thirty-five, or "junior," with high suitability and "fit" were considered as potential members.[18] A benefactor or sponsor, however, did not guarantee membership. An admissions committee voted by secret ballot to confirm that only the right type of women joined their ranks and that decisions were not challenged. The local Junior League used secret ballots until 1982, which coincidentally is also when their influence and power began to wane.

With funds raised through fashion shows, balls, and dances, the Junior League donated to and engaged in a variety of charitable causes. They regularly received attention in the local papers for hosting and attending galas, high-end parties and social events, often appearing in Mexican, Indian, or other "exotic" costumes. These moments, captured in both text and photographs, may have seemed trivial for a group that sought to be taken seriously as civic leaders. Yet major fundraising events such as the "Follies," learning to dance "the hustle," signaled that elite women and their husbands did indeed indulge in frivolous activities, but they did so in lavish settings and in the company of their own.[19]

The restoration of the Cordova house received heightened coverage in part because of this visibility. Photographs from the era show Junior League members in the latest fashions: wide-legged bell bottoms, styled hair, and confident postures. They looked modern, composed, and cool. Their involvement made the Cordova restoration as much about civic pride as about historical recovery.

The Decision to Go Back in Time

Although the Junior League coordinated the restoration, they still relied on experts and professionals for guidance. One of the defining decisions was to restore the Cordova home to resemble a nineteenth-century Mexican household. This idea had been proposed as early as 1966. At that time, popular Tucson Art Center Director Frank Sanguinetti suggested that the house might be restored "to illustrate family life as it was here 100 to 150 years ago."[20]

On September 26, 1972, representatives from the Junior League met with Sidney Brinckerhoff of the Arizona Historical Society. In local preservation circles, he was considered an expert on regional history.[21] At the time, María Cordova still lived in the house, and the TMA had not yet formally announced that it had tasked the Junior League with leading the restoration.

At that meeting, Brinckerhoff steered the League toward implementing his vision. He proposed that the front rooms be used as a Mexican shop and the back rooms as a typical 1850s Mexican home. He suggested removing the cooling unit and wood flooring so that the house would have dirt floors, and furnishing it only with pieces from the period. He disliked the idea of adding windows because they looked too contemporary but accepted that security made them a necessity. Brinckerhoff pointed to the "Old House" in Santa Fe as the model. That early meeting shows how professionals like Brinckerhoff influenced the Junior League's major decisions.[22]

Santa Fe's so-called "Oldest House," also known as the De Vargas Street House, was staged in a Spanish Colonial domestic style: adobe fireplaces, exposed vigas, and period furnishings meant to evoke the 18th century. Rather than highlight the lives of actual occupants, the restoration aimed to create an immersive environment that allowed visitors to "step back in time." The house itself became the artifact. Its rooms told a curated story of early Spanish and Mexican life in New Mexico. This approach reflected Santa Fe's early twentieth-century cultural agenda, when boosters and preservationists embraced a romanticized "Spanish Pueblo Revival" aesthetic to craft the city's identity as an ancient Hispano-American settlement.[23]

La Casa Cordova, like Santa Fe's 'Oldest House,' was transformed into a period museum meant to recapture a Mexican Territorial-era aesthetic rooted in architectural authenticity. Five rooms were furnished in what was considered a typical Sonoran style: sparse interiors, corner fireplaces, packed-earth floors, adobe walls, and exposed vigas. Curators from the Junior League placed objects throughout the home. While they researched the period extensively, their efforts reflected the constraints of the time. With no surviving photographs and little firsthand documentation, the final result reflected prevailing ideas of what a Sonoran-era home should look like.

Eleazar D. Herreras

Under the direction of architect Eleazar D. Herreras, La Casa Cordova was stabilized and restored to resemble its mid-nineteenth-century appearance. He was born in Tucson in 1897, on Meyer Street just south of downtown. Herreras was one of the earliest Mexican Americans to graduate from the University of Arizona with a degree in mathematics and went on to train as a civil engineer. Over the course of his career, he became the city's chief building inspector and later served as Tucson's official architect before opening his own firm in 1958. Although he would later claim that he "never thought much about racial discrimination," in the 1930s he founded the Hispanic American Democratic Club and served as its president from 1932 to 1938. He was also active in the Alianza

Hispano-Americana, a prominent fraternal organization, where he held membership from 1926 through 1966.[24]

Eleazar D. Herreras had built a reputation as an expert in adobe architecture by the time he was selected to lead the restoration of La Casa Cordova. He had previously supervised the restoration of San Xavier del Bac Mission for fourteen years, a project that required what he described as "intensive study of its structural system and the materials used in the building." He also worked on the restoration of the "Fremont" House south of downtown, further solidifying his role in Tucson's early preservation efforts.[25] In 1973, around the time he took on the Cordova restoration, Herreras was elected to the College of Fellows of the American Institute of Architects: a lifetime honor. By then, he was widely regarded as knowing adobe construction "as much as any architect alive."[26]

Herreras also knew which local contractors and craftspersons skilled in adobe restoration to include in the project (see Figure 6.2). Starting in early 1973, under his direction, the Cordova house's roof was replaced, the foundation stabilized, and materials like mud plaster and original woodwork were either conserved or carefully replicated. He and his crew produced new mud adobe bricks to match and replace those that had deteriorated in both the exterior and interior walls. The original dirt floors were exposed. New doors were crafted from rough planks and hand-forged nails to resemble the originals. Fireplaces were added to each room, even though the Cordova house had only one.

Staging the Mexican Museum

As the project moved forward, the restoration itself became indistinguishable from the museum. Reporter Edith Armstrong, in a full-page *Star* article, wrote, "Mexican heritage, the backbone of modern Tucson, is being commemorated in the restoration of La Casa Cordova, designated to be a Mexican museum." She quoted Bettina Lyons as saying, "Nowhere in Arizona is the story of our Mexican heritage being told—a part of Southwestern history of which Tucson is particularly proud."

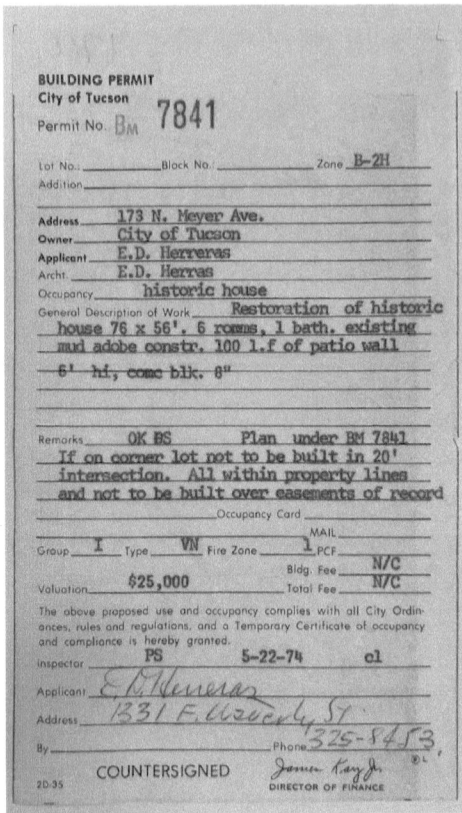

FIGURE 6.2 Building permit for the restoration of 173 North Meyer Avenue, issued May 22, 1974. Architect E. D. Herreras listed both as applicant and designer. Courtesy of the TMA Research Library.

Armstrong outlined plans for "a museum room" and "a shop that will make available reproductions of household items on display in the building." The Junior League also projected the inclusion of bilingual docents to lead visitors through the house in the future.[27]

La Casa Cordova was curated to celebrate a Mexican presence; however, preservationists stripped away any evidence of resistance or disruption. Prioritizing adobe bricks, packed earth floors, and antique furnishings over lived experience and community memory fits what scholars like Laurajane Smith call an "object-based" model of heritage, which privileges material evidence over intangible meaning and social context.[28] In that light, the Junior League's museum project offered a version of Tucson's past that allowed families descended from large landowners and successful merchants who arrived after the Gadsden

FIGURE 6.3 Exterior of the Cordovas' former home with plaster removed during its restoration as La Casa Cordova, 1975. Courtesy of the TMA Research Library.

Purchase to appear as stewards of culture rather than as beneficiaries of its erasure.

Rather than engage with the full history of the house, the Junior League concentrated on returning it to what they called its "original state." They described the restoration as "pure," explaining this as meaning "no concessions to modern comfort. There will be no heating, cooling or electricity . . . The idea is to experience how it was in Tucson between the 1850s and 1879," before the arrival of the railroad and Anglo influences.[29] A photograph caption in the *Star*, printed beneath an image of the home with its plaster stripped away to expose the adobe blocks, read "Originality returns" (see Figure 6.3). These descriptions suggested that the farther back in time the efforts reached, the more authentic the house became, even if that came at the expense of stripping away the layers of lived experience that had shaped La Casa Cordova. As museum theorist Barbara Kirshenblatt-Gimblett has argued, staging the past often becomes a substitute for actually recovering it.[30]

The exterior of La Casa Cordova was also modified. Workers built an adobe wall to enclose the patio. A wooden well, originally located elsewhere, was dismantled, moved to the site, and reassembled. To complete the look, plants, trees, herbs, and roses described as being from "the period" were added. A *Star* article covering the restoration featured a small

FIGURE 6.4 Photo by author. A similar image appeared in Edith Armstrong's "Casa Cordova—Restoring Tucson's Mexican Heritage," *Star*, May 26, 1974. The paper's caption read: "Indoor plumbing has no place in the 'pure' restoration of La Casa Cordova. This adobe building in the back of the house will be converted into an outdoor privy, in keeping with the genuine restoration."

adobe structure with the caption, "Indoor plumbing has no place in the 'pure' restoration of La Casa Cordova. This adobe building in the back of the house will be converted into an outdoor privy, in keeping with the genuine restoration."[31]

When the restoration was completed in 1975, plans included an air-conditioned display room meant to house exhibits that would "tell the story of Mexican Tucson." But that part of the vision proved harder to realize. Establishing what the Junior League had called Arizona's first Mexican Museum required continued investment and a willingness to engage histories that could not be conveyed through furniture and artifacts alone. Although Bettina Lyons and other Junior Leaguers devoted significant energy to researching La Casa Cordova and the surrounding Historic Block, turning the property into a meaningful museum ultimately proved far more difficult than restoring its physical structure.

Los Padrinos de la Casa Cordova

Two years after the Junior League announced they would spearhead the restoration of the house; they introduced a new partner. *Los Padrinos* was unveiled at a party on April 20, 1975, held in the patio of La Casa Cordova. The event drew over 200 guests. According to the newspaper, the atmosphere was set by "the fragrance of adobe walls . . . the feeling of dirt floors under foot . . . the emotion of Mexican music in the background" in the courtyard of what was described as "a historic home being converted into a Mexican museum."

"Padrinos" means godparents in Spanish, a term associated with support, guidance, and ceremonial sponsorship. By naming the group *Los Padrinos de la Casa Cordova*, the Junior League likely intended to signal cultural respect and community involvement. With the restoration still seven months from completion, forming and publicly presenting this group suggested an effort to appear more inclusive and to give the project a communal face, though it also served as another carefully staged moment.

By this point, it appears that the Junior League had realized that exposed adobe walls and period decorations alone did not constitute a museum. The aesthetic idealizations, including the antique furnishings, could set a scene, but they could not stand in for interpretation or meet the expectations of what a museum should offer.[32] And yet, their subsequent actions suggest that they did not put this understanding into practice.

For older, established Mexican Americans, joining Los Padrinos may have represented a meaningful, if limited, opportunity to claim space in Tucson's civic and cultural life. Unlike the "Frémont" House, which explicitly sidelined Tucsonense contributions and erased their connection to the very property it repurposed, La Casa Cordova, though flawed in its representation, was at least visibly framed as "Mexican." Joining Los Padrinos provided a way to participate in shaping public memory. Most were active in Tucson's civic and professional spheres and partnering with the TMA opened doors to fundraising networks and social capital. Whether driven by pride, obligation, or strategy, their involvement gave the project an appearance of inclusion.

Restoration Completed

Local newspaper columnist Sue Giles described the "excitement in the air" at a celebration on November 21, 1975, where the Junior League officially gifted the restored house to the TMA. "Few 'celebrations' in town have produced the electricity generated at a party Friday morning at La Casa Cordova." Socializing took place in the newly restored patio that city funds had donated $10,000 to construct, on a dirt floor enclosed by an adobe wall, with a relocated well and faux outhouse. Mariachis played Mexican tunes and guests were treated to coffee, small doughnuts, and tequila punch.[33]

On behalf of the Junior League, Bettina Lyons thanked everyone and offered a brief overview of the project. She added that, "When the Junior League first allocated $50,000 for this project, members had two goals—to restore the house as authentically as possible, and help bring about the establishment of a Mexican museum in the house."[34]

Giles named close to twenty people in attendance she felt merited recognition. Only two were Mexican American: Dan Valdenegro, the co-chair of Los Padrinos de la Casa Cordova, and project architect Ed Herreras. In recognition for his work, Herreras received a thank-you plaque and responded, "Next to my dear San Xavier, La Casa Cordova is my pride and joy because it's genuine."[35] What he meant by "genuine" is hard to determine. Was he referring to the materials, the restoration methods, or the adobe construction itself?

The handing over of the keys was symbolic, but it also marked a transition. Because the restoration had been completed, it allowed the Junior League to step aside, leaving the TMA and Los Padrinos to carry forward a vision for the Mexican Museum. Los Padrinos held a few receptions and events, and their involvement gave the project the appearance of cultural legitimacy. But the interpretation, programming, and maintenance needed to establish a Mexican Museum required resources and left the group little space to challenge its foundational premise.

Los Padrinos never extensively fundraised. Instead, they held open houses and hosted receptions to bring others to La Casa Cordova. In 1976, Alva B. Torres, who had been active in historic preservation, proposed "Cordova Sundays," saying, "We want people of the town to get a feel for the house; we hope they want to participate in the casa in an active way."[36]

A Heritage Site?

Two years after the house had been restored, in 1977, the TMA continued to promise something "unique to the city, state and region." One announcement declared, "When La Casa Cordova . . . becomes a Mexican Heritage museum it will be the first in the southwest." The phrasing marked a shift. The TMA was still promising a museum, but the addition of the word "heritage" suggested a growing awareness of audience and political context. Rather than referencing Mexico as a nation, the term pointed to cultural inheritance in a broader sense, one that acknowledged roots without insisting on a singular or national identity.[37]

The next year, the *Citizen* featured a half-page story titled, "La Casa Cordova Seeking Loan of Mexican Heritage." It included a photograph of one of the house's bedrooms, showing a large 1870s bed with fine pillowcases and spread, a chamber pot and wash basin, and a bureau. The article was an active appeal from the TMA for more heirlooms, clothes, shawls, serapes, and mantillas, traditional lace head coverings, or "what's left from Tucson's pioneer Mexican Families" to display in exhibits (see Figure 6.5).

FIGURE 6.5 Former curated exhibits and interior staging inside La Casa Cordova. Photographs downloaded from the Tucson Museum of Art website on July 14, 2014.

Another photograph featured Bettina Lyons, identified as the TMA's curator of historic sites. By this time, she was no longer working on behalf of the Junior League but had become part of the museum personnel, tasked with restoring the other houses in the Historic Block, including the Fish, Stevens, and the recently added Corbett Houses. In the image, Lyons was shown holding a decorative cross and standing near a deep windowsill with a teapot and pitcher. She shared that the TMA had received some donations but needed more to fill three new display cases: one for textiles, one for religious pieces, and one for clay cookware. At that point, three rooms in the house displayed period furniture, and the fourth was reserved for exhibits based on donated items that Lyons planned to curate. The focus remained on collecting artifacts to tell a story. Still missing, however, was any effort to narrate the house's history through the different waves of occupation or to connect its rooms to the lived experiences of those who had called it home.[38] That absence would soon be challenged by a new presence in the house itself. María Luisa Tena's artistic vision drew people in and offered them a different way to connect with La Casa Cordova.

More Than Decoration: María Luisa Tena's Nacimiento

María Luisa Tena arrived in Tucson from Guadalajara in 1968 and immediately became involved in several Mexican American groups and causes. She met María Cordova in 1972, while Cordova was still living in her house but was ill and dependent on her daughter's care. In addition to her fond memories of Cordova, Tena felt a deep connection to the house from the first time she stepped inside. She knew that María had been evicted and later reflected, "It was because she did not have papers . . . but in those times people didn't need or prepare official papers." After the restoration of La Casa Cordova, Tena became active in Los Padrinos and began spending more time with the group at the house. She recalled that the furniture in La Casa Cordova ". . . was from somewhere else [and] was not as beautiful or distinguished as María's."[39]

María Luisa Tena credited her mother, María Arredondo Leon, who made nacimientos, with sparking her interest in them. As a child, she watched and helped with the annual displays when her mother entered contests and won prizes for her nacimientos. After moving to Tucson, Tena began creating her own nativity scenes at home, but in 1978 she carried the tradition forward and built one for public display at La Casa Cordova. Her mother had recently passed, and she built it to honor her. The first was a modest scene that portrayed the manger, but the praise it received inspired her to expand the installation and add a new scene the next year, and again the year after that (see Figure 6.6).[40]

Tena built and curated the nacimiento in La Casa Cordova for thirty-one years. She traveled to nearby border towns, often with her good friend Alva Torres, to purchase more figurines. They were not averse to acquiring older, used pieces, since Tena enjoyed refurbishing them herself. Each year, she devoted at least two months to preparing the new display. According to Tena, she often worked late at night and took pride in her efforts "because it represented Mexico." She paid all the costs herself, donated her time, and appreciated how building the nacimiento brought life to the house, especially through the visitors it attracted.[41]

A few people helped her and built the tiered platforms, and over time, the settings became more elaborate. Tena remembered one scene, how-

FIGURE 6.6 María Luisa Tena standing in front of the nacimiento she created in 2007. Rachel Gross, "El Nacimiento: Tena's Work of Love," *Citizen*, December 14, 2007, 54. *Used with permission © Renée Bracamonte—USA TODAY NETWORK via Imagn Images.*

ever, always remained constant: "Since my mother, we always made a little ranch because Jesus was born in a humble place. This is a bit of folklore from Mexico, so I decided to include it."[42] Tena's creative scenes garnered increasing attention and more visitors to La Casa Cordova during the winter holiday months. Her nacimiento of approximately 800 pieces filled an entire room in La Casa Cordova. In 2009 the TMA decided to make it a permanent installation (see Figure 6.7). They added lighting and placed it behind glass. María Luisa Tena's labor was no longer needed to "dust and retouch nicks and change up some colors and reinstall her nacimiento." Putting it behind glass was "bittersweet" for Tena because her services were no longer needed. She shared, "This has been my life for 30 years."[43] In 2014, María Luisa remained resentful that she no longer had access to the house but proud of her work.[44]

Like the period furniture arranged by the Junior League to decorate La Casa Cordova, the figurines, props, and handcrafted elements in the Nacimiento, although much smaller, were still objects. Here, it is worth

FIGURE 6.7 María Luisa Tena's nacimiento includes several detailed scenes. This image shows a concentrated diorama within the larger display. Photo courtesy of prentiss wolfe.

asking how they differed. Foremost, the period furnishings used to decorate La Casa Cordova stayed the same and marked a frozen version of domestic life, curated to create the appearance of historical authenticity. María Luisa Tena's nacimiento, by contrast, is a living tradition built from memory, ritual, and cultural continuity. It evolved annually, drawing on her travels, her relationships, and her creative labor.

While the period pieces were carefully selected to recreate a time fixed in the past, the nacimiento reflects devotion, storytelling, and identity.

It is not merely an arrangement of objects, but an effort that connects past and present through personal and collective memory. Until 2009, when it was placed behind glass, the nacimiento was not a static display but part of a living tradition. Tena refurbished old figurines, updated scenes, and responded to praise to ensure her art evolved and remained dynamic. It represented a cultural practice rooted in lived experience, transmitted knowledge across generations, layered with meaning, and shaped by the specific cultural context of Mexicans and Mexican Americans in Tucson.

A Storied Property

The outcomes at La Casa Cordova were shaped by many actors. The Junior League of Tucson led the restoration of La Casa Cordova and made key decisions, but they did so while navigating the gender constraints of mid-twentieth-century civic life. These women held influence yet operated within systems built by and for men. The restoration reflected a series of choices: some driven by aesthetics, others by institutional priorities, and others still by a desire to quiet the injustice of urban renewal rather than confront it.

Together, these decisions weave the threads that form a *Storied Property*, layered with contested and constructed histories embedded in the walls and rooms of La Casa Cordova. Yet it will always be María Navarrete Cordova's casa—she who resisted removal, and who witnessed her home being turned into a museum while she was still inside it. She had no choice in the outcome, but her presence continues to haunt its edges. To understand La Casa Cordova fully is to reckon with those stories, even as we remain grateful that it survives.

Conclusion
Opening La Casa's Door Is Only the Beginning

Over the last six chapters, *Storied Property* has used a single adobe house as a window to illuminate broader battles over power, displacement, who gets to tell history and who gets edited out of it. The site, home to a transnational woman who told stories of the lavish parties once held there, who painted historical landscapes, played the piano, and tended to a business, was later recast to tell a harsher version of the past, one reduced to outhouses and dirt floors.

The structure at 173 North Meyer Avenue stands solely because of María Cordova. She recognized its value and began informing reporters as early as 1942 about its importance and her great-aunt Refugio Rambaud's role in making the house noteworthy. María's persistence and captivating presence brought more journalists to her door, and her version of history alerted preservationists and researchers to the house's historical significance. Before María's investment in telling its history, the house stood undistinguished and overlooked. She glorified the house's history and her family's connection to it, until she was forced to leave.

María insisted on being seen, even when others wanted her story to disappear. The museum that emerged, publicly framed as a celebration of Mexican heritage when it opened in 1975, ultimately stood in contradiction to that claim. When the museum's doors opened, María did not get the opportunity to welcome visitors, and neither did the members of her family. Any reminders of them were removed. The museum lacked the weight of lived experience and could not answer the elementary question of who once lived in the house and who María Cordova was.

La Casa Cordova's interpretive framework also remained static.[1] There was no space to account for María Cordova's resistance or the decades

FIGURE C.1 In 2013, with the exception of the nacimiento, the rest of La Casa Cordova was closed to visitors. Photo taken by the author.

of adaptation into apartments, a family home, and a smoke shop that shaped the house into what it became. Without evolving narratives or meaningful community involvement, the museum struggled to stay relevant. It existed as a display, and not a reflective space. Ultimately, it failed to resonate with the very community it was meant to represent. When this author first walked into the house in 2013 to explore the possibility of writing a book, all the rooms were used for storage. Except for the nacimiento, a "Do Not Enter" sign prevented visitors from walking through the house (Figure C.1).

The Burden of Stewardship

By the early 2010s, the museum had mostly abandoned its interpretive ambitions. This disengagement echoed a broader institutional fatigue that had begun decades earlier. The Tucson Museum of Art (TMA) had received leased city land for ninety-nine years at a dollar a year on the condition that it restore the houses. By 1979, tensions surfaced within the TMA as staff and leadership began to reckon with the burdens of preserving the houses in the Historic Block. Over time, the houses needed new roofs, windows, and repairs to heating and cooling systems. This ended up straining TMA resources and relationships. Criticism of preservationists, where "the goal was to get every last chimney, drainpipe, window, fireplace, door and floor to look like it did in the target years of 1850 and 1879," stood at the forefront.[2]

The historic homes had become financial liabilities. According to TMA director Paul Piazza, the projected cost was set at $60,000 to $70,000 in total for the Cordova, Romero, Fish and Stevens Houses in 1970. By 1974, the tab increased to $100,000 to $125,000 per building, and this did not include landscaping or other site improvements. Museum director Piazza shared with the *Citizen* that "if he had been around when the project started, he would not have attempted to go back to a particular year." Piazza also referred to previous TMA restoration efforts as "pointless in most cases because they wipe away years of intervening history."[3]

Shortly after intentionally removing the electricity, cooling, flooring, and stucco to make La Casa Cordova resemble a Mexican-period house, the TMA sought funds to reinstall these features. In 2016, the organization reported that between 1973 and 2012 it had spent $1.7 million repairing the five houses in the Historic Block, which were still in need of further work estimated at another $500,000.[4]

The relationship between the City of Tucson and the TMA had ebbed and flowed. The city never got around to fulfilling the promise they made in the early 1970s to build a pedestrian bridge across Alameda Street that would have connected the Historic Block to the underground parking garage. But in 1988, as city officials debated the fate of a 23,000-square-foot building located near the TMA that had served many municipal purposes, the latest being the city courts building, they approved an 85-year lease with the TMA.[5] It is now the TMA's Alice Chaiten Baker Center for Art Education building at 150 West Alameda

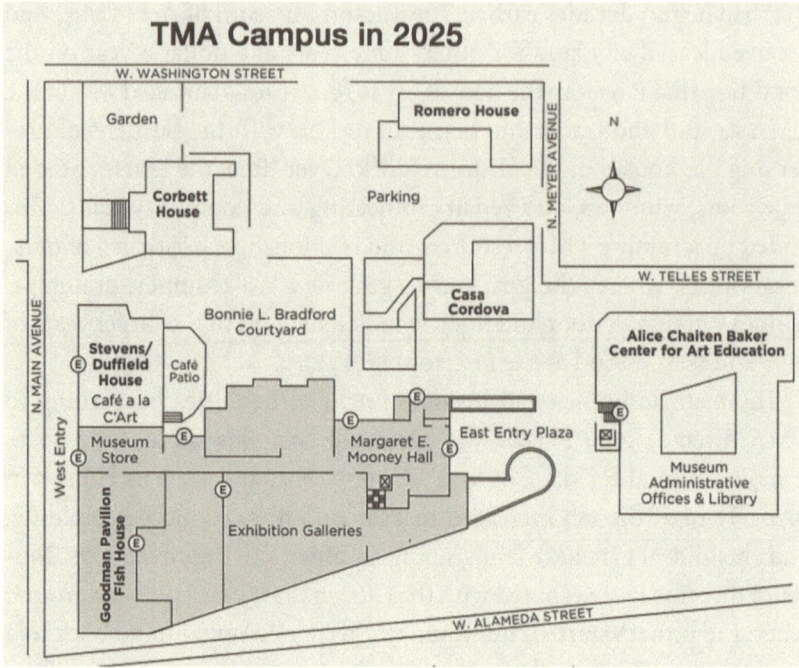

FIGURE C.2 Adapted from a 2025 version originally published on the Tucson Museum of Art website.

Street (see Figure C.2). In more recent years, the city and the TMA have not maintained the same level of collaboration. After the 2008 financial crisis, the city curtailed its annual allocation of $60,000 to the TMA for maintenance of the historic structures.[6]

From Contained Identity to Active Resistance

To a young Tucsonense in the early 1970s, the newly restored La Casa Cordova may not have held much appeal. The "Mexican heritage" museum, an adobe house without electricity, was less a source of pride and more a staged reminder of how dominant institutions chose to represent Mexican identity. Rather than offering dignity or recognition, the exhibit risked reinforcing stereotypes that cast Mexican Americans as relics of the past, confined to domestic spaces and folkloric displays.

At that time, many young Tucsonenses were looking forward to a new future, embracing the promises of civil rights, education, and the expanding influence of the Chicano Movement.[7] La Casa Cordova looked backward. It offered a quiet, apolitical version of Mexicanness that failed to reflect the urgency and political energy that others were fighting for. In contrast to the energy of César Chávez, Dolores Huerta, student walkouts, and grassroots organizing advocating for change, the museum's vision felt frozen, out of step with a generation that saw itself not in adobe walls but in possibility.

At the very moment the museum opened its doors, self-identified Chicanos and Chicanas in Tucson like Raúl M. Grijalva, Isabel Garcia, and Guadalupe Castillo were organizing around educational equity, access to public services, and labor rights. The El Pueblo Neighborhood Center on the southside also opened in 1975. As Grijalva recalled, the drive to build the center began in 1970 "when residents in the area saw a need . . . pushed and pushed—and pushed enough."[8] The local Chicano movement rejected symbolic inclusion and advocated for structural change, refusing to let others define the limits of their place in the city.

Was a Mexican museum the antidote for what city leaders and cultural brokers considered a radical identity and politics? This question gains weight when placed alongside the work of Franciscan priest and historian Kieran McCarty, who published *Desert Documentary: The Spanish Years, 1767–1821* in 1976, just one year after the Mexican Museum at La Casa Cordova opened. His perspective revealed how historians stealthily delegitimized Chicano identity while promoting a safer, more controlled version of Mexican heritage. He wrote, "It is sad indeed that modern Mexican-Americans have had to resort to the Aztlan myth to provide themselves with a past . . . a connection which lends itself readily to false patriotism, protest and violence."[9] The Mexican heritage curated at La Casa Cordova reflected a broader impulse to manage cultural identity through controlled narratives. But the cultural recognition it offered, especially in light of urban renewal, was no solution. La Casa Cordova offered heritage without accountability, memory without confrontation.

Other Properties in the Historic Block

We know the fate of the house at 173 North Meyer Avenue, but the Tucson Museum of Art also assumed responsibility for restoring several other structures in the Historic Block. The city acquired the property at 119–121 North Main Avenue, known as the Fish House, from Margaret M. Gates in August 1968.[10] Unlike other acquisitions in the Historic Block, this was a smooth transaction. Gates, a seasonal resident with financial interests in Tucson, did not contest the sale. It eventually served as a library and, in 2025, houses the TMA gift shop and exhibitions.[11] The city also acquired the Stevens-Duffield House at 155 North Main Avenue from Gates. It was restored and used as a restaurant by the TMA, and still serves that function in 2025.

The city acquired the Corbett House at 180 North Main Avenue through condemnation in 1970 and then gifted it to the TMA with no "strings attached and allowed the art center to decide whether to restore it or tear it down." Built in 1907, the Corbett House is a Mission Revival style stucco-covered brick structure. The museum chose to restore it minimally but promoted the house as a showcase of Tucson's elite past. In contrast to the Cordova property, preservationists associated the Corbett House with "remarkable activities and achievement's."[12] They curated it as the residence of a wealthy pioneer family. The two-story property once included separate servants' quarters at the rear of the house, but the TMA removed them to expand its patio. This decision erased a physical reminder of the domestic labor that made the Corbett family's comfort, status, and lavish social life possible.[13] The Corbett House was used for smaller galleries and educational classes. In 2024, a fire forced its closure, and as of 2025, it remains closed for repairs.

The Source Preservationists Hesitated to Cite

Although they never explicitly stated an intent to discredit María Cordova, the preservationists and researchers involved often centered voices that contradicted or cast doubt on her claims, timelines, and versions of events.[14] Yet, in doing so, they produced some of the most elaborate scholarships of the early 1970s preservation movement in Tucson. They conducted interviews, gathered documentation, and created a record that remains valuable for understanding mid-century Tucson and Arizona.

The Junior League's 1978 publication, *The Restoration of La Casa Cordova* stands out in that list.[15] Edited by Judith Brainerd Hunt, the formal and professional report includes archaeological findings, dendrochronology of the roof beams, and detailed information regarding the house's architectural features. Scholars from the University of Arizona and members of the Arizona Historical Society also contributed to the report. Together, these efforts produced a version of the Cordova house that fit within dominant preservation frameworks and aligned with national trends, but ultimately this report was shaped by the values of the preservationists who were invested in making La Casa Cordova into a period house.

Despite the depth of research and analysis, María Cordova herself was almost entirely absent from *The Restoration of La Casa Cordova*. The only mention reads: "La Casa Cordova has been continuously inhabited by Mexican families. The last family to have lived in the house was the family of María Navarrete Cordova, for whom La Casa is named." In doing so, the publication reduces María and her family to a name on a building, not a presence in its history.

When Legacy Did Not Fit the Profile

In 1972, the property at 102 West Washington Street and the corner of Meyer Avenue legally belonged to María Cordova. It was often referred to as the second Cordova House in early discussions of the Historic Block. The city acquired it through eminent domain and transferred it to the TMA for restoration. Although they studied the property extensively, they were unable to determine when the house was built. They did, however, locate a deed and decided to name the property the Romero House, after Leonardo Romero, its "first known resident."

The house did not appear on early maps, but the deed recorded in 1871 provided the earliest evidence of ownership that preservationists accepted. Early land records in Tucson were fractured and improvised. The fact that the property was recorded by William S. Oury, a Confederate sympathizer and convicted traitor, underscores how white settler control shaped which histories and claims to home ownership preservationists took seriously.

Deed transactions indicate that in 1884, Leonardo Romero moved to another location and sold it to Severin Rambaud for $700 in gold, which included the property and presumably a house. Severin married Refugio in 1892, and they made the house their home, remodeling it extensively and either adding or converting a section into apartments. When Severin died in 1918, ownership transfer to Refugio. When she died in 1934, she willed the property to her great-niece, María Cordova.[16]

Before her death, Refugio Rambaud owned three houses on North Meyer Avenue, including what would become La Casa Cordova. The chain of ownership was recorded, and she lived on and managed the entire block for more than forty years. During the late nineteenth and early twentieth centuries, very few Mexican or Mexican American women, if any, owned an entire block of houses that included apartments and housed multiple businesses.

It is not known whether preservationists ever considered naming the house on Washington Street the Refugio Rambaud House. She was a landholder, an investor, and an enterprising and ambitious woman. Recognizing a matrilineal chain of occupation and influence would have offered a welcome shift in the local historical record. Instead, preservationists reached back to the earliest name they could find in a deed book. Leonardo Romero offered a neutral, documentable male figure, free of complications. In choosing him, preservationists sidestepped the complexities of lived experience, especially when memory centered ambitious, independent women.

Beyond Deeds and Records

In tracing the chain of ownership for La Casa Cordova, preservationists again turned to deed books at the Pima County Recorder's Office. The following sequence appears in *The Restoration of La Casa Cordova* (see Figure C.3). Notably, when Severin Rambaud acquired the property in July 1896, he was already married to Refugio. Since Arizona has long been a community property state, the house at 173 North Meyer Avenue legally entered Refugio's family in 1896.

While these deeds establish a legal chain of ownership for La Casa Cordova, they do not confirm who actually lived in the house. Occupancy and title were not always aligned, particularly in nineteenth-century Tucson, where informal tenancy, extended family arrangements were common.[17] These records also raise questions that legal documents alone cannot answer: Why did Severin, who owned multiple properties, purchase this particular house at 173 North Meyer Avenue? Did Refugio share her and her family's earlier connection to the home? Could it have been a gift for her from Severin, a favor, or something else entirely? If we relied only on the deed records, the City of Tucson's 1972 acquisition of the Cordova properties through condemnation would be reduced to a single line. But as we have seen, *Storied Property* pushes against the

---

CHAIN OF OWNERSHIP

The Deed Books of the Pima County Recorder's Office record the chain of ownership of Lot 8, Block 183 as follows:

April 5, 1875 – The Corporation of Tucson to James Lee (James Lee was married to Maria Ramirez).

May 1, 1879 – James Lee to Gabino Ortega for $100.

September 1, 1883 – Gabino Ortega willed La Casa to Carmen Ortega, his wife.

July 11, 1896 – Carmen (Ortega) and Manuel Coronado (Carmen's second husband) to Severin Rambaud for $900.

February 8, 1919 – Severin Rambaud willed to Rufugio Diaz (Carrillo), his wife.

November 14, 1936 – Rufugio Rambaud willed to Arturo Cordova, a minor and her great nephew.

January 21, 1952 – Arturo to Raul Cordova, his older brother, for $10 and other considerations. (These are Maria Navarette Cordova's sons).

1972 – The City of Tucson acquired the property by condemnation, as part of a federally funded urban renewal project.

FIGURE C.3 Deed sequence of ownership for La Casa Cordova. From Judith Hunt and Junior League of Tucson, *The Restoration of La Casa Cordova* (Tucson: Junior League of Tucson, Inc., 1978), 7.

reductive tendencies often embedded in deed transactions. These official records tend to overlook the legal battles, challenges, and resistance involved. They also fail to capture the more personal aspects of ownership, including something as ordinary as a husband purchasing property as a gift for his wife.

In the 1978 Junior League publication, *The Restoration of La Casa Cordova*, they admitted, "The earlier history of the building now known as La Casa Cordova is somewhat uncertain and clouded by the lack of early record keeping."[18] But the historical gaps and lack of a paper trail did not prevent preservationists from claiming, "It was believed to be one of the oldest existing houses in Tucson, dating back to the Mexican period prior to the Gadsden Purchase (1854)."[19] The only person who had made this claim in the many newspaper stories that featured her was María Cordova. A portion of the house appears on the 1862 Ferguson Map, and experts consider this a record of existence. But the Junior League restored the house and turned it into a Mexican museum based on the belief that it predated 1862 and the Gadsden Purchase.

Preservationists considered María Cordova a disruptor, someone whose claims about a Spanish land grant were seen as irrational because she challenged settler colonial narratives and legal authority. Her refusal to heed an eviction notice and willingly leave her home was taken as further evidence of her defiance. No verified documentation links La Casa Cordova to the Mexican period before the Gadsden Purchase. Even the tree-ring analysis commissioned by preservationists in the 1970s dated the house to 1879, twenty-five years after the Gadsden Purchase.[20] Preservationists and experts dismissed María in every formal sense, yet built the house's historical significance on her words and proclamations.

If we begin the story of La Casa Cordova in 1875, with its first recorded deed, we lose Refugio Rambaud's account of the past, as preserved by María Cordova. This extended version, however, still overlooks the deeper Indigenous history that preceded it. Focusing on deeds obscures the ways land passed through hands informally, shaped more by power than legality. What would settler colonialism be without recorded deeds? The written record, shaped by those who benefited most from dispossession, became the basis for what is considered real, legitimate, and historical. At some point, we as a society and as a nation will have to confront the fallacy at the core of this logic, because we are living on Indigenous land. And while María Cordova's narrative pushes against one version of authority, it does not undo the deeper structures that erased the Indigenous presence long before she entered the story. Recognizing this does not diminish her voice. It situates her account within a longer history of exclusion, one that also depended on overlooking the Indigenous presence she did not name.

Bringing María Home

To their credit, over the last seven years the TMA has dedicated more attention to La Casa Cordova. On June 8, 2017, they opened the largest west-facing room, the one that had once housed the smoke shop, and installed new, updated exhibits (see Figure C.4). For the first time, photographs and images of María Cordova were displayed in her former home. This merits repeating. Since the Cordovas were evicted in 1972, this marked the first time a photographic image of María appeared inside La Casa Cordova. Some exhibits included her words, along with letters and newspaper articles about her placed inside a display case.

The exhibits also directly critiqued urban renewal. A looping video featured Tucsonenses who had lived through, witnessed, and recalled urban renewal, paired with photographs of the area and barrios being demolished. Anyone entering the main room would trigger the documentary, and voices speaking of the injustices wrought by urban renewal echoed through the house. The exhibit remained open until it was forced to close temporarily during the COVID years.

In 2022, after noting that sections of plaster had detached, the roof needed repair, parts of the adobe and foundation had deteriorated, and the walls were bowing out of plumb, the TMA invested in an extensive and costly $200,000 repair and stabilization of the house.[21] Undertaking this effort speaks to the current mindset of the leadership team, who have fully committed resources to La Casa Cordova. In 2024 the TMA opened two more rooms in La Casa Cordova. Exhibits included more about the

FIGURE C.4 The celebration and reopening of La Casa Cordova on June 9, 2017. The event featured Mariachi Milagro and a Borderlands Theater performance about urban renewal. Photos courtesy of the TMA Research Library.

Cordova family, a nearby restaurant, El Rapido and the cultural infusion introduced by Chinese American markets.[22]

Although no one associated with the TMA reviewed a draft of *Storied Property*, the museum has granted permission for its launch to be held at La Casa Cordova at the end of 2025. These actions suggest a willingness to confront the difficult and conflicting histories explored in these pages. As reflected in its recent exhibits, the TMA also appears ready to view the building as part of an ongoing story and to acknowledge its relationship to histories of exclusion, eviction, and removal.

It is evident that the TMA recognizes that if La Casa Cordova is to have a future, it must become more than a backdrop for nostalgia. Acknowledging its full story is critical, not just the imagined nineteenth-century version but also the life María Cordova built there, the fights her family endured, and the community that once surrounded it. This house can still serve Tucson, but only if it becomes a place where the community can gather, learn, and tell stories that have long been excluded. When reimagined, La Casa Cordova can be a means of connection: a place that belongs to the people, not just to institutions. By exploring new models of collective ownership, La Casa Cordova could become a bulwark against displacement and a catalyst for more equitable forms of civic engagement and belonging.

Ideally, those who walk through La Casa Cordova should recognize that they are stepping into a multilayered, unfinished story and see themselves as participants in a living history. *Storied Property* is purposefully local. If you live in or care about Tucson, this history belongs to you. Tucson has always been layered and complicated, beautiful and brutal at the same time. We need to pay closer attention to the everyday spaces we often take for granted because the past is everywhere in our city: embedded in buildings, street names, and in the absences that go unmarked. *Storied Property* reopened the door to María Córdova's casa, but other doors are calling to be unlatched, walked through, and reevaluated. We have reached the time to ask the harder questions about who belongs, who decides, and what kind of history this city wants to tell about itself.

ACKNOWLEDGMENTS

Storied Property has been in the making since 2012. I put it aside because I could not yet figure out how to write it. At the time, I was trying to tell María Cordova's story through the lens of historic preservation, which limited my understanding of her life because others were the ones preserving her story. The complexity of the stories María told about her life challenged me because I did not know how to contextualize them. I also had not yet learned how to write about someone else in a way that allowed for contradiction or uncertainty. Writing two memoirs since then has taught me how to write about another person by first learning how to write about myself. That work made me a better writer, and it helped me return to María's story with more clarity. I also gained the understanding that leaving readers with questions can sometimes be more fruitful than giving them definitive answers. History, like María Cordova's story, is still unfolding. Sometimes it takes time and new information to emerge before the answers can come.

In *Storied Property*, I draw extensively from newspapers, not only for textual references but also for photographs. It is surprising how often María Cordova appeared in the press, the media of its time, and yet most people know so little about her. The photographs in this book are not used decoratively. They contextualize historical moments, illuminate arguments, and support analysis by placing the visual record alongside written sources. Each image serves an interpretive function integral to the book's overall argument. Because I could not always locate the original photographs in archives or access higher-resolution versions, I chose to include newspaper images that are not visually sharp but remain important for understanding context. Unless otherwise noted, I created the maps and graphics that appear throughout this book.

Many have supported this book in recent years as I regrouped the energy and documentation needed to complete *Storied Property*. Foremost among them is the Southwestern Foundation for Education and Historical Preservation, whose funding made it possible to expand the project's reach through additional research and materials available on the companion website. Their commitment to local research is admirable, and I deeply appreciate the confidence the Trustees placed in me to complete and produce this work. While their support made this project possible, any errors or interpretations made throughout the book are mine alone.

Whenever I encountered a writing block or veered off course, I returned to the archives and relied on librarians to help me find my way back. The support of Marianna Pegno at the Tucson Museum of Art and Historic Block was instrumental in accessing the materials featured in this book. She answered numerous questions and provided access to specific photographs and court documents. All the archivists at the University of Arizona Special Collections, particularly Verónica Reyes-Escudero, have supported this work in one way or another since I began the project in 2012. Rachel Black at the Arizona Historical Society was also helpful and patient as I searched for rare and specific items.

The list of people who offered assistance, guidance and advice in the making of *Storied Property* is long, but I want to give special thanks to those who helped me work through ideas and walked with me through and around the La Casa Cordova area while I shared glimpses of the project. The conversations and assistance of the following people have resulted in a better book: Maureen Campesino, Fernando Cordova, Mauro Trejo, Aengus Anderson, Raúl "Netza" Aguirre Jr., Andrea Espinoza, Adam Schwartz, José Jiménez, Alisha Vásquez, Pedro and Leticia Gonzales, Charlene Mendoza, Betty Villegas, Desireé Aranda, Tina Mendoza, Jennifer Levstik and Andrew Brown. Lastly, I want to thank all the desert creatures who mostly remain hidden but sometimes, when least expected, make it a point to reveal themselves so we can witness their tremendous beauty. They are a reminder that Tucson is truly a place of wonder.

NOTES

Introduction

1. Throughout *Storied Property*, La Casa Cordova is referred to by the address 173 North Meyer Avenue. In various documents and accounts, the property was sometimes identified as 171 or 175 North Meyer Avenue. The use of 173 is intended to provide consistency and clarity.
2. This book does not focus on the house's architectural details but instead on its layered history. Architect Serena Huaraque, in a brief note to the author, described Casa Cordova as "a template for the classic presidio home. The facade displays the adobe construction; a method built from both the mud and the skilled hands of the land. The building's fenestration rhythmically guides the movement along the street edge, while the rooms inside orient around a quiet courtyard in the rear to allow more openings for life and light." Email to the author, May 27, 2025.
3. For a critical and incisive examination of historical markers and commemoration, see Laura Pulido, "Cultural Memory, White Innocence, and United States Territory: The 2022 Urban Geography Plenary Lecture," *Urban Geography* 44, no. 6 (2023): 1063.
4. The National Register of Historic Places was created in 1966 as part of the National Historic Preservation Act. For a list of Tucson's individually listed properties, see City of Tucson, "Individually Designated Historic Properties," Planning and Development Services, accessed May 20, 2025, https://www.tucsonaz.gov/Departments/Planning-Development-Services/Historic-Preservation/Individually-Designated-Historic-Properties.
5. For existing work on La Casa Cordova, see Bettina O'Neil Lyons, *A History of La Casa Cordova and the Gabino Ortega Family and the Cordova Family* (Tucson: Tucson Museum of Art, 1980); Heather N. McMahon, "Cordova House," *SAH Archipedia*, Society of Architectural Historians, https://sah-archipedia.org/buildings/AZ-01-019-0049; Judith Hunt and Junior League of Tucson, *The Restoration of La Casa Cordova* (Tucson: Junior League of Tucson, Inc., 1978); Lydia R. Otero, "La Casa Cordova: A Reimagining of Mexican Heritage," *History News* 73, no. 3 (Summer 2018); Tucson Museum of Art,

"La Casa Cordova," accessed May 6, 2025, https://www.tucsonmuseumofart.org/la-casa-cordova; and "Cordova House," *Wikipedia*, last modified April 2024, https://en.wikipedia.org/wiki/Cordova_House. Though not a scholarly source, the Wikipedia entry's brevity and omissions underscore how little public documentation exists about María Cordova and her role.

6. Although some sources list María Navarrete birth year as 1896, her death certificate indicates 1895, which is the date used throughout this book.
7. Diego Castañeda Garza and Alice Krozer, "Life on the Edge: Elites, Wealth and Inequality in Sonora 1871–1910," *Revista de Historia Económica / Journal of Iberian and Latin American Economic History* 41, no. 1 (2023): 34.
8. There is no comprehensive study or book dedicated to Tucson's role or connections during the Mexican Revolution. The most relevant context appears in Miguel Tinker Salas, *In the Shadow of the Eagles: Sonora and the Transformation of the Border During the Porfiriato* (Berkeley: University of California Press, 1997). Also see Thomas E. Sheridan, *Los Tucsonenses: The Mexican Community in Tucson, 1854–1941* (Tucson: University of Arizona Press, 1986), 166–167.
9. Although much has been published on settler colonialism since 2006, Patrick Wolfe's original framework continues to profoundly influence newer scholarship and remains one of the most cited works in the field. Patrick Wolfe, "Settler Colonialism and the Elimination of the Native," *Journal of Genocide Research* 8, no. 4 (2006): 388.
10. *Ibid.*
11. James E. Officer, "Sodalities and Systemic Linkage: The Joining Habits of Urban Mexican Americans" (PhD diss., University of Arizona, 1964), 57n.
12. For works on the dispossession of Mexican land and its effects, see Ned Blackhawk, *Violence over the Land: Indians and Empires in the Early American West* (Cambridge, MA: Harvard University Press, 2008); Rosaura Sánchez and Beatrice Pita, *Spatial and Discursive Violence in the U.S. Southwest* (Durham: Duke University Press, 2021); Richard Griswold del Castillo, *The Treaty of Guadalupe Hidalgo: A Legacy of Conflict* (Norman: University of Oklahoma Press, 1990); Karen R. Roybal, *Archives of Dispossession: Recovering the Testimonios of Mexican American Herederas, 1848–1960* (Chapel Hill: University of North Carolina Press, 2017); Natalia Molina, *How Race Is Made in America: Immigration, Citizenship, and the Historical Power of Racial Scripts* (Berkeley: University of California Press, 2014); Brian DeLay, *War of a Thousand Deserts: Indian Raids and the U.S.-Mexican War* (New Haven: Yale University Press, 2008).
13. Wolfe, "Settler Colonialism," 388.
14. "Tucsonense" is used as a marker of identity, not merely geography. It signals self-identification and cultural belonging in Tucson, where naming carries political and historical weight. For more, see Sheridan, *Los Tucsonenses*, 3. Sheridan explains that "Tucsonense" was used by members of Tucson's Mexican community to assert their rootedness in the city and to distinguish themselves

from both Anglo residents and more recent Mexican immigrants. See also Lydia R. Otero, *In the Shadows of the Freeway: Growing Up Brown & Queer* (Tucson: Planet Earth Press, 2019), which discusses how local Mexicans and Mexican Americans used the identifier to claim belonging, especially those intimately familiar with the city's pre-suburban landscape.

15. Tucson's urban renewal project, known as the Pueblo Center Redevelopment Project, demolished La Calle, a densely populated area south of downtown where many of Tucson's Asian, African American, and Mexican American residents lived. For a detailed analysis of these efforts, see Lydia R. Otero, *La Calle: Spatial Conflicts and Urban Renewal in a Southwest City* (Tucson: University of Arizona Press, 2010). This current work shifts focus to the area north of City Hall, where events surrounding María Cordova and her family offer a more nuanced understanding of the broader scope and complexity of urban renewal in Tucson.

16. Works focusing specifically on Latine/x/o conservatives remain limited. For historical and political context, see Geraldo Cadava, *The Hispanic Republican: The Shaping of an American Political Identity, from Nixon to Trump* (New York: Ecco, 2020), and *Standing on Common Ground: The Making of a Sunbelt Borderland* (Cambridge: Harvard University Press, 2013). While Leo R. Chavez's *The Latino Threat: Constructing Immigrants, Citizens, and the Nation* (Stanford: Stanford University Press, 2013) does not examine Latine/x/o conservatism directly, it analyzes the narratives and cultural pressures that have shaped Latine/x/o political responses, including a turn toward conservative ideologies.

17. For more on Juan Seguín, a Tejano leader who fought for Texas independence but was later marginalized, see Jesús F. de la Teja, *A Revolution Remembered: The Memoirs and Selected Correspondence of Juan N. Seguín* (Austin: Texas State Historical Association, 1991). Seguín's life is also dramatized in the PBS film *Seguin* (1982), which explores his role in the Texas Revolution and the racialized exile that followed.

Chapter 1

1. Rosa Linda Fregoso, *meXicana Encounters: The Making of Social Identities on the Borderlands* (Berkeley: University of California Press, 2003), xiv. Fregoso, a Chicana studies scholar, defines a transnational woman as one who "draw[ing] attention to the historical, material, and discursive effects of contact zones and exchanges among various communities on the Mexico-U.S. border, living in the shadows of more than 150 years of conflict, interactions, and tensions." See also Luin Goldring, "Disaggregating Transnational Social Spaces: Gender, Place and Citizenship in Mexico-US Transnational Spaces," in *New Transnational Social Spaces: International Migration and Transnational Companies in the Early Twenty-First Century*, edited by Ludger Pries (London: Routledge, 2001), 59–76.

2. Deni J. Seymour, "Unveiling Tucson's Namesake: The Sobaipuri O'odham Village of San Cosme del Tucsón," *Journal of Arizona History*, 63, no. 2 (Summer 2022): 115–117.
3. Regarding the inclusion of this statement in Polk's message to Congress on May 11, 1846, historian Amy S. Greenberg states that "None of it was true—but Polk didn't consider it lies. There was a greater truth at stake . . ." See *A Wicked War: Polk, Clay, Lincoln, and the 1846 U.S. Invasion of Mexico* (New York: Vintage, 2013), 104.
4. While newer research rightly credits Native Americans with establishing Tucson, this book focuses on the narratives that were dominant from the early to late twentieth century, shaped by settler colonial frameworks that largely erased Indigenous contributions. By exploring these narratives, *Storied Property* aims to reveal how the achievements of white settlers, and to a lesser extent, Spanish colonizers in sites such as the presidio, were constructed and centered, often at the expense of acknowledging the foundational role of Indigenous peoples.
5. U.S. mercenary William Walker's 1853 expedition added greatly to the instability by attempting to "free" Baja California and Sonora from what he claimed were the "neglect and tyranny" of the Mexican government, with the goal of establishing a new republic he intended to claim as his own. See Scott Martelle's *William Walker's Wars: How One Man's Private American Army Tried to Conquer Mexico, Nicaragua, and Honduras* (Chicago: Chicago Review Press, 2018), 59–92. Adding to the chaos were gold discoveries in the region as outlined in Lawrence D. Taylor's, "The Mining Boom in Baja California from 1850 to 1890 and the Emergence of Tijuana as a Border Community," *Journal of the Southwest* 43, no.4 (Winter 2001): 463–492.
6. Adrián Valadés, *Historia de la Baja California, 1850—1880. Prólogo de Miguel León Portilla* (México: UNAM, 1974),156. Valadés also asserts that Navarrete was from South America. The family name appears with various spellings in historical records, including Navarrete, Navarette, and Navarrette. María Cordova and her children consistently used the spelling Navarrete.
7. Ibid., 165.
8. The most informative book on Californios remains an old one, Leonard Pitt, *The Decline of the Californios: A Social History of the Spanish-Speaking Californians, 1846–1890* (Berkeley: University of California Press, 1966).
9. Antonio A. Navarrete's birth year is listed as 1862 in several genealogical sources. As will be discussed later in this chapter, he signed an affidavit affirming this date.
10. Albert R. Buehman, ed., "Arizona Album: 1887 Bridal Gown from Spain," *Tucson Daily Citizen* (hereafter *Citizen*), July 25, 1952, 8; reprinted June 29, 1960,10. The information and photograph were provided by María Cordova, referred to as "Mary" in the article. It is important to acknowledge that the age difference between twenty-five-year-old Antonio and fifteen-year-old Telesfora raises

questions about the appropriateness of the union. While such arrangements were not uncommon at the time, societal norms and legal standards have since changed. As of 2024, the legal age for marriage in both Mexico and the U.S. is generally eighteen, with some jurisdictional exceptions.

11. *Ibid.*
12. A "Help Wanted" advertisement stated that George E. Baker, referred to as a railroad expert in Tucson, was seeking men aged 18 to 35 with "good sight," and emphasized "No strike." *Citizen*, May 20, 1911, 9. See also "Strike Situation in Nogales, Sonora: Yards Filled with Freight Cars but Cannot Be Moved Due to the Strike," *Star*, January 20, 1911, 2.
13. Gloria Anzaldúa, *Borderlands/La Frontera: The New Mestiza* (San Francisco: Spinsters/Aunt Lute, 1987), 3.
14. Manuel Gamio, *The Mexican Immigrant: His Life-Story* (Chicago: The University of Chicago Press, 1931), viii.
15. Sheridan, *Los Tucsonenses*, 166. He cites data compiled by James Greenberg, Tucson Project Research, Bureau for Applied Research in Anthropology, Department of Anthropology, University of Arizona.
16. In contrast, many working-class Mexican people faced severe discrimination and barriers, such as inadequate educational resources in the United States, and often had to overcome internalized social stigmas to openly express and embrace their identities. These barriers, which endured well into the twentieth century, are illuminated in Lydia Otero's, "A Journey of Combating Language Insecurity: Parts 1, 1C, 2 and 3," in *Aquí se habla: Centering the Local and Personal in Spanish Language Education*, ed. Adam Schwartz, Dalia Magaña, Devin Grammon, and Sergio Loza, vol. 7 of *Critical Approaches in Applied Linguistics* (Berlin and Boston: De Gruyter Mouton, 2025), chap. 17.
17. Birth records indicate that María Refugio Díaz was born in San Miguel Horcasitas to José María Díaz and Jesús Cesma on April 10, 1855. *San Miguel Arcángel, Navojoa, Sonora, México, Matrimonios 1853–1864; Bautismos 1853–1856*, entry 462, page 48, FamilySearch. Accessed October 12, 2024.
18. An Arizona Department of Health Services Genealogical Record Search revealed that at least two of Refugio's siblings also lived in Tucson: Manuel, who spelled his last name "Diez," and Theresa Díaz Benson. *Arizona Department of Health Services Genealogical Record Search*. Accessed May 26, 2025.
19. *Las Dos Repúblicas* and *El Fronterizo* are part of the Historic Mexican and Mexican American Press collection available at University of Arizona Libraries Special Collections.
20. As will be discussed in the final chapter, preservationists focused much of their effort on researching María Cordova's claims. "Marriage Certificate" of Manuel Carrillo and Refugio Díaz, November 21, 1877, performed by Justice of the Peace Joseph Neugass, Precinct No. 1, Pima County, Arizona Territory. Certified copy obtained through correspondence from Arturo Jacobs to Bettina

Lyons, November 18, 1977. On file at the Tucson Museum of Art and Historic Block Research Library (hereafter TMA Research Library), from the Office of the Superior Court, Pima County, Arizona.
21. Dale Wittner, "Downtown Land Title Action Filed: Family Claims Key Sites," *Citizen*, November 9, 1965, 1.
22. Correspondence from Bettina Lyons to Arturo Jacobs, December 19, 1977, TMA Research Library.
23. A brief history of why Arizona is a community property state, linking it to Spanish and Mexican legal traditions, is available in "Arizona Is a Community Property State: A Brief History," *State 48 Law,* accessed May 21, 2025, https://state48law.com/arizona-is-a-community-property-state-a-brief-history/.
24. Edith Sayre Auslander, "Pioneer Family: 'Panchanga' Will Pay Tribute to Carrillos," *Star*, October 16, 1977, H-2.
25. Researching property and family records across different eras presents significant challenges, especially when names change, individuals disappear from the record, and documentation is inconsistent. Historian Mike Speelman determined that Leopoldo had been born Leopoldo Martines, the son of María Martines, and at some point acquired the Carrillo surname for reasons that remain unclear. See Mike Speelman, "Incident at Altar: The Ransoming of Leopoldo Carrillo," *The Journal of Arizona History* 59, no. 1 (Spring 2018): 35.
26. TMA Research Library, *Finding Aid: Historic Block Collection*, inventory of records related to the Historic Block holdings at the Tucson Museum of Art. Arizona Memory Project, accessed May 26, 2025, https://azmemory.recollectcms.com/nodes/view/90668. This is an important site for readers looking to learn more about the houses that survived urban renewal and now sit in the Tucson Museum of Art's Historic Block.
27. Lyons, *A History of La Casa Cordova*, 4.
28. "District Court," *Arizona Weekly Citizen* (Tucson, AZ), October 31, 1885, 3. Newspapers.com. Accessed July 30, 2024.
29. Bettina Lyons, *A History of the Leonardo Romero House and the Leonardo Romero Family and the Severin Rambaud Family,* (Tucson: Tucson Museum of Art, 1980), 3. Also available at https://azmemory.azlibrary.gov/nodes/view/90666.
30. Ibid., 13.
31. Ibid., 13–15
32. "Interview with Mrs. Jose Miranda nee Antonia Pascale," January 17, 1978, by Bettina Lyons. TMA Research Library. The interviews conducted by Lyons are not transcribed and include only notes summarizing the information she considered pertinent.
33. An Arizona Department of Health Services Genealogical Record Search, *Death Certificate for T. Navarrete*, July 20, 1923. Accessed February 27, 2018.
34. "Marriage Licenses," *The Arizona Republic* (Phoenix), December 25, 1924, 17.

35. Arturo Jacobs to Bettina Lyons, November 8, 1977. A copy of the affidavit is enclosed with the letter at the TMA Research Library.
36. *Ibid.*
37. The address was 108 W. Washington Street. Information gathered from the Arizona Department of Health Services Genealogical Record Search, *Death Certificate for Antonio A. Navarrete*, July 13, 1932. Accessed February 27, 2025.
38. "Mrs. Refugio Rambaud, Tucson Pioneer Dies," *Citizen*, October 15, 1934, 7.
39. "Mrs. Rambaud Dies at Sister's Home," *Arizona Daily Star* (hereafter *Star*), October 15, 1934, 5.
40. Refugio Rambaud's death certificate was difficult to locate using the Arizona Department of Health Services Genealogical Record Search. To access it, one must enter the first name "Refugio" and the year of death, 1934. Accessed May 26, 2025.
41. "Cases in Superior Court Carry Over," *Star*, November 14, 1934, 2. The will that would be given more credence was drafted on July 13,1933.
42. Letter from Bettina Lyons to Arturo Jacobs dated December 19, 1977, TMA Research Library.
43. Lyons, *A History of La Casa Cordova*, 12. The restaurant was located at 197 N. Meyer Avenue.
44. Four months later, the property was listed as available for a new business. "Business Opportunities," *Star*, February 10, 1940, 16.
45. "Former Band Leader F.M. Quintero Dies," *Star*, April 2, 1972, 11.
46. The site became Old Tucson Studios that remains operational as a theme park in the Tucson Mountains near Saguaro National Park. See David Leighton's "Street Smarts: Tucson Enticed Stars in '30s," *Star*, March 4, 2024, B1 and B2 for more background information. Paul J. Lawton, ed. *Old Tucson Studios* (South Carolina: Arcadia Publishing, 2008) has an interesting array of photographs.
47. "Novel Who's Who Contest Is Sponsored by Film Company," *Star*, April 14, 1940, 2; Clarence Budington Kelland, *Arizona* (New York: Harper & Brothers, 1939).
48. "Columbia Still Seeking for Descendants of the Pioneers," *Star*, April 17, 1940, 16.
49. "Descendants' List Grows in Star-Columbia Pioneer Derby: New Addition Include Woman Who, If Not Related to Character, Is Definitely Related to The Set, Itself," *Star*, April 19, 1940, 3.
50. *Ibid.*
51. "Tucson a Century and a Half Ago," *Citizen*, January 5, 1919, 7. Reprinted from the *Citizen* of June 21, 1873.
52. Richard L. Zijdeman and Filipa Ribeiro de Silva, "Life Expectancy Since 1820," in *How Was Life? Global Well-Being Since 1820*, ed. Jan Luiten van Zanden, Marco Joerg Baten, Auke Rijpma, Mira d'Ercole, and Marcel P. Timmer (Paris: OECD Publishing, 2014), 109, Table 6.3, "Life Expectancy at Birth in Selected

Countries, 1820s–2000s," accessed May 26, 2025, https://www.oecd.org/en/publications/how-was-life_9789264214262-en.html.
53. "Anecdotes of the Early Days: Tucson a Century and a Half Ago," *Citizen*, January 5, 1919, 7.
54. In "Amendment of Housing Act Urged," *Star*, September 6, 1957, 9, Raul Cordova is identified as a law student at the University of Arizona who spoke before the Pima County Young Republican Club.
55. For discussions of placemaking in Latino communities and how spatial practices intersect with cultural identity and resilience, see Michael Rios and Leonardo Vazquez, eds., *Diálogos: Placemaking in Latino Communities* (New York: Routledge, 2012); and Jesus J. Lara, ed., *Latino Placemaking and Planning: Cultural Resilience and Strategies for Reurbanization* (New York: Routledge, 2021).
56. "Descendants' List Grows," *Star*, April 19, 1940.

Chapter 2

1. Tucson's presidio exemplifies intentional colonial planning, influenced by previous Spanish experiences in the Americas. For more on plazas as a blending of indigenous and colonial forms see, Setha Low M., *On the Plaza: The Politics of Public Space and Culture* (Austin: University of Texas Press, 2000).
2. Cynthia Radding, *Bountiful Deserts: Sustaining Indigenous Worlds in Northern New Spain* (Tucson: University of Arizona Press, 2022), 11–12.
3. "Historic Courthouse," *Desert.com*, accessed June 20, 2023, https://desert.com/historic-courthouse/. Excavations determined that ". . . between AD 750 and 1150, Hohokam people lived in a large, sprawling village built where the courthouse now stands," a location that likely included the site where the Spanish later built their presidio.
4. For more detailed information on the presidio, see J. Homer Thiel, "In Search of El Presidio de Tucson," *Archaeology in Tucson Newsletter* 12, no. 3 (Summer 1996): 1–5, https://www.archaeologysouthwest.org/pdf/ait/arch-tuc-v12-no3.pdf. For a description of life inside the presidio, see Sheridan, *Los Tucsonenses*, 16. Nina Veregge analyzes how five towns including Santa Fe, Albuquerque, Socorro, Las Vegas in New Mexico, and Tucson in Arizona evolved from their Spanish colonial roots through the Mexican period and into the era of U.S. rule. "Transformations of Spanish Urban Landscapes in the American Southwest," *Journal of the Southwest* 35, no. 4 (1993): 378–398.
5. Kieran McCarty, *A Frontier Documentary: Sonora and Tucson, 1821–1848* (Tucson: University of Arizona Press, 1997).
6. For more on this era, see Sheridan, *Los Tucsonenses*, 23; and David J. Weber, *The Mexican Frontier, 1821–1846: The American Southwest Under Mexico* (Albuquerque: University of New Mexico Press, 1982), 207–241.
7. Thomas Edwin Farish, *History of Arizona, Volume 1* (San Francisco, California: Filmer Brothers Electrotype Company, 1915), 321; Sheridan, *Los Tucsonenses*, 30, 275n24.

8. Hilario Gallego, *Reminiscences of an Arizona Pioneer; Personal Experiences of Hilario Gallego. Related at Tucson: April 22, 1926*, copy of transcript provided by Charles Morgan Wood, 3, accessed July 25, 2024, https://azmemory.azlibrary.gov/nodes/view/310066.
9. Thomas F. Saarinen, John Crawford, and Karen Thomas, "Street Patterns and Housing as Ethnic Indicators," in Saarinen and Lay J. Gibson, eds., *Territorial Tucson*, unpublished manuscript in possession of T. F. Saaringen, 6–4.
10. According to the *Citizen*, the importance of this map was not recognized and "kicked" around until the 1940s. It got "frayed at the edges and several very definite tears began to appear" until someone at City Hall framed it. See "80-Year-Old Map First of Tucson," *Citizen*, January 11, 1943, 9.
11. "Old Timers' Tales" *Arizona Weekly Citizen*, April 7, 1891,1.
12. For further exploration of the racial ideologies and expansionist motivations driving Manifest Destiny, see Reginald Horsman, *Race and Manifest Destiny: The Origins of American Racial Anglo-Saxonism* (Cambridge, MA: Harvard University Press, 1981), 95–101; David J. Weber, *Foreigners in Their Native Land: Historical Roots of the Mexican Americans* (Albuquerque: University of New Mexico Press, 2003), 133–132; and Laura E. Gómez, *Manifest Destinies: The Making of the Mexican American Race* (New York: New York University Press, 2018).
13. Pulido, "Cultural Memory, White Innocence,"1063.
14. Bernice Cosulich, *Tucson* (Tucson: Treasure Chest Publications,1953), 12.
15. Ibid., 124.
16. "Tucson—20 Years Ago: From the Citizen, this Date, 1890," *Citizen*, November 14, 1910, 4. For more on Meyer, see David Leighton, "Street Smarts: Meyer Named For Pioneer Who Knew Little of Law," *Star*, February 4, 2014, A2, A5.
17. Micheline Keating, "The Old Drugstore Corner," *Citizen*, August 5, 1967, 31, claims that Meyer established the drugstore in 1858. Also see Don Schellie, "Pills And Justice Were Meyer's Game," *Citizen*, March 24, 1966, 22.
18. "From the Arizona Citizen: An Interesting Landmark," *Citizen*, December 24, 1971, 18. Also see Don Schellie, "Congress Hall Saloon Was Tucson Showplace," *Citizen*, November 4, 1968, 19.
19. "First Tucson Map Shows Mexicans Named Streets," *Citizen*, February 4, 1923, 2
20. Lester N. Inskeep, "City Hall Shuffle: Recreation Department Among 'Most Moved,'" *Star*, October 12, 1963, 15. This article includes a map of all municipal buildings downtown and indicates that the Police Services Building was located directly across the Cordova Home.
21. In 2025, the City of Tucson formally recognized the importance of community corridors in promoting transit-oriented development, walkable neighborhoods, and sustainable growth. Under the leadership of Mayor Regina Romero, the City Council approved the Community Corridors Tool (CCT), a zoning initiative designed to revitalize underutilized spaces along major streets into vibrant, livable communities. The CCT simplifies infill development, particu-

larly affordable housing, by updating zoning regulations to allow for a broader range of housing types and mixed-use developments. For more information, see City of Tucson, "Community Corridors Tool," accessed May 30, 2025.
22. Jimmy's, known for its food and as an entertainment venue, was located at 275 South Meyer Street.
23. Author Melani Martinez provides insightful information about her family that owned and ran the El Rapido restaurant. Her book also illustrates the strong and intimate connections families and individuals form with their neighborhoods. See *The Molino: A Memoir* (Tucson: University of Arizona Press, 2024).
24. Although self-fashioning is often associated with bodily presentation and fashion, it also applies here, offering insight into how Cordova, a transnational woman, positioned herself and her material belongings in her domestic or private space. As Latinx/o/e Studies scholar Marci R. McMahon surmises, "With various representational practices, Mexicanas and Chicanas fashion their identities to negotiate multiple national, regional, and cultural contexts." See Marci R. McMahon, *Domestic Negotiations: Gender, Nation, and Self-Fashioning in US Mexicana and Chicana Literature and Art* (New Brunswick: Rutgers University Press, 2013), 4. For more on self-fashioning, see Amalia Mesa-Bains, "Domesticana: The Sensibility of Chicana Rasquachismo," in *Chicana Feminisms: A Critical Reader*, ed. Gabriela F. Arredondo, Aída Hurtado, Norma Klahn, Olga Nájera-Ramírez, and Patricia Zavella (Durham, NC: Duke University Press, 2003), 298–315; and Jennifer A. Gonzales, "Invention as Critique: Neologisms in Chicana Art Theory," in *Chicana Feminisms: A Critical Reader*, ed. Gabriela F. Arredondo, Aída Hurtado, Norma Klahn, Olga Nájera-Ramírez, and Patricia Zavella (Durham, NC: Duke University Press, 2003), 313–323.
25. Albert R. Buehman, ed., "Arizona Album: Mary Navarette Cordova," *Citizen*, October 18, 1951, 12. The same photograph and story appeared again with a different title and her maiden name spelled as "Maria Navarrete Cordova" in the *Citizen*, October 17, 1957, 8. The "Arizona Album" columns that featured María and members of her family indicate that she willingly shared her history and rare family photographs with Buehman and the newspaper. None of the original photographs can be located in local archives.
26. Ibid.
27. Carolyn C. Robbins, "A Century of Arizona Women Artists," *Traditional Fine Arts Organization*, accessed January 19, 2025, https://www.tfaoi.org/aa/8aa/8aa413.htm.
28. Ibid.
29. Lew McCleneghan, "Painting Points Up Old Wall," *Citizen*, October 18, 1951, 25.
30. Lew McCleneghan wrote another article based on one of María's paintings. The paper included a photo of the painting, but it was too small to make out much detail of her home in Carbó, Sonora. See "Early Hacienda Wall Yields Huge Store of Secret Gold," *Citizen*, June 9, 1952, 2.

31. Most books on women painters from the past focus on those who were more professional and whose works were preserved and appreciated in their time. See, for example, Patricia Trenton, Sandra D'Emilio, and Autry Museum of Western Heritage, *Independent Spirits: Women Painters of the American West, 1890–1945* (Los Angeles: Autry Museum of Western Heritage in association with the University of California Press, 1995).
32. Albert R. Buehman, ed., "Arizona Album: Front of Home Was Part of Old City Wall," *Citizen*, January 22, 1952, 6.
33. J. Homer Thiel, "In Search of *El Presidio de Tucson*," *Archaeology in Tucson* 12, no. 3 (Summer 1996): 1. https://www.archaeologysouthwest.org/pdf/ait/arch-tuc-v12-no3.pdf.
34. "Notice: Public Hearing," *Star*, January 24, 1952, 10.
35. "Advertisement," *Citizen*, July 16, 1926, 4.
36. "Toy S. Don," obituary, *Star*, September 5, 1952, 25.
37. "Notice: Public Hearing," 10.
38. "High-Rise Tops City Agenda," *Citizen*, November 21, 1964, 10.
39. "Harry A. Sellers," Obituary, *Star*, April 10, 1967, 14.
40. "$3.2 million Pima County Office Center Proposed," *Star*, January 30, 1953, 19.
41. "Civic Square Federal Aid Questioned," *Citizen*, January 31, 1953, 1.
42. "Low-Rent Housing Debate Held Here," *Citizen*, September 22, 1950, 8.
43. According to the *Citizen's* editor, the initiative faced "a trouncing defeat." See Editorial, "Election Lessons," *Citizen*, September 28, 1950, 16.
44. For more on federal housing policy and exploitative systems that benefited real estate interests while undermining public housing, see Keeanga-Yamahtta Taylor, *Race for Profit: How Banks and the Real Estate Industry Undermined Black Homeownership* (Chapel Hill: University of North Carolina Press, 2019); Gail Radford, *Modern Housing for America: Policy Struggles in the New Deal Era* (Chicago: University of Chicago Press, 1996); Richard Rothstein, *The Color of Law: A Forgotten History of How Our Government Segregated America* (New York: Liveright Publishing Corporation, 2017).
45. "Civic Square Federal Aid Questioned," *Citizen*, January 31, 1953, 1.
46. "Drachman Brought Hughes, Spring Training to Growing City," *Citizen*, December 27, 1999, Special Section "Trend$," 1, 4. The deals Drachman brokered as a real estate developer are lauded, but his role in leading urban renewal is not mentioned other than crediting him for "shaping" the city.
47. Roger O'Mara, "Progress Threatens Storied Past: Civic Center Will Mean Razing of Historic Homes," *Star*, February 6, 1953, 4
48. "Republican Women Hit Plan to Seek Federal Aid for Civic Center," *Star*, February 10, 1953, 2.
49. "Meeting Planned to Form Plans of Civic Center," *Star*, February 20, 1953, 2. The article also notes that the Chamber had been "notified" that no federal money was available, though it does not elaborate further.

50. "Horan To Hear Proposal: Civic Center's Aid Pan Draws Protests from Group of Women," *Star,* February 17, 1953, 6. "Mrs. Roca, Local Artists Dies At 74," *Citizen*, April 21, 1954, 40.
51. Roger O'Mara, "Progress Threatens Storied Past," *Star*, February 6, 1953, 4. To get an idea of the stature and influence Sedgwick held, see Massachusetts Historical Society, "Atlantic Harvest: Ellery Sedgwick and *The Atlantic Monthly*," https://www.masshist.org/news/story.php?entry_id=174.
52. Norman Harrington, "Federal Help for Civic Center Impossible: Aid for County 'Out of Window,'" *Citizen*, February 18, 1953, 34.
53. More on how this voting restriction advanced urban renewal in *La Calle*, see page 115–117. For additional context, see "The History of the Bond Election Law," *Star*, January 22, 1966, B-14. For a more comprehensive discussion, see Katherine Levine Einstein and Maxwell Palmer, "Land of the Freeholder: How Property Rights Make Local Voting Rights," *Journal of Historical Political Economy* 1, no. 1 (2021): 1–31. On page 20, they assess that "The federal government granted its enormous land holdings in the West to loggers, miners, ranchers, and homesteaders, disposing of almost 1.3 billion acres of public land. Migration to the American West was inextricably linked with the acquisition of land and homeownership. It is perhaps unsurprising that the region formalized the connection between property rights and voting rights." A series of Supreme Court decisions in 1969 and 1970 declared such voting requirements unconstitutional under the Equal Protection Clause of the Fourteenth Amendment.
54. Editorial, "Big Project, Think Big," *Citizen*, March 12, 1953, 36.
55. "Downtown City Block Acquired: Property West of Stone May Be Developed for Luxury Apartments, Purchaser Hints," *Star*, May 12, 1960, 13. The target area was one block west of Stone Avenue. It was bounded on the east by North Church Avenue, On the south by W. Council Street, on the west by Court Avenue, and on the North by Franklin Street.
56. B.J. Sigesmund, "Obituaries: Land Entrepreneur, Lyle R. Palant, 54," *Citizen*, April 24, 1991, 35.
57. "'Nucleus' Of Downtown: Office Complex Planners Seek Zoning Change," *Star*, August 17, 1961, 17.
58. *Ibid.*
59. "Notice of Public Hearing," *Star*, December 1, 1961, 65.
60. "Ex-Land Tycoon Lyle Palant Files for Bankruptcy," *Star,* February 5, 1969, 1; "Palant Placed on Probation in Fraud Case," *Citizen*, April 2, 1981, 24.
61. "Arizona Runs Out of License Plates," *Star*, May 7, 1950, 11.
62. "Motor Vehicle Total Mushrooms," *Citizen*, October 10, 1951, 2.
63. "Over Half of People Licensed as Drivers," *Citizen*, July 24, 1958, 6.
64. "22 Downtown Stores Vacant; Realtor Blames It on Parking," *Star*, June 9, 1951, 9. Most of the vacant stores were newly constructed and faced the typical challenges that new businesses encounter when they first open.

65. "Work Begun on New Parking Space for Sheriff's Vehicles," *Star*, May 22, 1953, 13.
66. "Wrecking Crews Chipping Away at Another of City's Memories," *Citizen*, August 13, 1958, 24. Also see, Ray Halvorsen, "Tucson Landmark to Be Destroyed: City Building to Fall Under Hammers; New Parking Lot Seen," *Star*, July 9, 1953, 18; "Demolition of Russel House Spells End for Old Landmark," *Star*, July 4, 1951, 14.
67. "Parking lots To Open at City Hall," *Citizen*, August 1, 1962, 15.
68. William Mathews, editorial, "Urban Renewal in Tucson," *Star*, April 8, 1958, 24. Mathews refers to the battles between those who argued that parking should be handled by private enterprise and those who believed it should be a city responsibility as "... all this hullabaloo."

Chapter 3

1. While informed by scholarship on settler colonialism, this book does not approach it as a theoretical abstraction. Instead, it examines how María Cordova was shaped by and responded to its structures in the specific context of Tucson. See Wolfe, "Settler Colonialism and the Elimination of the Native," 388.
2. Albert R. Buehman, ed., "Arizona Album: The First Railroad in Sonora," *Citizen*, September 1, 1952, 8. The *Citizen* printed the story again on September 21, 1954, 10; July 21, 1959, 12; June 24, 1964, 16
3. *Ibid.*
4. Thomas Faist, "Transnationalization in International Migration: Implications for the Study of Citizenship and Culture," *Ethnic and Racial Studies* 23, no. 2 (2000): 196.
5. Alan Rosenus, *General Vallejo and the Advent of the Americans: A Biography* (Berkeley: Heyday Books/Urion Press, 1999), xiv.
6. Diego Navarette interview with author, November 16, 2013.
7. "Tucson Youth Had Part in Final Battle," *Citizen*, September 29, 1945, 2. A syndicated national radio that featured "Letters from Home" featured Raul Cordova's exploits. Its byline read, "NEWS! From our fighting men ... what they're doing ... where they are...." "Advertisement," *Citizen*, October 8, 1945, 8.
8. "Why Not Have Five Birthdays Every Year?" *Star*, February 24, 1960, 17.
9. Maria Navarrete Cordova, "Letter to the Editor: Tubac and Tucson," *Star*, February 27, 1960, 28. In her letter, Cordova provides book titles and specific page numbers to support her claims, modeling the conventions of historical citation. While some of the works she references could not be located in major library catalogs, this approach underscores her effort to establish credibility and authority in public discussions of local history.
10. Raul followed in María's footsteps to tell the family's story. Either he or María drafted a handwritten account, more than thirty pages long, recounting María's relationship with Refugio and claiming that María moved to Tucson to take her

place as heir to the Tucson Presidio Land Grant. An undated narrative written in the style of a children's story, in the author's possession, portrays María as a young woman destined to fulfill her legacy, it reflects the family's ongoing efforts to assert a connection to the land grant. Though highly stylized, the account reflects the family's efforts to assert historical connection to the property.

11. Although it would further elaborate Cordova's land claim, The City of Tucson clerk has been unable to locate this letter. The Webster quote is from Dale Wittner, "Downtown Land Title Action Filed: Family claims Key Sites," *Citizen*, November 9, 1965, 1.
12. Don Robinson, "Relic of Presidio Days: Cordova Home Survives Century of Changes," *Star*, December 18, 1960, 39.
13. Ibid.
14. Martha Buddecke, "Today's Citizen: 150 Years Live Vividly in Memory of Pioneer," *Citizen*, February 15, 1963, 12.
15. Steve Emerine, "Urban Renewal Area, Plan Ok'd: City Requests U.S. Allocation," *Citizen*, February 1, 1965, 1. Interestingly, although the urban renewal news dominated the front page of the *Citizen*, a small box article appeared titled "Dr. King Arrested in Selma."
16. Raul Navarrete Cordova, "Letters to the Editor," *Citizen*, February 4, 1965, 14.
17. *Raul Navarrete Cordova v. United States of America and the City of Tucson*, "Court Docket Sheet," November 4, 1965, Pima County, Arizona. On file at the TMA Research Library.
18. Documents associated with *Raul Navarrete Cordova v. United States of America and the City of Tucson*, Civ. No. 2104, United States District Court for the District of Arizona, 1965–1966, available at the TMA Research Library.
19. The headline referred to the official adoption of an urban renewal plan by the City Council. A news story by Peter Starrett, "Vote will probably be Dec.28," *Citizen*, November 9, 1965, 1, explained the public hearing that ultimately convinced the council to embrace the program. That story also included a photograph of Roy Drachman with the caption "Get on with the job" under it.
20. Dale Wittner, "Downtown Land Title Action Filed: Family Claims Key Sites," *Citizen*, November 9, 1965, 1.
21. Ibid.
22. Dale Wittner, "Tucson Land Claim: Cordova Says He Seeks Only to Clear Home Title," *Citizen*, November 10, 1965, 3.
23. Don Bufkin, "From Mud Village to Modern Metropolis: The Urbanization of Tucson," *Journal of Arizona History* 22, no. 1 (1981): 68–70. See also Gilbert J. Pedersen, "'The Townsite Is Now Secure': Tucson Incorporates, 1871," *Journal of Arizona History* 11, no. 3 (1970).
24. John C. Lacy, "Original Land Titles in Tucson," *The Journal of Arizona History* 56, no. 3 (2015), 327.

25. Lacy, "Original Land Titles in Tucson," citing Sidney B. Brinckerhoff and Odie B. Faulk, *Lancers for the King: A Study of the Frontier Military System of Northern New Spain* (Phoenix: Arizona Historical Foundation, 1965), 34–35.
26. McCarty, *A Frontier Documentary*, xiii. The Catholic Diocese has retained some records, but these are mostly baptismal, marriage and death records. The San Xavier Mission's archives were also a separate collection from the presidio's civil, military and religious records.
27. Arizona Historical Society (hereafter cited as AHS), MS 1155, Officer, James E., Papers, 1950–1995, Box 39, folder 523, "Speeches—Research on Hispanic Arizona," paper titled "Hispanic Arizona: Research Perspectives and Challenges," 3.
28. Ibid., 7. In *Hispanic Arizona, 1536–1856* (Tucson: University of Arizona Press, 1987), xv. Officer attributes this story to Juan Bojórquez, a corporal in the Mexican military, and cites Atanacia Santa Cruz Hughes as the source. Officer claims to have found it in "The Mexican Troops' Departure from Tucson, 1856," as told in Spanish to Donald W. Page, May 12, 1929, with translation, introduction, and notes by Donald W. Page at AHS. However, it appears that the file is not located in the source Officer cited. The document can actually be found in Microfilm Case 309, Dr5 0300 in MS 641 Capt. Donald W. Page. Page's original transcript, not the translation, of his conversation with Atanacia Santa Cruz indicates that she was not present when Juan Bojórquez told the story. At some point, her husband Sam Hughes conveyed to her that Bojórquez had shared the story with him in the company of Hiram Stevens. She later recounted it to Page in 1929 when she was 79 years old. While it is impossible to cross-check the details of this account with other sources or evidence, the story has been repeatedly cited, suggesting it offered a possible and expedient explanation for the fate of the presidio archive.
29. More about Bancroft's expansive research collection is available at https://guides.lib.berkeley.edu/BancroftNativeAmericanCollections/HHBancroft.
30. Ibid., 8. James Officer wrote that "Father Keiran McCarty persuaded the Bancroft Library folks to microfilm all of Pinart's Sonoran documents and provide copies to the Sonora Historical Society. The originals remain, however, at Berkeley." Pinart's collection forms part of the Hubert Howe Bancroft collection. See the *Alphonse Louis Pinart Papers*, BANC MSS Z-Z 17, The Bancroft Library, University of California, Berkeley at https://oac.cdlib.org/findaid/ark:/13030/tf5g5004kl/entire_text/.
31. Ibid., 7.
32. J. Homer Thiel and Tucson Presidio Trust for Historic Preservation, *Pioneer Families of the Presidio San Agustin del Tucson, 1775–1856* (Tucson: Tucson Presidio Trust for Historic Preservation, 2016), 146.
33. Ibid., 149.

34. Regarding the Oury and León's connection, Thiel writes that, "In 1861 the Confederate Army occupied Tucson for a few months. By February 1862 the California Union soldiers had recaptured Tucson. William Oury, a prominent Confederate sympathizer, came to the León house and asked Francisco to hide money and medicines. At first, he hesitated but then took the items and hid them in a cellar. The Oury family were near neighbors of the Leóns at the time." *Ibid.*, 146. Also on this page, Thiel estimates that León owned 360 acres of land.
35. Paul L. Allen, "Leon Family Artifacts Span 1840s to the 1920s," *Citizen*, May 9, 2000, 20. Thiel adds more to our knowledge of León: "In 1870, León was listed as a farmer worth $15,000, placing his family among the elite of Tucson. Few other Mexican families had attained financial wealth after the arrival of the Anglos, and Francisco was one of the wealthiest native Tucsonans;" Thiel, *Pioneer Families*, 148.
36. Sonnichsen, *Tucson*, 43. William S. Oury was appointed the local agent for the Butterfield Overland Stage, acting as an intermediary by facilitating accommodations for guests, storing cargo, and providing corrals for livestock.
37. The presidio's church chaplain took the survey on August 6, 1820, and he counted 395 persons. See Victor R. Stoner and Henry F. Dobyns, "Fray Pedro Antonio De Arriquibar, Chaplain of the Royal Fort at Tucson.," *Arizona and the West* 1, no. 1 (1959): 75. See Sheridan, *Los Tucsonenses*, 3, for the population in 1860, of which 653 were Tucsonenses, making up 70.6 percent of the population.
38. Sheridan, *Los Tucsonenses*, 38.
39. Sonnichsen, *Tucson*, 48–49.
40. Cornelius Cole Smith, *William Sanders Oury: History-Maker of the Southwest* (Tucson: University of Arizona Press, 1967) 85–86. Oury is Smith's great-grandfather.
41. Sonnichsen, *Tucson*, 61.
42. Smith, *Oury*, 132.
43. Jay J. Wagoner, *Arizona Territory, 1863-1912: A Political History* (Tucson: University of Arizona Press, 1970),16. Thomas H. Pederson, Curator of Collections at the Arizona Historical Society, notes that "The actual confiscation cases against the property of the Ourys and several other Confederate sympathizers lingered on, never coming to trial until November 12, 1870. Judge John Titus, Chief Justice of the U.S. Court, Judicial District 1, heard the cases and granted a dismissal." See, Thomas H. Pederson, "The Buckley House: Tucson Station for the Butterfield Overland Mail," *Journal of Arizona History* 7, no. 4 (1966): 166, n.41. For more on this episode regarding the conviction of Civil War secessionists, see the notable case of Sylvester Mowry: Bert Fireman, "'What Comprises Treason?' Testimony of Proceedings Against Sylvester Mowry." *Arizoniana* 1, no. 4 (1960): 5–10.

44. Sue Smith, "The First Property Recordings in Tucson, by Wm S. Oury, Recorder," in *Copper State Bulletin*, Spring/Summer 1985, vol.20, nos.1–2, 1. Found in AHS, MS 1072, "Property Records, 1862–1864," Box 1.
45. Sonnichsen, *Tucson*, 66.
46. *Ibid.*, 66–69. Tucson's next mayor, Mark Aldrich, also acquired a sizable number of properties once he arrived. He moved to Tucson to escape a wife and six children and a past that included an indictment for killing Joseph Smith, the founder of Mormonism. See Paul L. Allen, "Tucson's First Mayor Came with Extremely Checkered Past," *Citizen*, December 20, 2004, 9A.
47. For more on the Camp Grant Massacre, see Chip Colwell-Chanthaphonh, *Massacre at Camp Grant: Forgetting and Remembering Apache History* (Tucson: University of Arizona Press, 2007) and Karl Jacoby, *Shadows at Dawn: A Borderlands Massacre and the Violence of History* (New York: Penguin Press, 2008).
48. Lacy, "Original Land Titles in Tucson," 334.
49. AHS, MS 1155, Officer Papers, Box 48, folder 642, "Research—Oury Property Record, 1862–1863." A review of the titles Officer complied shows that William S. Oury purchased Lot 73, 74, 75, 76 and 77. Regarding Lot 72, issued to John Sweeny, the record states that "Sweeny apparently out of the territory at this time." No lot number was assigned to the Meyer property, but the filing date is listed as "3/3/64"
50. Lacy, "Original Land Titles in Tucson," 332–333.
51. *Ibid.*, 337–340.
52. *Raul Navarrete Cordova v. United States and City of Tucson*, "Court Docket Sheet."
53. *Raul Navarrete Cordova v. City of Tucson*, No. CIV-2104-TUCSON (D. Ariz. 1965), "Answer," filed November 15, 1965, 2.
54. *Raul Navarrete Cordova v. United States of America*, No. CIVIL-2104-TUCSON (D. Ariz. 1965), "Motion to Dismiss, Notice and Memorandum," filed December 29, 1965, Memorandum, 2.
55. See "It's Not Often That You Can Sue the U.S. Government," *Citizen*, June 19, 1969, 3.
56. "U.S. Files for Dismissal of Tucsonans' Land Suit: Cordova Claims City Hall Property," *Star*, December 29, 1965,18; "U.S. Requests Dismissal of Downtown Land Suit," *Citizen*, December 29, 1965, 4.

Chapter 4

1. "New Shows Rate Interest," *Citizen*, February 21, 1959, 16. The former Tucson Art Center was once housed in what is now known as Kingan Gardens, a venue that hosts many weddings and celebrations, accessed February 5, 2025, https://www.kingangardens.com/.
2. "Kingan Museum Loaned to TFAA, Rent Free," *Star*, September 29, 1955, 24.

3. "New Century Society," *Tucson Museum of Art*, 2023, 5, LINK https://tucsonmuseumofart.org/wp-content/uploads/2023/12/new-century-society-booklet_2023.pdf.
4. "Cities Given Break in Government Program for Urban Renewal," *Star*, January 2, 1955, 15. Clarksville, Tennessee, and New Orleans, Louisiana, had already recently submitted their urban renewal programs for approval, and at least eight more cities were considering similar projects.
5. Arizona H.B. 94 in *Session Laws, State of Arizona, 1954, Twenty-First Legislature, 2nd Regular Session*, Chapter 128, 217. Arizona Legislature. See Arizona Memory Project, accessed November 24, 2024, https://azmemory.azlibrary.gov/nodes/view/252937.
6. This special bond election is discussed in *La Calle*, 115–117. Voters were asked to mark yes or no on permitting the city to borrow up to $14 million in short-term, low-interest loans from the federal government. Their approval would allow the city to acquire properties in the designated eighty-acre renewal area through negotiated purchase or condemnation under the power of eminent domain.
7. "CAA to Put $47,933 for Airport Development," *Citizen*, July 17, 1958, 17. It is interesting that the first act by the Mayor and Council to move on urban renewal did not attract that much attention or even a headline. The Old Pueblo District project area ballooned to 416 acres in 1961, see "Tucson Urban Renewal Plan Okayed by P&Z," *Star*, June 14, 1961, 10. "Unrealistic" expectations eventually chipped the area down to less than 100 acres, see, Pete Cowgill, "City Gets Report on Renewal," *Star*, September 24, 1963, B-1.
8. "CAA To Put Up" *Citizen*, July 17, 1958, 17.
9. These statistics were provided in the following, Peter Starrett, "Tucson's Slum Clearance Program is the Most Ambitious in the Nation," *Citizen*, August 26, 1958, 19. This project area was known for its diversity and included many Chinese and Chinese Americans.
10. "Study Opens on Urban Renewal," *Citizen*, July 14, 1958, 28. Also see Tucson (Ariz.) Urban Renewal Office, *History of Slum Clearance and Redevelopment Programs in the City of Tucson, Arizona, Old Pueblo District, Project No. Ariz. R-6* (Tucson: Urban Renewal Office, March 1959), 18–22.
11. Peter Starrett, "Most Families Seek to Stay in Urban Renewal Area," *Citizen*, August 25, 1958, 1.
12. *Ibid*.
13. *Ibid*. The $200 down payment in 1958 is equivalent in purchasing power to about $2,500.00 in 2025.
14. *Ibid*.
15. Hummel and other city officials balked at the idea of building a large auditorium or civic center because they could not figure out how to secure federal funding; without such support, the city would have to cover the entire cost. See

Peter Starrett, "Urban Renewal Plan May Reveal Hassle Over Land for Auditorium," *Citizen*, September 28, 1960, 1.
16. "5,500 Dwell in Unfit Quarters: U.S. Agency Clears Way for Building of 200 Housing Units to Replace Homes," *Star*, October 3, 1958, 13.
17. The 76 acres is mentioned in an editorial that declared, "The federal urban renewal project is dead, and remains only to be laid away by the mayor and Council" in "Urban Renewal Plan Should Be Dropped—Now," *Citizen*, May 04, 1962, 10. Also see City of Tucson, "Redevelopment Plan: Southwestern Section Central District Development Plan" (Old Pueblo Project, Arizona R-6; City of Tucson: March 22, 1962), unpaginated.
18. David Leighton, "Street Smarts: Midtown Subdivision Developer Would Go on to Be Tucson Mayor," *Star*, March I, 2021, B-1.
19. Peter Starrett, "Homer to Take Rochester Post," *Citizen*, February 26, 1962, 1.
20. Sanguinetti's formal appointment with the TAC began in August 1964, but he had already started performing related duties beforehand. A profile published that summer provides additional personal and professional background. See Gene Brooks, "Today's Citizen: Tucson's Rarity Says Rarity in the Field of Art," *Citizen*, July 17, 1964, 16.
21. "Frank Sanguinetti: 1917–2002," *The Salt Lake Tribune*, April 4, 2002, 20. According to his obituary, Sanguinetti ran his family's department stores between 1948 and 1959. He served on the board of the Arizona Savings & Loan between 1950 and 1955 and moved to Tucson in 1960 to pursue his graduate degree. He also taught art at the University of Arizona. This obituary mistakenly states he was hired by the TAC in 1962. Considering his love of art and professional position, he was most likely an active TAC member since his 1960 move to Tucson.
22. "180-Degree Turn: City Council Embraces Federal Urban Renewal," *Star*, December 1, 1964, 15.
23. Steve Emerine, "City Reopens Study of Urban Renewal: Area Now Increased in Size," *Citizen*, November 30, 1964, 1.
24. See Roy P. Drachman and Vincent L. Lung, *The Pueblo Center Redevelopment Project: Report presented to the Central City Council of the Urban Land Institute, April 23, 1965,* by Roy Drachman, Chairman, Citizens Committee on Municipal Blight and Vincent L. Lung, Assistant City Manager and Coordinator of Community Development (Tucson: City of Tucson, 1965).
25. Steve Emerine, "Urban Renewal Action Set: City Bond Election Slated for May," *Citizen*, December 7, 1964, 1.
26. Steve Emerine, "Urban Renewal Area, Plan Ok'd: City Requests U.S. Allocation," *Citizen*, February 1, 1965, 1.
27. Charles Turbyville, "Group Gets Historic Sites List: 'Must Save' Tag Put on Homes," *Citizen*, April 30, 1965, 13. The list of structures that deserved to be "pardoned" would grow to about forty. Research by the Historic Sites Committee found its way into a valuable book which provides detailed historical and archi-

tectural background on sixty-nine buildings that, it concluded, merited restoration. See Historic Areas Committee, *Historical Sites* (Tucson, 1969). Although currently included as part of the Historic Block, the J. Knox Corbett House was not included in the conversations regarding historic homes until the 1970s.

28. For more regarding the committee's role in urban renewal, see Bob Thomas and Pete Cowgill, "Old Pueblo's Historical Heritage May Not Fall Victim to Progress: Site Committee Outlines Plan," *Star*, April 23, 1965,13. Relevant to this issue, also see an eight-page booklet, Emil W Haury and Isabel Fathauer, *Tucson From Pithouse to Skyscraper* (Tucson: The Committee, 1975). Born in Bisbee in 1909, Fathauer's father was one of the leading businessmen in Bisbee. See "Tucson, Bisbee Legend Isabel Fathauer, 88," *Star*, September 4, 1997, 8.
29. Don Robinson, "Full Block is Called 'Historic': Group Asks Pardon for Pioneer Area," *Star*, May 7, 1965, B-1.
30. Charles Turbyville, "Group Gets Historic Sites List: 'Must Save' Tag Put on Homes," *Citizen*, April 30, 13.
31. Robinson, "Full Block is Called 'Historic': Group Asks Pardon for Pioneer Area," *Star*, May 7, 1965, 15. Directly after receiving the report, COMB's Planning and Land Use Subcommittee recognized the "possibilities of a graceful mixture of modern and historic sites" and recommended preserving the block. See "Preservation of Area Urged," *Citizen*, May 7, 1965, 7.
32. Edward N. Fish, "'Forty-Niner' Passes Away," *Star*, December 19, 1914, 8; Bettina Lyons, *A History of the Edward Nye Fish House and Edward Nye Fish Family* (Tucson: Tucson Museum of Art, 1980), 10. For perspective, Fish's wealth in 1870 would be worth more than $3 million in 2025.
33. Today, the Fish House is home to the TMA's Museum Store and houses exhibits.
34. Bettina Lyons, *A History of the Edward Nye Fish House*, 1–2. $3000 in 1868 would be worth around $120,000 in 2025.
35. Colwell-Chanthaphonh, *Massacre at Camp Grant* ; Jacoby, *Shadows at Dawn*.
36. Known as the Stevens/Duffield House, it now is home to the TMA's restaurant Café à la C'Art. See Bettina Lyons, A History of the Hiram Stevens House and the Hiram Stevens Family and U.S. Marshal Milton B. Duffield (Tucson: Tucson Museum of Art, 1981). It is also available at https://www.tucsonmuseumofart.org/stevensduffield-house/.
37. Eric Cavaliero, "Hospitable Home: Hiram Stevens Entertained in Western Style," *Citizen*, May 3, 1965, 2.
38. Frank C. Lockwood and Donald W. Page, *Tucson—The Old Pueblo* (Phoenix, AZ: Manufacturing Stationers, Inc., 1930), 53.
39. Margaret Regan, "A Short History of the Stevens House," *Tucson Weekly*, April 5, 2001, accessed January 17, 2025, https://www.tucsonweekly.com/tucson/a-short-history-of-the-stevens-house/Content?oid=1068170.
40. "Broadlands Farm," *Carroll County Farm Museum*, accessed December 29, 2024, https://www.ccfarmmuseum.org/about-us/broadlands-farm.

41. Cavaliero, "Hospitable Home," *Citizen*, May 3, 1965, 2. Also see Don Schellie, "Hiram Stevens—Man of The West," *Citizen*, November 9, 1977, 29. Lyons, *A History of the Hiram Stevens House*, 8.
42. "Home of Pioneer Merchant Proposed as Historical Site," *Citizen*, April 29, 1965, 15. This article also features a photograph of the interior of Frank Sanguinetti's well styled 13-foot-high living room ceiling.
43. Cordova, "Historical Heritage to Be Destroyed," *Citizen*, February 4, 1965, 14. Previously cited and discussed in Chapter 3.
44. Raul Navarrete Cordova, "Letter to the Editor: Save Historical Buildings," *Star*, March 8, 1965, 22.
45. Edited by Albert R. Buehman, "Arizona Album: Homes in Tucson's History: Home Once Inside City Wall," *Citizen*, May 11, 1964, 14.
46. Bernice Johnston, "City's Mexican Heritage Captured by Paintings," *Star*, May 2, 1965, 11. Edwin "Ted" Booth Sayles was the first Curator at the Arizona State Museum and served in that capacity for twenty years until 1963. He rented the house on Meyer Avenue and Washington Street from María. Sayles must have appreciated Cordova's paintings and used his connections to arrange an exhibition. See Bruce B. Huckell, Darrell C. Creel and G. Michael Jacobs, "E.B. 'Ted' Sayles, Pioneer Southwestern Archaeologist." *Kiva*, Vol. 63, No. 1 (Fall, 1997), 77. Also see Charlotte Cardon, "Renewal Casts Pall on Landmarks Rooted Deep in Tucson History," *Star*, July 18, 1965, 11 where Sayles claims that the house on the corner of Washington and Meyer "was part of the soldier's barracks within the [presidio] enclosure."
47. Eric Cavaliero, "On North Meyer: Her 117-Year-Old House Still Home," *Citizen*, April 26, 1965, 2.
48. *Ibid*. María Cordova explained an aspect that causes problems for researchers regarding Tucson's ever-changing addresses in its more established areas. She said, "The house where my great-aunt lived is now No. 199. But it used to be 203, and this one [the current Casa Cordova] used to be 201."
49. *Ibid*.
50. *Ibid*.
51. *Ibid*.
52. Eric Cavaliero, "The Old Lady Had a Story to Tell," *Citizen*, June 26, 1965, 21. Although it includes a photo of María Cordova, the article primarily conveys knowledge gathered over time about life in the presidio and its construction. The "old lady" referenced in the title was Mariana Diaz, who was born in the presidio around the 1770s.
53. The Arts Center hired its first executive director in 1959, and subsequent hires were always male in the 1960s and 1970s. Before 1959 the task of directing the group fell on two executive secretaries, Ynida Smalley Moore (1951–1953) and Winifred Wise (1953–1959). See J.C. Martin, "Tucson Art Center: Its Beginnings: What Direction?: At What Pace?" *Star*, May 20, 1973, D-3.

54. "Fine Arts Picks Nelson President," *Citizen*, March 30, 1960, 3.
55. The Civic Center group also included leaders from the Chamber of Commerce, Women's Clubs, and dozens of civic and fraternal organizations. See S.C. Warman, "Report Points Out Need for Big Convention Center," *Citizen*, March 9, 1960, 13.
56. "Editor's Urban Renewal Opinions are Disputed: Architect Nelson Defends 'Center,'" *Star*, February 23, 1966, 5.
57. "Art Center Would Take Over Block: Offers to Save Old Buildings," *Citizen*, July 2, 1965, 1: "Museum Sought in Renewal Area: Art Center Director Sanguinetti Would Relocate His Facility at Improved Site," *Star*, August 27, 1965, 5.
58. "Museum Sought in Renewal Area: Art Center Director Sanguinetti Would Relocate His Facility at Improved Site," *Star*, August 27, 1965, 5.
59. "Historic Sites May Be Doomed: Some on 'Save' List Don't Meet Criteria," *Citizen*, August 25, 1965, 3. Sanguinetti imagined the historic adobe structures to be recreated to an architectural museum covering the range of Arizona and Sonora and another as a "typical dwelling of the period of the Mexican occupation with characteristic exterior paintings and interior furnishings." Also see "Annual Report of the Historical Committee of the City of Tucson to the Mayor and Council and Sub-Committee Report on Historical Aspects of the Proposed Tucson Art Center," 7 September–15 March 1972, 15, available at the TMA Research Library.

Chapter 5

1. Urban renewal was not unique to Tucson but played out most acutely here in ways shaped by local conditions and histories. While many other cities saw similar federal and municipal partnerships targeting inner-city and ethnic communities for "rehabilitation," this book remains focused on how those forces unfolded in Tucson. In addition to Otero, *La Calle*, there are a few historical works on urban renewal that focus on Tucson. Michael Logan, *Fighting Sprawl and City Hall: Resistance to Urban Growth in the Southwest* (Tucson: University of Arizona Press, 1995), focuses on Tucson and Albuquerque and sheds light on the conservative politics associated with growth issues. Sarah Anne Launius, "The Streetcar Effect: Capital, Revitalization, and the Battle over Gentrification in a Sunbelt City" (PhD diss., University of Arizona, 2018), examines how state intervention and public incentives fueled downtown Tucson's redevelopment and gentrification, particularly in connection with the modern streetcar project, and highlights historical patterns of displacement and racialized property dispossession. Juan Gomez-Novy and Stefanos Polyzoides, "A Tale of Two Cities: The Failed Urban Renewal of Downtown Tucson in the Twentieth Century," *Journal of the Southwest* 45, no. 1/2 (2003): 87–119, highlights urban renewal as a form of violence. Margaret Regan, "There Goes the Neighborhood: The Downfall of Downtown," *Tucson Weekly*, March 6–12, 1997, addresses what ur-

ban renewal meant to Tucson's Mexican American community and critically examines the process. Regan makes use of a variety of interviews to highlight residents' attachment to their neighborhoods and to argue that city planners failed to achieve their goal of revitalizing the downtown area. Keith Carew, Adolfo Quezada, and Priscilla Altuna, "Urban Renewal's Dispossessed," *Citizen*, December 12, 1970, A-1, and "¡Ole!" section, pp. 1–12, stands out as a valuable, timely investigation of urban renewal in Tucson, including interviews with those relocated and some city officials that were conducted shortly after relocation and demolition had taken place. See also "Tucson's Barrios: A View from the Inside," special report, *Star*, July 16, 1978, 1–27, which includes Tucsonenses' reflections about urban renewal and the area destroyed; Janet Mitchell, "Vanished Tucson," *City Magazine*, May 1989, 44–48; Bufkin, "From Mud Village to Modern Metropolis;" and Patricia J. Clark and Martha M. Fimbres, "A Study to Identify and Access the Psychological Ramifications Inherent in the Process of Relocation Regarding Census Tract I in Downtown Tucson, Arizona" (master's thesis, Arizona State University, 1978), which illuminates the more human aspects of urban renewal. Though not a study of urban renewal, Sunaura Taylor's *Disabled Ecologies: Lessons from a Wounded Desert* (Berkeley: University of California Press, 2024) offers a valuable framework for considering how environmental harm, settler logics, and bodily vulnerability are intertwined in southern Arizona.

2. Discussions about a new art center were secondary to that of building a civic-community center south of downtown. See "Civic Center Is Renewal 'Must,'" *Star*, May 20, 1965, 16.
3. Marin, "Tucson Art Center," *Star*, May 20, 1973, D-3.
4. "Citizens Group Asked to Pick Building Sites," *Citizen*, November 4, 1966, 13.
5. As for the historic houses, Sanguinetti proposed, without naming a specific house, that one would be restored beyond the Territorial period "to illustrate family life as it was here 100 to 150 years ago" in "Citizens Group Asked to Pick Building Sites," *Citizen*, November 4, 1966, 13.
6. "Just in Passing," *Citizen*, December 10, 1966, 11. Sanguinetti went to work at the Utah Museum of Fine Arts. For more, see "Frank Sanguinetti:1917–2002," *The Salt Lake Tribune*, April 4, 2002, 20. Talks regarding planetarium continued; see "Murphy Asks Catalyst Role: Trade Unity Hears Planetarium Plea," *Star*, April 11, 1969, 11.
7. "Home Of Pioneer Merchant Proposed as Historical Site," *Citizen*, April 29, 1965, 15.
8. Mindy Fullilove, *Root Shock: How Tearing Up City Neighborhoods Hurts America, and What We Can Do About It* (New York: One World/Ballantine, 2004), 68.
9. "Pueblo Center Project: Urban Area Property Acquisition Initiated," *Citizen*, April 4, 1967, 15.

10. *Ibid.*
11. Resolution No. 6874, Mayor and Council of the City of Tucson, April 3, 1967, Pueblo Center Redevelopment Project (No. Ariz. R-8), obtained from the City Clerk's Office, City of Tucson, June 20, 2025. The resolution was signed by Lew Davis (Mayor)
12. "Pueblo Center Project: Urban Renewal Acquisition Initiated," *Citizen*, April 4, 1967, 15.
13. Don Robinson, "$15 Million Area Improvement Plan: Tucson's Urban Renewal Is Fast: Land Use Expected by November 1970," *Star*, May 16, 1968, 13.
14. "Director Cites Other Cities: Art Center Seeks City Government Backing," *Citizen*, October 27, 1967, 6.
15. "Art Center Director Tells Plans," *Star*, October 27, 1967, 13.
16. Urban renewal officials purchased the home for $127,000 from the individuals who owned it in 1968. See Don Robinson, "Revered City Landmark Will Yield to Progress," *Star*, December 29, 1967, 19; also see, Dan Pavillard, "Jacobs Mansion Comes Down: Old Showplace Demolished," *Citizen*, January 5, 1969, 3.
17. The *Citizen* featured the photograph with the caption titled "Jacobs Mansion Falls to Progress" on its front page on January 5, 1968, 1.
18. "Art Center Likely to Drop Site Downtown for Randolph Park," *Citizen*, February 28, 1968, 11. Patricia Ann Murphey Groom was married to Barrick Groom and the daughter of real estate developers, Helen and John W. Murphey.
19. *Ibid.*
20. *Ibid.* Also see, "Planned Museum May Be Shifted: Art Center Advises City Financial Snag Makes Urban Renewal Area Site Impossible," *Star*, February 21, 1968, 19.
21. "Art Center Likely to Drop Site Downtown," *Citizen*, February 20, 1968, 11.
22. Civil 108818, *City of Tucson v. Raul Navarrete Cordova et al.*, condemnation complaint, July 31, 1968, microfilm, Legal Records, Pima County Superior Court and Consolidated Justice Court, Clerk's Office, 110 W. Congress, Ste. 241, Tucson, AZ 85701. Interpretations of case records are based on the author's reading of the legal documents. The author is not an attorney.
23. Civil 108822, *City of Tucson v. Raul Navarrete Cordova et al.*, condemnation complaint, July 31, 1968, microfilm, Legal Records, Pima County Superior Court and Consolidated Justice Court, Clerk's Office, 110 W. Congress, Ste. 241, Tucson, AZ 85701. Unless otherwise noted, all references to this case and Civil 108818, *City of Tucson v. Raul Navarrete Cordova et al.*, are drawn from files housed in this archive.
24. "City Council Again Rejects Proposal: Reid: Art Center Will Fit in Park," *Citizen*, September 17, 1968, 12.
25. "Irked Art Center Members Ask Voice in Site Selection," *Citizen*, October 10, 1968, 10.

26. Cathryn McCune, "'Not Interested in Culture': Art Center Head Quits, Scores [sic] City Officials," *Star*, April 2, 1969, 19.
27. "City Fathers Deny They Scorn Culture," *Star*, April 3, 1969, 4. The remarks directed at TAC were made by Councilperson Richard Kennedy.
28. "Art Center May Accept City Plan," *Star*, May 6, 1969, 12; "Art Museum to Get Civic Center Site," *Citizen*, September 19, 1969, 1.
29. In February 1970, Wilde's architectural firm had been in business for twenty-five years and he had established a working relationship with finance and construction executives on the committee and who admired his architectural designs. Wilde had recently been selected to design the city's new police and fire buildings in the urban renewal area and had completed the Solar Laboratory and Space Center at the University of Arizona. "Wilde Chosen to Design Museum at Art Center; Architect to Shun 'Warehouse' Idea," *Star*, February 18, 1970, 16; "Architect Wilde Engaged to Design New Art Center," *Citizen*, February 17, 1970, 7.
30. "Fish-Stevens Home: Joyner Proposes Mayor's Mansion," *Citizen*, May 20, 1969, 2. Also see Nancy Sortore, "Whither Goest We Now? City Has Saved the Territorial Buildings: Their Final Disposition Now the Problem," *Star*, May 25, 1969, 44.
31. Arizona Foundation for Legal Services & Education: The Legal Bar Foundation, "James M. Murphy," *Legal Legacy Project*, accessed March 15, 2025, https://legallegacy.org/13-attorneys/61-james-m-murphy.
32. Civil 108818 *City of Tucson v. Cordova*, microfilm, Legal Records, Pima County Superior Court and Consolidated Justice Court.
33. "Homes Tour To Give Glimpse into Old Pueblo's Historic Past," *Star*, October 5, 1965, 12.
34. "Heritage Tour Set This Afternoon," *Star*, January 31, 1971, 59.
35. Arrangements between the anonymous donor and TAC were more involved and outlined in greater detail in the "Annual Report of the Historical Committee of the City of Tucson to the Mayor and Council," 7 September–15 March 1972, available at the TMA Research Library.
36. "Agreement with City: Art Center Settles Problems of Sites," *Star*, June 9, 1970, 4-A.
37. Ibid.
38. Resolution No. 7886, "Relating to Community Development: Proposing Intention to Enter into Lease Agreement with the Tucson Art Center" appeared in the "Legal Notice" section of the *Star*, August 10, 1970, 18.
39. Ibid.
40. "Council Oks Lease for Art Museum," *Star*, October 23, 1973, 3.
41. While this book does not typically use bullet points, they are included here to clearly present the legal inconsistencies and contradictions the Cordovas'

defense exposed in court. The structure highlights the complexity and significance of their argument, as laid out in the Defendant's Memorandum, filed on May 21, 1971, which directly challenged the City of Tucson's justification for condemning their properties. Legal Records, Pima County Superior Court and Consolidated Justice Court.
42. Notice of Appeal, July 19, 1971, Legal Records, Pima County Superior Court and Consolidated Justice Court.
43. Designation of Additional Portions of Record, filed July 23, 1971, Legal Records, Pima County Superior Court and Consolidated Justice Court.
44. Notice of Taking Deposition, *City of Tucson v. Maria Cordova et al.*, Consolidated Cases No. 108822 and 108818, filed August 4, 1971, Legal Records, Pima County Superior Court and Consolidated Justice Court.
45. Alec Lamis, "'Holdout' Determined to Resist City," *Star*, November 8, 1971,13.
46. Ibid.
47. The city's payout check, after subtracting property taxes, was delivered and made payable to the Cordovas' attorneys. $1,500.73 was deducted for María Cordova's property taxes, and $1,408.22 was deducted for Raul Cordova's. Legal Records, Pima County Superior Court and Consolidated Justice Court.
48. Interview: Soledad (Perez) Tarazon, Angela Peyron by Bettina Lyons, January 25, 1978, TMA Research Library. Several archival materials cited from this collection were accessed prior to their 2024 cataloging update. As a result, file names and folder numbers may have changed. Researchers are encouraged to consult library staff for assistance in locating referenced materials.
49. María Luisa Tena, telephone conversation with the author, October 6, 2014.
50. Pam Engebretson, "Two Old Bedrooms Spark Furor," *Citizen*, December 23, 1971, 23.
51. The National Register of Historic Places is the official list of the United States' historic buildings, districts, sites, structures, and objects deemed worthy of preservation. Established under the National Historic Preservation Act of 1966, it is overseen by the National Park Service. The Register recognizes properties significant in American history, architecture, archaeology, engineering, and culture. See "National Register of Historic Places," U.S. General Services Administration, accessed March 20, 2025, https://www.gsa.gov/real-estate/historic-preservation/historic-building-stewardship/national-register-of-historic-places. See also "Historical Society Joins Cordova Houses Battle," *Citizen*, January 15, 1972, 6. The article, which is unattributed, accuses Raul Cordova "of adding another lump to the adobe [by] . . . seeking court actions to keep his property despite efforts by the city to buy it."
52. Pam Engebretson, "New Delays May Plague Art Museum," *Citizen*, February 18, 1972, 26.
53. "Cordova House Condemnation OK," *Citizen*, March 2, 1972, 12; "Condemnation of Cordova House Upheld," *Star*, March 1, 1972, 12.

54. Mandate from the Court of Appeals, *City of Tucson v. Maria Cordova et al.*, Consolidated Cases No. 108822 and 108818, issued April 28, 1972, Legal Records, Pima County Superior Court and Consolidated Justice Court. Also see, Engebretson, "New Delays May Plague Art Museum," *Citizen*, February 18, 1972, 27.
55. *National Register of Historic Places Inventory—Nomination Form: Cordova House*, prepared by Robert Fink, April 18, 1972. National Park Service, accessed June 06, 2024, https://npgallery.nps.gov/GetAsset/e701d353-4c3c-41b1-896b-129446e23d2a.
56. Ibid.
57. Ibid.
58. Ibid.
59. Despite the prominent role of women in Tucson's preservation efforts, and although many major projects in the 1970s were led by women, all the experts enlisted to assess the Cordova house were men. Those who toured the property included archaeologist James E. Ayres, Dr. Raymond Thompson of the Arizona State Museum and head of the University of Arizona's Anthropology Department, Gordon Heck, a professor in the UA's School of Architecture, and Dennis McCarthy and Robert Fink from the Arizona State Parks Board. "Evaluators Study Cordova House Significance," *Star*, April 20, 1972, 5.
60. "Removal Of Cordova House Could Hurt Historic Grants," *Citizen*, May 4, 1972, 36. Also see, Judy Donovan, "Wing Threatened by Art Center: Council to Weight Fate of Cordova House," *Star*, May 7, 1972, 8.
61. "Register Picks Cordova Home," *Star*, May 4, 1972, 1.
62. Art Arguedas, "Council Oks Art Center Site: Historic House to be Kept," *Star*, May 9, 1972, 19.
63. "Cordova Shift Put At 2 Feet," *Citizen*, May 9, 1972, 27.
64. Tena, telephone conversation with the author, October 6, 2014.
65. "February 6, 1973, Board Meeting: Cordova House," 1; Lyons, *A History of La Casa Cordova*, 14. Both items are available at the TMA Research Library.

Chapter 6

1. The demolition of structures began in May 1967. Over the next two years, the city's urban renewal program destroyed 269 structures, some of them multiple-occupancy dwellings or businesses. See Don Robinson, "Barren Land Near City Hall to Mark Progress: Cultural Center to Spring Up," *Star*, January 2, 1969, A1.
2. The phrase comes from historian David Lowenthal, who explored how societies reconstruct the past to serve present needs. David Lowenthal, *The Past Is a Foreign Country* (Cambridge: Cambridge University Press, 1985).
3. "Community Arts Committee Meeting," dated November 10, 1972, TMA Research Library. The minutes are written in a timeline format, and the information referenced is from the entry dated October 5, 1972. In Lyons, A History of

La Casa Cordova, it reads, "Maria Cordova continued to live in the house until 1973, when she was moved by her family to a nursing home."
4. "February 6, 1973, Board Meeting: Cordova House," 1, TMA Research Library.
5. Lyons, *A History of La Casa Cordova*, 14.
6. Christina Collins, "New Art Museum Plans Unveiled," *Citizen*, January 25, 1973, 29.
7. "Council Oks Lease for Art Museum," *Star*, October 23, 1973, 3. The City of Tucson also pledged $60,000 a year to the museum for operations.
8. Sue Giles, "Throng Marks Start of New Art Museum," *Citizen*, November 21, 1973, 17.
9. "Community Arts Committee Meeting," Dated November 10, 1972, 3. TMA Research Library.
10. Defendant's Memorandum, filed on May 21, 1971.
11. "Cordova House: Grant to Help in Restoration," *Citizen*, February 1, 1974, 20; "Jr. League To Restore Old House," *Star*, February 4, 1974, 9. Dennis McCarthy who helped drafted the application to the National Register of Historic Places for the Cordova house the previous year oversaw and issued these grants.
12. "Junior League to Aid in Historic Restoration," *Star*, April 21, 1973, 24.
13. Archaeologist James E. Ayres made this assessment. See "Evaluators Study Cordova House Significance," *Star*, April 20, 1972, 5.
14. "Society Assumes Ft. Lowell Museum Control Saturday," *Citizen*, November 12, 1963, 28.
15. The Tucson chapter was admitted to the Association of Junior Leagues in 1933. See "JTL History," accessed April 12, 2016, https://www.juniorleagueoftucson.org/about/jlt-history/. Most of what we know about the Tucson chapter has been written by members with commemorative and celebratory intentions. See Dawn Cole and Catherine Mendelsohn eds., *As I Recall: Recollections from the Junior League of Tucson, 1933–1993* (Tucson: The League, 1993) and *Grand Dames & Great Causes: The Way We Were . . . A History of the Junior League of Tucson, 1933–2013* (Tucson: Junior League of Tucson, Inc, 2013).
16. Susan Ostrander, *Women from the Upper Class* (Philadelphia: Temple University Press, 1984), 139.
17. Helen Brooks, quoted in Cole and Mendelsohn, *As I Recall*, 35.
18. *Ibid.*, Brooks also added that "To become a member, a young woman was supposed to be under 35 years of age."
19. Sue Giles, "Around Town: Davis Party a Real 'Hustle,'" *Citizen*, February 22, 1977, 2B.
20. "Citizens Group Asked to Pick Building Sites," *Citizen*, November 4, 1966, 13.
21. Sidney Brinckerhoff exemplified the professionalization of preservation in Arizona. He was well-versed in contemporary preservation frameworks established by the National Historic Preservation Act of 1966 and was part of a

broader network of preservationists who drew lessons from national projects like Colonial Williamsburg and restorations in Santa Fe. By the early 1980s, he was serving on Governor Bruce Babbitt's Task Force on Historic Preservation, where he helped shape statewide policy and advocated for historically grounded approaches to restoration. See "Sidney Brinckerhoff Research Materials," AHS, Tucson, Arizona.

22. "Community Arts Committee Meeting." Dated November 10, 1973. TMA Research Library. The notes are arranged in a timeline fashion and indicate that this meeting with Brinckerhoff took place on September 26, 1972.
23. For more regarding how adobe facades and stereotypes were marketed to appeal to tourists, see Chris Wilson, *The Myth of Santa Fe: Creating a Modern Regional Tradition*, 1st ed. (Albuquerque: University of New Mexico Press, 1997).
24. Layla Cattan, "Former City Architect, San Xavier Mission Restorer Deserves Recognition," *Star*, February 21, 1988, 40.
25. See Otero, *La Calle*, chapter 7, "The Politics of Memory," for a discussion of how homes that once belonged to the Sosa and Carrillo families were restored and named after explorer and settler colonialist John C. Frémont.
26. Geraldine Sullivan, "Architect Master of Restoration: Herreras . . . Southwest Beauty Reborn," *Citizen*, May 24, 1973, 33. Also see Philip Garcia, "Barrio Childhood Spurred Architect's Pride in Area's Buildings—and History," *Star*, November 2, 1980, 20.
27. Edith Armstrong, "Casa Cordova—Restoring Tucson's Mexican Heritage," *Star*, May 26, 1974, G-1.
28. Laurajane Smith, *Uses of Heritage* (London: Routledge, 2006), 29. Smith writes, "The dominant Western heritage discourse is concerned with aesthetically pleasing material objects, sites, places and landscapes. It privileges monumentality and grand scale, innate artefact/site values and visually based experiences."
29. Armstrong, "Casa Cordova" *Star*, May 26, 1974, G1. In addition to interviewing Lyons, the reporter took information from a press release, "La Casa Cordova: Restoration Project of the Junior League of Tucson: For the *Tucson Daily Citizen*." Dated November 22, 1974. Found at TMA Research Library.
30. Barbara Kirshenblatt-Gimblett argues that "staged authenticity" often replaces deeper historical engagement in heritage work. See *Destination Culture: Tourism, Museums, and Heritage* (Berkeley: University of California Press, 1998), 3–7. On the role of forgetting in shaping modern memory and suppressing historical complexity, see Paul Connerton, *How Modernity Forgets* (Cambridge: Cambridge University Press, 2009), 2–3, 59–60.
31. "Historic La Casa Cordova's Restoration Complete," *Citizen*, November 14, 1975, 17.
32. "Cordova Padrinos Party in Patio," *Star*, April 21, 1975, 8.

33. Sue Giles, "Art Museum Gets 'Keys' To La Casa Cordova," *Citizen*, November 10, 1975, 10.
34. *Ibid.*
35. *Ibid.*
36. Sue Giles, "Su Casa," *Citizen*, November 17, 1976, 18.
37. "Tucson Museum of Art Has Roots That Date to 1924," *Star*, August 11, 1977, 22.
38. Marian Lucas, "La Casa Cordova Seeking Loan of Mexican Heritage," *Citizen*, November 16, 1978, 25.
39. According to Tena, Los Padrinos held their meetings in the room where the nacimiento was installed. She also recalled that Hector Laos made some of the pieces used in the nacimiento.
40. Lucas, "La Casa Cordova."
41. Tena, telephone conversation, October 6, 2014.
42. Alva B. Torres, "Maria Luisa Tena's Nacimiento," in *Notitas: Select Columns from the Tucson Citizen by Alva B. Torres*, compiled by Lydia R. Otero (Tucson: Planet Earth Press, 2021), 71–73.
43. Natalia Lopera, "Nativity Scene, or Nacimiento, at TMA Now Encased in Glass," *Star*, November 29, 2009, E4.
44. Tena, telephone conversation, October 6, 2014.

Conclusion

1. In the 1970s, preservationists often locked buildings into a single time period, creating static versions of the past that ignored a structure's layered history. La Casa Cordova is a case in point. Today, preservation practices are shifting. There is growing recognition that historic spaces carry multiple meanings and should reflect community input and the ongoing relevance of place. See Stephanie Meeks and Kevin C. Murphy, *The Past and Future City: How Historic Preservation is Reviving America's Communities* (Washington, DC: Island Press, 2016); Max Page and Randall Mason, eds., *Giving Preservation a History: Histories of Historic Preservation in the United States* (New York: Routledge, 2004); Erica Avrami, ed., *Preservation and Social Inclusion* (New York: Columbia Books on Architecture and the City, 2020); Kenneth C. Turino and Max A. van Balgooy, eds., *Reimagining Historic House Museums: New Approaches and Proven Solutions* (Lanham, MD: Rowman & Littlefield, 2019); Ned Kaufman, *Place, Race, and Story: Essays on the Past and Future of Historic Preservation* (New York: Routledge, 2009); Erica Avrami, Randall Mason, and Marta de la Torre, eds., *Values in Heritage Management: Emerging Approaches and Research Directions* (Los Angeles: Getty Conservation Institute, 2019).
2. "Glance," *Citizen*, January 20, 1979, 42.
3. *Ibid.*
4. Maggie Driver, "Museum of Art needs $500K to Repair Buildings It Oversees," *Star*, March 28, 2016, A1.

5. "Art," *Star*, August 2, 1988, 2.
6. Driver, "Museum of Art needs $500K," *Star*, March 28, 2016, A1.
7. While I use the term "Chicano Movement" here to reflect the language of the period, I acknowledge that terms such as Chicanx and Chicane have since emerged to more fully include gender-diverse and nonbinary people within the movement's legacy.
8. "Many Services Offered: Fiesta Opens El Pueblo Neighborhood Center," *Star*, October 19, 1975, 24. Grijalva served as El Pueblo's first director and had already been elected to the Tucson Unified School District's School Board.
9. Kieran McCarty, *Desert Documentary: The Spanish Years, 1767–1821* (Tucson: Arizona Historical Society, 1976), 2. McCarty dedicates the book to "Sidney B. Brinckerhoff, friend and mentor."
10. Pima County Recorder, *Deed Indexes, 1866–1976*, City of Tucson (Grantee) from Margaret M. Gates (Grantor), two separate transactions dated August 22, 1968, Book 3332, pages 33 and 35, entry numbers 56632 and 56635, microfilm page 224, A–H Index (Nov. 1966–June 1969), Pima County Recorder's Office, Tucson, Arizona. The City of Tucson acquired the Fish and Stevens properties on the same day.
11. "Old Fish Home Resumes Role as TMA Library," *Citizen*, April 10, 1980, 3B.
12. Bettina Lyons, *The J. Knox Corbett House and the J. Knox Corbett Family* (Tucson: Tucson Museum of Art,1981), 21.
13. *Ibid.*, 6.
14. *Ibid.*, 14. A section subtitled "Biography of Maria Navarrette Cordova 1896–1975" oddly highlights Cordova's inconsistencies and eccentricities. For example, in a 1977 interview with María's nephew, Diego Navarrete, the only detail deemed important to include was that he "remembers as a boy that his aunt would direct the children where to look for buried gold and Spanish treasure." In 2013, Diego Navarrete recalled a phone conversation with Lyons and claims to have offered more extensive information about his aunt "Yita," whom he held in high esteem. The last paragraph in this section is also baffling. Instead of a summary of the home's historical value or notable highlights, the final paragraphs return to the theme of treasure hunting. Ending a professional report in this way encourages readers to see Cordova as someone preoccupied with fantasy, an impression that preservationists seemingly wanted to promote.
15. Hunt and Junior League of Tucson, *Restoration*, 1978.
16. Lyons, *A History of the Leonardo Romero House*, 6. Pages 14–16 in the report cast suspicions on María Cordova, how she came to acquire the property, and Refugio's personal belongings.
17. For discussion of informal tenancy and non-aligned occupancy and title in nineteenth-century Tucson and the U.S. Southwest, see Eric V. Meeks, *Border Citizens: The Making of Indians, Mexicans, and Anglos in Arizona* (University of Texas Press, 2007); Otero, *La Calle*; and María E. Montoya, *Translating Prop-*

erty: *The Maxwell Land Grant and the Conflict over Land in the American West, 1840–1900* (University of California Press, 2002).
18. Hunt and Junior League, *Restoration*, 7.
19. *Ibid.*, 1.
20. *Ibid.*, 11.
21. This is the estimate price for repairs over the next ten years. Bob Vint, *Field Inspection & Preservation Recommendations: Casa Córdova, Tucson Museum of Art & Historic Block, 181 N. Meyer Ave., Tucson, AZ* (Tucson: Vint & Associates Architects, Inc., November 27, 2022), unpublished report provided to the author via email.
22. Tucson Museum of Art. "La Casa Cordova." *Tucson Museum of Art and Historic Block*. Accessed June 16, 2025. https://www.tucsonmuseumofart.org/la-casa-cordova/.

SELECTED BIBLIOGRAPHY

Newspapers
Arizona Daily Star (Tucson)
Arizona Weekly Citizen (Tucson)
Tucson Citizen (Tucson)
Tucson Weekly (Tucson)
Arizona Republic (Phoenix)

Unpublished Materials
Saarinen, Thomas F., and Lay J. Gibson, eds. *Territorial Tucson*. Tucson, n.d. Unpublished manuscript in possession of Thomas F. Saarinen.

Vint, Bob. *Field Inspection & Preservation Recommendations: Casa Córdova, Tucson Museum of Art & Historic Block, 181 N. Meyer Ave., Tucson, AZ*. Tucson: Vint & Associates Architects, Inc., November 27, 2022. Unpublished report.

Books, Articles and Online Sources
Anzaldúa, Gloria. *Borderlands/La Frontera: The New Mestiza*. San Francisco: Spinsters/Aunt Lute, 1987.

Avrami, Erica, ed. *Preservation and Social Inclusion*. New York: Columbia Books on Architecture and the City, 2020.

Blackhawk, Ned. *Violence over the Land: Indians and Empires in the Early American West*. Cambridge, MA: Harvard University Press, 2008.

Bufkin, Donald H. "From Mud Village to Modern Metropolis: The Urbanization of Tucson." *Journal of Arizona History*, 22 (Spring 1981), 63–81.

Cadava, Geraldo L. *The Hispanic Republican: The Shaping of an American Political Identity, from Nixon to Trump*. New York: Ecco (an imprint of HarperCollins Publishers), 2021.

———. *Standing on Common Ground: The Making of a Sunbelt Borderland*. Cambridge, MA: Harvard University Press, 2013.

Carew, Keith, Adolfo Quezada, and Priscilla Altuna. "Urban Renewal's Dispossessed." *Tucson Citizen*, December 12, 1970, A-1, "¡Ole!" section, 1–12.

Castañeda Garza, Diego, and Alice Krozer. "Life on the Edge: Elites, Wealth and Inequality in Sonora 1871–1910." *Revista de Historia Económica / Journal of Iberian and Latin American Economic History* 41, no. 1 (2023): 7–38.

Chavez, Leo R. *The Latino Threat: Constructing Immigrants, Citizens, and the Nation.* Stanford: Stanford University Press, 2013.

City of Tucson. "Redevelopment Plan: Southwestern Section Central District Development Plan" (Old Pueblo Project, Arizona R-6). Tucson, March 22, 1962.

Clark, Patricia J., and Martha M. Fimbres. "A Study to Identify and Access the Psychological Ramifications Inherent in the Process of Relocation Regarding Census Tract I in Downtown Tucson, Arizona." Master's Thesis, Arizona State University, 1978.

Cole, Dawn, and Catherine Mendelsohn, eds. *As I Recall: Recollections from the Junior League of Tucson, 1933–1993.* Tucson: The League, 1993.

Colwell-Chanthaphonh, Chip. *Massacre at Camp Grant: Forgetting and Remembering Apache History.* Tucson: University of Arizona Press, 2007.

Connerton, Paul. *How Modernity Forgets.* Cambridge: Cambridge University Press, 2009.

Cosulich, Bernice. *Tucson.* Tucson: Treasure Chest Publications, 1953.

DeLay, Brian. *War of a Thousand Deserts: Indian Raids and the U.S.-Mexican War.* New Haven: Yale University Press, 2008.

de la Teja, Jesús F., ed. *A Revolution Remembered: The Memoirs and Selected Correspondence of Juan N. Seguín.* Austin: Texas State Historical Association, 1991.

Drachman, Roy P., and Vincent L. Lung. *The Pueblo Center Redevelopment Project. Report presented to the Central City Council of the Urban Land Institute, April 23, 1965, by Roy Drachman, Chairman, Citizens' Committee on Municipal Blight, and Vincent L. Lung, Assistant City Manager and Coordinator of Community Development.* Tucson: City of Tucson, 1965.

Einstein, Katherine Levine, and Maxwell Palmer. "Land of the Freeholder: How Property Rights Make Local Voting Rights." *Journal of Historical Political Economy* 1, no. 1 (2021): 1–31.

Faist, Thomas. "Transnationalization in International Migration: Implications for the Study of Citizenship and Culture." *Ethnic and Racial Studies* 23, no. 2 (2000): 189–222.

Farish, Thomas Edwin. *History of Arizona.* Vol. 1. San Francisco: Filmer Brothers Electrotype Company, 1915.

Fregoso, Rosa Linda. *meXicana Encounters: The Making of Social Identities on the Borderlands.* Berkeley: University of California Press, 2003.

Fullilove, Mindy. *Root Shock: How Tearing Up City Neighborhoods Hurts America, and What We Can Do About It.* New York: One World/Ballantine, 2004.

Gamio, Manuel. *The Mexican Immigrant: His Life-Story.* Chicago: The University of Chicago Press, 1931.

Goldring, Luin. "Disaggregating Transnational Social Spaces: Gender, Place and Citizenship in Mexico-US Transnational Spaces." In *New Transnational Social Spaces: International Migration and Transnational Companies in the Early Twenty-First Century*, edited by Ludger Pries, 59–76. London: Routledge, 2001.

Gómez, Laura E. *Manifest Destinies: The Making of the Mexican American Race*. New York: New York University Press, 2018.

Greenberg, Amy S. *A Wicked War: Polk, Clay, Lincoln, and the 1846 U.S. Invasion of Mexico*. New York: Vintage, 2013.

Griswold del Castillo, Richard. *The Treaty of Guadalupe Hidalgo: A Legacy of Conflict*. Norman: University of Oklahoma Press, 1990.

Gomez-Novy, Juan, and Stefanos Polyzoides. "A Tale of Two Cities: The Failed Urban Renewal of Downtown Tucson in the Twentieth Century." *Journal of the Southwest* 45, no. 1/2 (2003): 87–119.

Gonzales, Jennifer A. "Invention as Critique: Neologisms in Chicana Art Theory." In *Chicana Feminisms: A Critical Reader*, edited by Gabriela F. Arredondo, Aída Hurtado, Norma Klahn, Olga Nájera-Ramírez, and Patricia Zavella, 313–323. Durham, NC: Duke University Press, 2003.

Horsman, Reginald. *Race and Manifest Destiny: The Origins of American Racial Anglo-Saxonism*. Cambridge: Harvard University Press, 1981.

Hunt, Judith, and Junior League of Tucson. *The Restoration of La Casa Cordova*. Tucson: Junior League of Tucson, Inc., 1978.

Kaufman, Ned. *Place, Race, and Story: Essays on the Past and Future of Historic Preservation*. New York: Routledge, 2009.

Jacoby, Karl. *Shadows at Dawn: A Borderlands Massacre and the Violence of History*. New York: Penguin Press, 2008.

Kirshenblatt-Gimblett, Barbara. *Destination Culture: Tourism, Museums, and Heritage*. Berkeley: University of California Press, 1998.

Lacy, John C. "Original Land Titles in Tucson." *The Journal of Arizona History* 56, no. 3 (Autumn 2015): 323–352.

Lara, Jesus J., ed. *Latino Placemaking and Planning: Cultural Resilience and Strategies for Reurbanization*. New York: Routledge, 2021.

Launius, Sarah Anne. *The Streetcar Effect: Capital, Revitalization, and the Battle over Gentrification in a Sunbelt City*. PhD diss., University of Arizona, 2018.

Lawton, Paul J., ed. *Old Tucson Studios*. Charleston, S.C.: Arcadia Publishing, 2008.

Lockwood, Frank C., and Donald W. Page. *Tucson—The Old Pueblo*. Phoenix, AZ: Manufacturing Stationers, Inc., 1930.

Logan, Michael F. *Fighting Sprawl and City Hall: Resistance to Urban Growth in the Southwest*. Tucson: University of Arizona Press, 1995.

Low, Setha M. *On the Plaza: The Politics of Public Space and Culture*. Austin: University of Texas Press, 2000.

Lowenthal, David. *The Past Is a Foreign Country*. Cambridge: Cambridge University Press, 1985.

Martelle, Scott. *William Walker's Wars: How One Man's Private American Army Tried to Conquer Mexico, Nicaragua, and Honduras*. Chicago: Chicago Review Press, 2018.

Martinez, Melani. *The Molino: A Memoir*. Tucson: University of Arizona Press, 2024.

McCarty, Kieran. *Desert Documentary: The Spanish Years, 1767–1821*. Tucson: Arizona Historical Society, 1976.

———. *A Frontier Documentary: Sonora and Tucson, 1821–1848*. Tucson: University of Arizona Press, 1997.

McMahon, Marci R. *Domestic Negotiations: Gender, Nation, and Self-Fashioning in US Mexicana and Chicana Literature and Art*. New Brunswick, NJ: Rutgers University Press, 2013.

Meeks, Eric V. *Border Citizens: The Making of Indians, Mexicans, and Anglos in Arizona*. Austin: University of Texas Press, 2007.

Meeks, Stephanie, and Kevin C. Murphy. *The Past and Future City: How Historic Preservation is Reviving America's Communities*. Washington, DC: Island Press, 2016.

Mesa-Bains, Amalia. "Domesticana: The Sensibility of Chicana Rasquachismo." In *Chicana Feminisms: A Critical Reader*, edited by Gabriela F. Arredondo, Aída Hurtado, Norma Klahn, Olga Nájera-Ramírez, and Patricia Zavella, 298–315. Durham, NC: Duke University Press, 2003.

Molina, Natalia. *How Race Is Made in America: Immigration, Citizenship, and the Historical Power of Racial Scripts*. Berkeley: University of California Press, 2014.

Montoya, María E. *Translating Property: The Maxwell Land Grant and the Conflict over Land in the American West, 1840–1900*. Berkeley: University of California Press, 2002.

Morrison, Emily, Carrie Durham, and Angela DiFuccia. *Grand Dames & Great Causes: The Way We Were . . . A History of the Junior League of Tucson, 1933–2013*. Tucson: Junior League of Tucson, Inc., 2013.

Officer, James E. *Sodalities and Systemic Linkage: The Joining Habits of Urban Mexican-Americans*. PhD diss., University of Arizona, 1964.

———. *Hispanic Arizona, 1536–1856*. Tucson: University of Arizona Press, 1987.

O'Neil Lyons, Bettina. *A History of La Casa Cordova and the Gabino Ortega Family and the Cordova Family*. Tucson: Tucson Museum of Art, 1980.

———. *A History of the Leonardo Romero House and the Leonardo Romero Family and the Severin Rambaud Family*. Tucson: Tucson Museum of Art, 1980.

———. *A History of the Edward Nye Fish House and Edward Nye Fish Family*. Tucson: Tucson Museum of Art, June 1980

Ostrander, Susan. *Women from the Upper Class*. Philadelphia: Temple University Press, 1984.

Otero, Lydia R. *La Calle: Spatial Conflicts and Urban Renewal in a Southwest City*. Tucson: University of Arizona Press, 2010.

———. "La Casa Cordova: A Reimagining of Mexican Heritage." *History News* 73, no. 3 (Summer 2018): 1–24.

———. *In the Shadows of the Freeway: Growing Up Brown & Queer*. Tucson: Planet Earth Press, 2019.

———. "A Journey of Combating Language Insecurity: Parts 1, 1C, 2 and 3." In *Aquí se habla: Centering the Local and Personal in Spanish Language Education*, edited by Adam Schwartz, Dalia Magaña, Devin Grammon, and Sergio Loza, vol. 7 of *Critical Approaches in Applied Linguistics*, chap. 17. Berlin and Boston: De Gruyter Mouton, 2025.

Page, Max, and Randall Mason, eds. *Giving Preservation a History: Histories of Historic Preservation in the United States*. New York: Routledge, 2004.

Pedersen, Gilbert J. "'The Townsite Is Now Secure': Tucson Incorporates, 1871." *Journal of Arizona History* 11, no. 3 (Autumn 1970): 151–174.

Pitt, Leonard. *The Decline of the Californios: A Social History of the Spanish-Speaking Californians, 1846–1890*. Berkeley: University of California Press, 1966.

Pulido, Laura. "Cultural Memory, White Innocence, and United States Territory: The 2022 Urban Geography Plenary Lecture." *Urban Geography* 44, no. 6 (2023): 1059–1083

Radding, Cynthia. *Bountiful Deserts: Sustaining Indigenous Worlds in Northern New Spain*. Tucson: University of Arizona Press, 2022.

Radford, Gail. *Modern Housing for America: Policy Struggles in the New Deal Era*. Chicago: University of Chicago Press, 1996.

Regan, Margaret. "There Goes the Neighborhood: The Downfall of Downtown." *Tucson Weekly*, March 6–12, 1997. Accessed February 21, 2023. http://www.tucsonweekly.com/tw/03-06-97/cover.htm.

———. "A Short History of the Stevens House." *Tucson Weekly*, April 5, 2001. Accessed January 17, 2025. https://www.tucsonweekly.com/tucson/a-short-history-of-the-stevens-house/Content?oid=1068170.

Rios, Michael, and Leonardo Vazquez, eds. *Diálogos: Placemaking in Latino Communities*. New York: Routledge, 2012.

Robbins, Carolyn C. "A Century of Arizona Women Artists." *Traditional Fine Arts Organization*. Accessed January 19, 2025. https://www.tfaoi.org/aa/8aa/8aa413.htm.

Rosenus, Alan. *General Vallejo and the Advent of the Americans: A Biography*. Berkeley: Heyday Books/Urion Press, 1999.

Rothstein, Richard. *The Color of Law: A Forgotten History of How Our Government Segregated America*. New York: Liveright Publishing Corporation, 2017.

Roybal, Karen R. *Archives of Dispossession: Recovering the Testimonios of Mexican American Herederas, 1848–1960*. Chapel Hill: University of North Carolina Press, 2017.

Sánchez, Rosaura, and Beatrice Pita. *Spatial and Discursive Violence in the U.S. Southwest*. Durham: Duke University Press, 2021.
Seymour, Deni J. "Unveiling Tucson's Namesake: The Sobaipuri O'odham Village of San Cosme del Tucsón." *Journal of Arizona History* 63, no. 2 (Summer 2022): 115–152.
Sheridan, Thomas E. *Los Tucsonenses: The Mexican Community in Tucson, 1854–1941*. Tucson: University of Arizona Press, 1986.
Smith, Cornelius Cole. *William Sanders Oury: History-Maker of the Southwest*. Tucson: University of Arizona Press, 1967.
Smith, Laurajane. *Uses of Heritage*. London: Routledge, 2006.
Smith, Sue. "The First Property Recordings in Tucson, by Wm S. Oury, Recorder." *Copper State Bulletin* 20, nos. 1–2 (Spring/Summer 1985): 1–6.
Sonnichsen, C. L. *Tucson: The Life and Times of an American City*. Norman: University of Oklahoma Press, 1987.
Speelman, Mike. "Incident at Altar: The Ransoming of Leopoldo Carrillo, August 1875." *The Journal of Arizona History* 59, no. 1 (Spring 2018): 31–50.
Taylor, Lawrence D. "The Mining Boom in Baja California from 1850 to 1890 and the Emergence of Tijuana as a Border Community." *Journal of the Southwest* 43, no. 4 (Winter 2001): 463–492.
Taylor, Keeanga-Yamahtta. *Race for Profit: How Banks and the Real Estate Industry Undermined Black Homeownership*. Chapel Hill: University of North Carolina Press, 2019.
Thiel, J. Homer. "In Search of El Presidio de Tucson." *Archaeology in Tucson Newsletter* 12, no. 3 (Summer 1996): 1–5. https://www.archaeologysouthwest.org/pdf/ait/arch-tuc-v12-no3.pdf.
——— and Tucson Presidio Trust for Historic Preservation. *Pioneer Families of the Presidio San Agustín del Tucson, 1775–1856*. Tucson: Tucson Presidio Trust for Historic Preservation, 2016.
Tinker Salas, Miguel. *In the Shadow of the Eagles: Sonora and the Transformation of the Border During the Porfiriato*. Berkeley: University of California Press, 1997.
Torres, Alva B. *Notitas: Select Columns from the Tucson Citizen*. Compiled by Lydia R. Otero. Tucson: Planet Earth Press, 2021.
Trenton, Patricia, Sandra D'Emilio, and Autry Museum of Western Heritage. *Independent Spirits: Women Painters of the American West, 1890–1945*. Los Angeles: Autry Museum of Western Heritage in association with the University of California Press, 1995.
Turino, Kenneth C., and Max A. van Balgooy, eds. *Reimagining Historic House Museums: New Approaches and Proven Solutions*. Lanham, MD: Rowman & Littlefield, 2019.
Valadés, Adrián. *Historia de la Baja California, 1850–1880*. Prólogo de Miguel León Portilla. México: UNAM, 1974.

Veregge, Nina. "Transformations of Spanish Urban Landscapes in the American Southwest, 1821–1900." *Journal of the Southwest* 35, no. 4 (Winter 1993): 371–459.

Wagoner, Jay J. *Arizona Territory, 1863–1912: A Political History.* Tucson: University of Arizona Press, 1970.

Weber, David J. *The Mexican Frontier, 1821–1846: The American Southwest under Mexico.* Albuquerque: University of New Mexico Press, 1982.

———. *Foreigners in Their Native Land: Historical Roots of the Mexican Americans.* Albuquerque: University of New Mexico Press, 2003.

Wilson, Chris. *The Myth of Santa Fe: Creating a Modern Regional Tradition.* Albuquerque: University of New Mexico Press, 1997.

Wolfe, Patrick. "Settler Colonialism and the Elimination of the Native." *Journal of Genocide Research* 8, no. 4 (2006): 387–409.

INDEX

African Americans, 48, 95, 117
Angulo, Margarita, 19
Apache, 12, 17, 34, 35, 42, 43, 85, 87, 106
architecture, Sonoran Row, 5, 49–50
Arizona (film), 33–35
Arizona Album (column), 21, 51–52, 70, 71, 109
Arizona Court of Appeals, Division Two, 134
Arizona Superior Court (Pima County), 133, 137
Arizona Historical Society, 6, 51, 88, 128, 137, 147, 149, 169
Arizona Savings and Loan, 100
Arizona State Museum, 110
Arizona State Parks Board, 138–47
Arizona Territory, 18, 34, 35
Arizona Zarape Restaurant, 32
Anzaldúa, Gloria, 22
automobile culture, 65
Ayres, James E., 130

bail bonds, 32, 135
Bancroft, Hubert Howe, 82
Barron Jacobs Mansion, 3, 123–24
Baja California, Navarrete family connections to, 18–20
"blight," 98, 101, 102,
bond initiatives, 62; Pima County, 60–61, 63; urban renewal, 192n53, 198n6
Brinckerhoff, Sidney B., 149

Buehman, Albert R., 21, 51–54, 56, 70–71, 109

Calle de la Alegría. *See* Congress Street
Camp Grant Massacre, 87, 106
Catalina Foothills, 125, 127, 131
Catalina Junior Women's Club, 130
Carleton, James H., General, 86
Carrillo, Manuel, 24–26, 52–53, 76, 109, 111
Carrillo, Leopoldo, 24–25
Chamber of Commerce, 58, 60, 61, 62
Chicano/x/e Movement, 15, 167
Chinese Americans, 48, 58, 117, 174
citizens' committees (City of Tucson): COMB (Committee on Municipal Blight), 101–3, 104, 114; CURE (Citizens' Urban Renewal Enterprise), 115; Historical Sites Committee, 104, 114
citizenship, 30, 62, 88
City Hall, 119; hub of civic and political power, 8, 48, 100–101, 124; informal information networks, 8, 100–101, 124–25; linked to conversations about parking, 65–66; location, 2; north/south of, as spatial marker, 77, 102, 104, 108, 115, 117, 128
City of Tucson v. Raul Navarrete Cordova and María Cordova, 125–26, 128–29, 132–35, 137–38
Columbia Pictures, 33

COMB (Committee on Municipal Blight), 101–3, 104, 114
Congress Street (*Calle de la Alegría*), 47–48
community property law (Arizona), 24–26
Corbett House, 168
Corbett, James ("Jim") (mayor), 122, 124, 126, 127
Cordova, Alfred, 29
Cordova, Arturo, 29, 31, 36
Cordova, Fernando, 29
Cordova, María Dolores, 29, 142
Cordova, María Navarrete: artistic work and exhibitions, 53–56, 109–10, 113; birth, 9; business ventures, 32, 36; children, 10, 31; class background, 9, 13, 17, 20, 23, 69; conservation leanings, 13, 15; death, 8; eviction, 126, 139, 142, 144; family background, 9; gender expectations, 50; interviews, 19, 51, 75–77, 110–12, 115; letter to the mayor, 24; marriage and divorce, 29, 31; migration to Tucson/U.S., 10, 21; naming of house, 6, 14; racial perceptions of, 13; relationship to Raul Navarrete Cordova, 72–73; role in preservation debates, 7–8; source of claims that house was built before 1854, 7, 52, 53, 75, 80, 136, 163, 168–69, 172; transnational identity, 18–20. See also *City of Tucson v. Raul Navarrete Cordova and María Cordova*; historic preservation; La Casa Cordova
Cordova's neighborhood, 108; home tours, 104, 130
Cordova, Raul H., 29
Cordova, Raul Navarrete: background and education, 36, 69, 73; interviews and media presence (including statements on historic preservation), 78, 108–9, 112; Presidio Title land grant claim, 77–80, 89–91, 94; legal battle against urban renewal (court cases and land title disputes), 115, 125–26, 132–36; owner of La Casa Cordova, 36, 140. See also *Raul Navarrete Cordova v. United States of America and the City of Tucson*
Cordova Brothers Smoke Shop, 36, 49, 53, 55, 58, 77, 109, 126, 130, 131, 135, 136, 142, 144, 164
Cosulich, Bernice, 46
CURE (Citizens' Urban Renewal Enterprise), 113

Davis, Lew (mayor), 98; Pueblo Center Redevelopment Project, 101–3, 117, 120, 126, 143; Resolution 6874, 121, 204n11
deeds, 15, 26, 80, 86–89, 170
DeLong, Sidney R. (mayor), 80
Dias, Mariana, 35–36
Dias, Refugio: born, 10; familial connection to María Cordova, 10, 19, 24, 109; marriage to Manuel Carrillo, 24–25, 76; marriage to Severin Rambaud, 26–27; migration to Tucson, 23. See also Rambaud, Refugio
Dobyns, Henry F., 81
Drachman, Roy P.: advocate for downtown parking, 65–66; appointed to lead urban renewal (1964), 101; Chair of COMB, 101; early resistance from women in the Republican Party, 61–63; opposition to public housing, 59–60, 102; power of, 60; relationship with Frank Sanguinetti, 99–100; role in 1953 proposed Pima County Civic Center, 59–61
Duffield, Milton B., 107

El Rapido Tortilla Factory, 3, 48, 174
eminent domain, 79, 95, 117, 120–22, 128, 129, 132–35, 144, 146, 169, 198n6

Federal Housing Administration (FHA), 97–98
Fathauer, Isabel, 104, 136
Fergusson, David, 1862 map, 44–45, 47, 86–87
Fink, Robert, 138
Fish, Edward Nye (E.N.), 3, 61, 104, 105–6, 107–8, 128, 158, 165, 168
Foreman, Sidney W., map, 80, 89, 90
Fort Lowell Museum, 147
Fullilove, Mindy, 120

Gadsden Purchase (Tratado de la Mesilla), 6–7, 10, 11, 18, 22, 24
Gamio, Manuel, 22
Gates, Hoagland, 107
Gates, Margaret, 107, 168
Giles, Sue, 156
Girl Scouts, 55
Gold Rush: Baja, 19; California, 20, 72, 85, 105
Goldwater, Barry, 13
Grijalva, Raúl M., 167
Guadalupe Hidalgo, Treaty of, 18, 83

Huaraque, Serena, 181n2
Herreras, Eleazar D., 150–51, 152, 156
historic block, 93, 108, 124–25, 131, 133, 144, 168; definition and boundaries, 104, 105, 117; restoration debates, 114–15, 119, 120, 127–28, 136, 146, 158, 165; tours of, 130
historic plaques and markers, 5–7
historic preservation: authority of, 3, 38, 45, 104, 149; financial burden of, 165; framing of María Cordova's legacy, 24, 111, 152, 172; gender, 8, 130; preventing demolition of Cordova home, 136–41; Raul Cordova's perspective of, 108–9; supporting land use policies, 11, 15, 24, 170; urban renewal, 62, 102, 114–15, 119, 143, 146, 157, 168; values,

151. *See also* Historical Sites Committee; Junior League; La Casa Cordova; National Register of Historic Places
Historical Sites Committee, 104, 114
Hispanics: *See* Tucsonenses
Homer, Porter W. (city manager), 95–99
housing: close to downtown, 97–98; public, 98, 102; renters, 62
Hughes, Samuel, 25, 61, 62
Hummel, Don (mayor): Old Pueblo District (urban renewal plan), 95–98
Hunt, Judith Brainerd, 45, 169, 171

Imuris, Sonora, 82–84
Indigenous peoples: adaptation to desert, 42; Apache, 12, 17; Opata, 9, 12; Pima, 12; Sobaipuri O'odham, 17, 42; Tohono O'odham, 12, 17, 34, 42

Jacobs, Arturo W., 30–31
John C. Frémont House. *See* Sosa-Carrillo House
Junior League of Tucson, Inc.: framing of Mexican heritage, 151, 154, 157, 163, 166–67; involvement in La Casa Cordova restoration, 6, 8, 146–47, 149–50; membership, 147–49; partnership and relationship with Tucson Museum of Art, 143, 157–58; "period" furnishings and decor, 153–55, 157–58; relationship with experts, 8, 149, 169; symbolic inclusion of Los Padrinos, 155–56. *See also* historic preservation; Lyons, Bettina O'Neil

Kingan Gardens, 93
Kirshenblatt-Gimblett, Barbara, 153

La Calle, 48–49, 183n15
La Casa Cordova: claims about age, 172; early announcements as museum, 8, 14, 118, 146, 149; historic marker,

La Casa Cordova (*continued*) 5–8; located inside presidio, 17; recent exhibits, 173; restoration, 5–8, 146–55; temporary closing, 164. *See also* historic block; historic preservation; Junior League; Maria Cordova; Tucson Museum of Art
La Plaza de La Mesilla, 43, 44
La Reforma, 98
Lacy, John C., 81, 88
Laidlaw, Don, 122, 124
Lawson, Edward, 122, 127
León, Francisco S., 83–84
Lockwood, Frank C., 43
Los Padrinos de la Casa Cordova, 155–56
Lyons, Bettina O'Neil: chair, La Casa Cordova restoration, 146–47, 151–59; Fort Lowell Museum, 147; Junior League, 147; statements about María Cordova, 144. *See also* historic preservation; La Casa Cordova

Main Avenue, 93, 106, 107, 168
manifest destiny, 33, 44, 72
Mathews, William, 66
McCarthy, Dennis, 140, 167
McCarty, Kieran, 81
McCleneghan, Lew, 53–54
Meyer Avenue: as community corridor, 48–50; Barron Jacobs Mansion, 3, 123–24; La Casa Cordova, 5, 31, 36, 41, 44, 66–67, 77, 109, 111, 125–26; named after Charles H. Meyer, 46–47; Refugio Rambaud, 26–31
Meyer, Charles H., 44–46; drugstore, 47; Meyer street, 46–47
Meyer Street. *See* Meyer Avenue
Mexican Americans. *See* Tucsonenses
Mexican land titles, 80–85
Mexican Revolution, 10, 21, 23
Mexican War of Independence, 9, 17, 43

Miller, Pitt & Feldman, 134–35
Murphy, Helen, 145
Murphy, James M., 128

nacimiento, 144, 159–62, 164
National Register of Historic Places, 6, 8, 137, 138–42
Navarrete, Antonio Angulo: born, 20; citizenship, 30; death, 31; railroad, 20, 21, 70–71, 72
Navarrete family: connections to California, 18–20, 30; origins in Mexico, 18–20
Navarrete, Margarita Angulo, 19
Navarrete, Pedro Magaña, 19
Navarrete, Telesfora Forte: wedding gown imported from Spain, 20–21
Nelson, Edward H., 113–14

Ochoa, Estevan, 34
Officer, James E., 82–83
Ostrander, Susan, 148
Oury Property Records, 80
Oury, Granville, 86
Oury, William S., 80, 84, 85–89, 106, 107, 170

Palant, Lyle, 63–65
Piazza, Paul, 165
Pima County Civic Center complex (proposed), 58–63
Pima County Historic Courthouse, 3, 66, 78, 80, 188n3
Pima County Women's Republican Club, 61–62, 104
Pioneer Derby, 33, 39
placemaking, 7
Polk, James K., 18
Presidio Title Land Grant: early claims, 24; María Cordova's claims, 74, 76, 77; Raul Cordova's legal efforts to assert claim, 77–80, 89–92, 135. *See also Raul*

Navarrete Cordova v. United States of America and the City of Tucson public housing: Federal Housing Administration (FHA), 97–98; La Reforma, 98; plans to establish, 59–60, 95–98
Pueblo Center Redevelopment Project. *See* urban renewal
Pulido, Laura, 45–46

Quintero, Filiberto M., 32

Radding, Cynthia, 42
railroad, 18, 20, 21, 34, 47, 87, 153
Rambaud, Refugio: bequest of property to Cordovas, 31–32; house she built on Meyer Avenue, 3, 27–28; life on Meyer Avenue, 29–31; marriage to Severin, 26–27; overlooked by preservationists, 169–70. *See also* Dias, Refugio
Rambaud, Severin, 26–28, 30, 76, 111, 170–71
Randolph (Reid) Park, 124, 125
Raul Navarrete Cordova v. United States of America and the City of Tucson, 77–80, 89–92, 135
Republican Party, 13, 63, 98; opposition to federal funding, 61–63
Resolution 6874 (City of Tucson), 120–23
Roca, Stella, 61
Rosenus, Alan, 73
Robbins, Carolyn C., 53
Romero, Leonardo, 3, 28, 30, 169–70
Romero, Regina (mayor), 189n21

Safford, A. P. K. (governor), 35
St. Augustine Cathedral (formerly San Agustín Church), 111
San Miguel de Horcasitas (Sonora), 9, 10, 20, 23
San Xavier Mission, 147, 151, 156
Santa Cruz River, 42, 44, 83, 106

Seasonal residents, 107, 168
Seguín, Juan, 13–14
settler colonialism: fabrication of war, 18; Indigenous peoples, 12–13; in Mexico, 9; local intermediaries, 11, 84; María Cordova's place in, 10, 70; post–World War II, 12; racial ordering and exclusion, 11; relevance to preservation, 11; relevance to Tucson, 11, 13, 15; role in urban renewal, 12, 13, 15; Wolfe, Patrick (theoretical framework), 11, 12. *See also* urban renewal; white supremacy
Sanguinetti, Frank (E. F.), 99–101, 102, 108, 114–15, 117–19, 130, 149
Sellers, Harry A., 58
Sheridan, Thomas E., 22, 85, 182n14
slum clearance, 60–62, 95–98, 114, 121–22, 132–33
Smith, Laurajane, 152
Smoke Shop. *See* Cordova Brothers Smoke Shop
Sobaipuri O'odham, 17, 42
Sonora (Mexico): Álamos, 20; architecture, 5, 128, 181n2; Carbó, 20; Guaymas, 20, 30; Imuris, 82–84; Indigenous adaptation to, 42; Magdalena, 82, 84; Navarrete family origins, 18–20; Nogales, 20; San Miguel de Horcasitas, 9, 10, 20, 23; settler colonialism, 9
Sosa-Carrillo House (formerly John C. Frémont House), 104, 151, 155
Snob Hollow, 108
Southern Pacific Railroad, 21
Spanish colonial art, 118, 122
Spanish land titles, 80–83
Spanish language newspapers, 23
Stevens, Hiram, 106–7
Stevens, Petra Santa Cruz, 107
Stone Avenue, 48, 95, 111

Tena, María Luisa, 143; nacimiento creator, 160–62; relationship with Alva B. Torres, 159; relationship with María Cordova, 142
Thiel, J. Homer, 56
Tohono O'odham, 12, 17, 34, 42
Torres, Alva B., 157, 159
tourism, 99, 100, 103, 113, 122
TMA. *See* Tucson Museum of Art
Transnational ties (U.S.–Mexico): fluidity of borders, 19–21, 41; identity, 17, 18–19; mobility, 20–22; solidarity, 71–72
Tubac, 74
Tucson presidio, 24, 33, 34, 35, 41–43, 44, 66, 76, 77, 78, 95, 109, 112, 119; boundaries, 56–57, 106; documents associated with, 80–85; founding, 9, 17–18; interpretations of, 43, 53–56; location of historic block, 104, 114
Tucson (City of): citizen committees, 101–3, 104, 113, 114, 115, 121; city council, 95, 101, 106, 127; leasing or gifting of land to Tucson Museum of Art, 119, 131–32, 143, 145, 165, 168; letter from María Cordova (reported), 24; Resolution 6874, 120–23; role in evicting Cordovas, 126, 139, 142, 144. See also *City of Tucson v. Raul Navarrete Cordova and María Cordova;* historic preservation; La Casa Cordova; *Raul Navarrete Cordova v. United States of America and the City of Tucson*; Tucson Museum of Art; urban renewal
Tucson Art Center. *See* Tucson Museum of Art
Tucson Community (Convention) Center, 98, 101, 105, 113, 117, 127
Tucson Fine Arts Association. *See* Tucson Museum of Art
Tucson Museum of Art: art collections rhetoric, 118; assigned responsibility for restoring historic houses, 132, 164–66, 168; collaboration with City of Tucson, 108–9, 112–15, 131–32; connection to Junior League, 143, 146–47, 156–58; early institutional identities, 83, 93, 94; nacimiento, 151–62; new art center, 118, 136, 136–37, 144–45; request to be included in urban renewal, 114–15; role in La Casa Cordova restoration, 6, 143, 146–47, 156–58; temporary falling out with City, 119–20, 122–25, 126–28, 131–32. *See also* historic preservation; La Casa Cordova; urban renewal
Tucson–Pima County Historical Commission, 6
Tucsonenses, 11, 23, 29, 43–44, 45, 70, 155, 159; displacement of, 13, 95, 117, 118, 173; identity, 167, 182n14; settler colonialism, 11–13, 44

Udall, Morris K., 140
U.S. Housing Act of 1949, 94
urban renewal: boundaries, 50, 105, 108; citizen committees: COMB (Committee on Municipal Blight), 101–3, 104, 114; CURE (Citizens' Urban Renewal Enterprise), 113; Historical Sites Committee, 104, 114; critique of, 173; displacement and property condemnation, 13, 28, 62, 117, 118, 143, 173; framed as progress, 120, 123–24; impact on Cordova home, 13, 74, 77, 95, 117, 118, 125–26, 131, 133–36, 138; plans, 95; 1950s plan (Old Pueblo District), 76, 93, 95–98, 107; 1964 plan (Pueblo Center Redevelopment Project) ,77, 101–2, 117, 120–22, 137, 138, 143; office, 67; pace of, 122; partnership with the Tucson Museum of Art, 94, 99, 113–14, 122–25, 126–28, 131–32, 136; prelude to, 65–66; Resolution 6874, 120–23; role of Roy

Drachman, 100, 101–2; responses by María and Raúl Cordova, 77–79, 91, 128–29, 135–36; settler colonialism, 12, 15; Urban Renewal Act of 1954, 95. *See also* historic preservation; *Raul Navarrete Cordova v. United States of America and the City of Tucson*; Tucson (City of)

vacant lots north of City Hall, 58, 63–65
Vallejo, Mariano, 20, 71–72
Vint, Bob, 212n21

Warner, Solomon 34, 88
Washington Street, 26, 28, 30, 31, 32, 56, 110, 126, 134, 169–70
white supremacy, 11, 33–34, 39, 44–46, 70, 72, 86–89
Whitmore, Phillip B., 122, 135
Wilde, William, 128, 136, 140
wills, 9, 26, 31
Wolfe, Patrick. *See* settler colonialism

ABOUT THE AUTHOR

Lydia R. Otero, born and raised in Tucson, Arizona, revisits an era marked by displacement and sweeping redevelopment to build on themes first explored in *La Calle: Spatial Conflicts and Urban Renewal in a Southwestern City* (2010). More than fifteen years later, they return to examine the meanings of property ownership, memory, displacement, and preservation through the lens of a single house. These questions have become more urgent in Tucson, where debates over land, development, and representation remain unsettled, and where celebrations meant to honor local communities and histories are often shaped by economic priorities designed to attract tourists to a city built in the Sonoran Desert.

With each book, Otero's fascination with archives has deepened, along with a commitment to ensuring that readers have access to the documents, maps, and photographs that informed their research and writing. Earlier works include *L.A. Interchanges: A Brown & Queer Memoir* (2023), which reflects on the cultural shifts of 1980s and early 1990s Los Angeles, and *In the Shadows of the Freeway: Growing Up Brown & Queer* (2019), a memoir often referred to as a prequel to *La Calle* that traces the impact of urban development, environmental injustice, and intergenerational trauma. *Notitas: Select Columns from the Tucson Citizen* (2021) features the work of Alva B. Torres, whose columns ran from 1984 to 1993 in what was then one of the city's major newspapers.

They live in Tucson but continue to visit Los Angeles, refusing to let ICE raids and surveillance disrupt the friendships they have built there over the years.

www.lydiaotero.com

www.ingramcontent.com/pod-product-compliance
Lightning Source LLC
Chambersburg PA
CBHW060558080526
44585CB00013B/609